Aiming to

The Ethics of Suicide and Euthanasia

NIGEL BIGGAR

DARTON·LONGMAN+TODD

First published in 2004 by
Darton, Longman and Todd Ltd
1 Spencer Court
140-142 Wandsworth High Street
London SW18 4JJ

ISBN 0-232-52406-8

A catalogue record for this book is available from the British Library.

Phototypeset by Intype Libra Ltd
Printed and bound in Great Britain by
The Cromwell Press, Trowbridge, Wiltshire

Aiming to Kill

Contents

Contents

Acknowlegements

THIS BOOK HAS only one author, but it has many contributors. Most of it was written during a period of sabbatical leave in the first half of 2003 that was granted me by the School of Theology and Religious Studies at the University of Leeds, and which was supported by the University itself. My first debt of thanks, then, is to my colleagues in the School who shouldered the extra burden of my normal administrative and supervisory responsibilities, so as to set me free to write. My second debt is to Andrew and Catherine Dilnot and their family, who with unhesitating open-handedness allowed me to haunt the capacious upper reaches of the Principal's Lodgings of St Hugh's College, Oxford during the first two months of my leave. Throughout that same period the Provost and Fellows of Oriel College, Oxford welcomed me back to their common table; and I am pleased to record my gratitude to them here.

In the course of writing, several people gave me helpful advice on a number of particular matters: Professor Robert Gibbs of the Department of Philosophy at the University of Toronto; Dr Suzanne Kite, Consultant in Palliative Care at the Leeds General Infirmary; and Dr Lynne Russon, Palliative Care Consultant at Bradford Teaching Hospitals Trust. Professor Werner Jeanrond of the Department of Theology at the University of Lund kindly vetted my translations of French and German.

Next let me thank those who devoted considerable time to reading and commenting on penultimate drafts of chapters: my colleagues from the School of Philosophy at Leeds, Christopher Coope and Dr Chris Megone; Dr Theo Boer of

Acknowledgements

the Department of Systematic Theology at the University of Utrecht; and Professor Jan Jans of the Department of Moral Theology in the Tilburg Faculty of Theology.

Dr Margaret Atkins of Trinity and All Saints College, Leeds read a draft of the whole book and offered characteristically careful comment, which has made a substantial impression on the final version. Simon Walters, commissioned to play Man on the Clapham Omnibus and to hunt down reader-unfriendly passages, spent several flights on Foreign Office business also making his way through a complete draft. I only hope that it entertained him as much as he improved it.

Parts of Chapter Two have been taken, with revisions, from an article that first appeared in *Studies in Christian Ethics*, volume 11, number 1 (1998) under the title of 'God, the Responsible Individual, and the Value of Human Life and Suffering'. I am grateful to T. & T. Clark for granting me permission to re-use this material.

Finally, and above all else, I publish my deep gratitude to Virginia Dunn, my wife. The topic of this book lies very close to the heart of her professional life in palliative care. Through frank observation and astute advice, through constant patience and cheerful support, the achievement of this book is her achievement, too. Here, as everywhere, she has been my mainstay.

Basic Terms

IN THIS BOOK *euthanasia* refers to one person's deliberate killing of another, not because they are threatening injury or have committed a crime, but because their lives are reckoned not to be worth living.

Euthanasia that is *voluntary* is conducted at the request, or with the consent, of the person to be killed.

Non-voluntary euthanasia is conducted without such a request or such consent, because the person to be killed is not *competent* – that is, not capable of expressing his or her wishes. Non-voluntary euthanasia is conducted on the ground of an estimate of what the person to be killed would have wanted, had he been able to communicate his wishes.

In contrast to this, euthanasia that is *involuntary* is performed against the express wishes of the person to be killed, perhaps for the sake of economic efficiency or social 'hygiene'.

(One minor fly in this definitional ointment is that in Dutch discussions, about which we will have much to say in Chapter Four, 'euthanasia' always means 'voluntary euthanasia'.)

Suicide obviously differs from all forms of euthanasia in that the killing is performed, not by someone else, but by the one to be killed.

Where suicide is *assisted*, another person provides help – for example, instructions about how to commit suicide efficiently, or the means with which to do it – but the act of killing is still performed by the one to be killed.

Where the assistance is given by a doctor, we speak of *physician-assisted* suicide.

Explanations of other specialist terms may be found in the Glossary.

Introduction

THE DEBATE ABOUT the morality of euthanasia and assisted suicide and their legalisation has been running for at least a generation. The main arguments for and against have all been put through their paces, and their general profiles are by now widely familiar. In some quarters there are even signs of weariness, for the battle-lines appear thoroughly entrenched and there seems little prospect of any decisive advance by either side.

Stalemate, however, is not the only alternative to grand breakthrough. Progress can yet be made by some careful probing of each of the opposing fronts. That is the service that this book will attempt. It takes up a position in no man's land, in order to review as judiciously as possible the main lines of argument for and against the moral and legal permissibility of euthanasia and assisted suicide. It aspires to negotiate a way through to a mature judgement by taking account of the three basic elements of the controversy – the value of human life, the morality of acts of killing, and the fear of slippery slopes – and by running a coherent argument through all of them.

In moving into no man's land, the book – or, lest he be thought to hide, its author – does not pretend to dispassionate neutrality. I have my prejudices, not uninformed, which on these matters tend to be conservative. On the other hand, for some time I have also had doubts about certain arguments offered in defence of the traditional position; and I am prepared to discover that its critics speak more truth than I have generally supposed. So: no pretence to neutrality here, only an aspiration to heed of the claims of charity – and of the truth.

Introduction

Much of what follows takes the form of the presentation and analysis of other people's opinions. I trust that the results are as accurate as the process has been painstaking. For sure, this is not the stuff of a dramatic intellectual *tour de force*. In the course of a well developed debate on a complex set of moral issues, however, it would be foolish to presume to speak without first coming to close grips with what has already been said. There is no point in opening one's mouth unless one has something worthwhile to add; and one cannot discern what that might be without first having acquired a clear idea of what has gone before, and having attempted to identify its important elements. So, consider the prolonged moments of presentation and analysis as exercises in careful listening.

These, of course, are not the only moments. Were that so, I would not achieve the dialogue that I want. So, after the analytical presentation of the traditional position in Chapter One come those of its critics in Chapters Two to Four; and in each of these the moment of presentation is followed by one of critical response, culminating in an evaluative conclusion that summarises my own judgement.

Some readers might find the discussion that follows excessively theological. In these pages non-theists will encounter references to God, human creaturehood, divine vocation, and life beyond death; and they might be tempted on that account to dismiss the argument as vitiated by arbitrary appeals to incredible religious authorities. If so, I ask for their patience. Why? Let Jeremy Waldron, a political philosopher hitherto not famous for his religious convictions, make the point:

> Secular theorists often assume that they know what a religious argument is like: they present it as a crude prescription from God, backed up with threat of hellfire, derived from general or particular revelation, and they contrast it with the elegant complexity of a philosophical argument by Rawls (say) or Dworkin. With this

image in mind, they think it obvious that religious argument should be excluded from public life . . . But those who have bothered to make themselves familiar with existing religious-based arguments in modern political theory know that this is mostly a travesty . . .[1]

As in political theory, so in ethics.

Besides, not everything that a Christian theist affirms will every kind of agnostic or atheist feel the need to deny. Not everything that a moral theologian has to say will depend at all, or depend directly, on theological premises. Moreover, while an ethical work such as this is not the occasion to offer a comprehensive justification of all the theological beliefs that it invokes, there are moments when it seeks to show how such beliefs make better sense of certain widely held anthropological views – in particular, the value of the human *individual* – than certain non-theological alternatives. To that extent it offers reasons for theological belief that should interest everyone who *really* cares about that value; and it invites them to consider whether they know of a better framework of intelligibility.

What appears excessively theological to some, of course, could appear insufficiently theological to others. Readers of a certain Barthian[2] disposition, for example, might find the dialogical structure of this book suspect. They might fear that it takes the liberalising point of view far too seriously, that the move into no man's land already involves the surrender of basic Christian premises and the adoption of alien ones. If so, I share their general concern, but not their particular fears. As I have said, my position is not neutral, although it is one from which I can spy strengths and weaknesses on both sides; and it is also one from which I entertain the possibility that views of euthanasia and assisted suicide that are less morally restrictive than those traditionally dominant are indeed compatible with a properly Christian vision of things. In other words, the question of whether and to what extent a more permissive view is necessarily anchored in non-Christian premises is one of the things under consideration in this book. I may suspect that it is, but I do not assume so.

Some who consider themselves Barthian might also be disturbed by the fact that my discussion does not limit itself to theological considerations, but strays very far indeed into philosophical ones. They might imagine that a genuinely Christian ethic should operate in purely theological terms. If so, they will find such Christian ethics to be extremely thin on the ground, and those that they do find will not be adequate as ethics. Not everything that needs to be said about the kind of people we should be, or about the kinds of act that we should and should not do, can be said in terms that refer directly to God. Moreover, I doubt that Barth's authority can be invoked in defence of such a conception. What he contended for – and rightly so, in my opinion – is that a Christian ethic be appropriately *governed* by theological considerations, not that it be *limited* to them.[3]

Maybe, however, this is to play at knocking down a straw man. Perhaps the complaint is more subtle: namely, that it is the proper role of a moral theologian to work out the general ethical implications of theological doctrines, but to leave to others the task of bringing them to bear on concrete situations. Certainly, this has greater claim to Barth's authority.[4] In my opinion, however, it has little justification. If the moral theologian is not willing to carry through to completion the task of thinking from theological premises, through ethical concepts, to a moral judgement about a particular case, then who exactly is supposed to do it instead? Further, if the moral theological operation is separated from the casuistical one, the danger of the detachment of the latter stages of Christian moral reasoning from its theological principles will be so much the greater.

Certain kinds of Barthian are not the only Christians in whose minds I can imagine this book raising methodological doubts. Evangelicals might be distressed to find here barely a single handful of direct references to the text of the Bible. As a consequence they might doubt that my discussion is 'biblical'; and if it is not biblical, then it can hardly be truly Christian. If so, I would ask them to consider that references to the surface of the text of the Bible are not the only – and not even the main – index of Christian authenticity. Much more important is the invocation and deployment, at crucial points, of theological and anthropological concepts with deep rootage in biblical tradition – for example, the concept of God as a superhuman agent, benevolently intent upon bringing the world to its fulfilment; of human being as creaturely in its responsibility and its limited power; of human individuality as constituted by a vocation from God to play an inimitable part in the world's salvation; and of the valuable service that even hindered, dependent human life can render in its prophetic witness to what is good and beautiful.[5] It is quite true, as Richard Hays has pointed out, that ethical concepts that are abstracted from the biblical narrative are vulnerable to being understood in ways that are alien to fundamental Christian presuppositions.[6] I do not agree with Hays, however, that such concepts must be so misunderstood, and that therefore Christian ethics should only reason by means of 'imaginative analogies' between the biblical stories and our own situations.[7] Nor do I think that making such analogies – as distinct from mere copies – can avoid abstraction. Nor, further, do I see how Christian ethics could begin to do more than a fraction of the analytical work that needs to be done, if it is not permitted to travel some distance from the biblical text (albeit on a leash). I do believe that my discussion of the ethics of euthanasia and assisted suicide has been formed by the biblical narrative at the appropriate points, via certain theological and anthropological concepts. It may be that the Bible's information of what I say here is inadequate in either depth or breadth, or that closer attention to biblical stories would have yielded valid insights that require significant changes to my argument. If so, I must wait for others to show me where and how.

Enough has been said in methodological apology. To say

more at this stage would be to trade circumspection for para-
noia. So, leaving behind the how and pressing toward the
what, we begin with a presentation of the traditional
legal prohibition of suicide and euthanasia and its moral
rationale.

chapter one

The Traditional Position and the Pressures for Change

The Western legal position

HISTORICALLY, THE Western world has outlawed both euthanasia and suicide. Take English law, for example. Here 'it has always been murder for a doctor . . . intentionally to hasten a patient's death', however compassionate the motive of the doctor and whatever the condition and wishes of the patient; and it is no defence for a doctor to plead 'necessity' – namely, that terminating a patient's life was a reasonable way of securing a higher good recognised by the law (e.g. relief from unbearable suffering).[1]

This is not to say that all conduct foreseen to shorten life is deemed criminal; for, incorporating the principle of double effect (about which we shall have more to say in the next section), the law generally distinguishes between intention and foresight. Accordingly, a doctor may lawfully administer palliative drugs to a dying patient with the intention of alleviating his suffering – even if this has the foreseen result that the patient dies – but not with the intention of killing him. This was the reasoning behind the acquittal of Dr David Moor in 1999:

> Dr Moor was tried for murdering one of his elderly patients, 85-year-old George Liddell, who was dying from cancer, by injecting a fatal dose of diamorphine. Dr Moor denied the charge, claiming that he had

administered the drug to ease pain not to shorten life.
The trial judge directed the jury that they had to decide
whether Dr Moor was trying to ease pain or whether he
had set out to end his patient's life. The jury acquitted.[2]

It was also the reasoning behind the conviction of Dr Nigel
Cox in 1992:

> One of his elderly female patients, a Mrs Boyes, was
> dying from rheumatoid arthritis. She was in consider-
> able pain, and pleaded with Dr Cox to end her life. He
> injected her with potassium chloride and she died
> minutes later . . . Dr Cox was charged with . . .
> attempted murder rather than murder because . . . it
> was not possible to prove that the potassium chloride
> had actually caused the victim's death because her
> corpse had been cremated. The judge directed the jury
> that it was common ground that potassium chloride
> has no curative properties and is not used to relieve
> pain; that injected into a vein it is lethal; that one
> ampoule would certainly kill, and that Dr Cox had
> injected two . . . Dr Cox was convicted.[3]

Not only is it illegal for a doctor to kill a patient intentionally, it is also illegal for a patient to kill himself intentionally. Up until 1961 suicide was a criminal act under
English law. In that year it was decriminalised but, as John
Keown convincingly argues, it nevertheless remains 'unlawful'. Decriminalisation was not intended to grant permission
for suicide or a right to commit it; it was undertaken out of
recognition that criminal sanction is not an effective way to
discourage suicidal conduct. As the government minister
who steered the legislation through the House of Commons
stated:

> Because we have taken the view, as Parliament and the
> Government have taken, that the treatment of people
> who attempt to commit suicide should no longer be
> through the criminal courts, it in no way lessens, nor

should it lessen, the respect for the sanctity of human life which we all share. It must not be thought that because we are changing the method of treatment for those unfortunate people we seek to depreciate the gravity of the action of anyone who tries to commit suicide.[4]

In substantiation of this, the Suicide Act 1961 lays it down that anyone who assists or encourages another person to carry out a suicide should be punished, suffering a maximum penalty of 14 years imprisonment.[5]

The illegality of euthanasia and suicide does not imply a duty to preserve life at all costs. As we have seen, it is lawful to perform acts of pain-relief that risk death – provided that *death* is not what is intended. It is also lawful for a competent adult patient to refuse life-saving treatment, and it is obligatory for doctors to respect such a refusal. This need not be read as permitting suicide and obliging assistance. In his refusal, the patient does not necessarily intend his own death so much as the avoidance of treatment that is either futile or too burdensome; and in his withholding or withdrawing treatment, the doctor might only intend to respect the patient's proportionate refusal. It is true that the courts seem to have granted patients an *unconditional* right to refuse treatment, that sometimes this right might be exercised with suicidal intent, but that doctors are still required to respect it. Nevertheless, this need not be taken as a legal permission of suicide and assistance in it, for 'it is arguable that, in order to avoid the injustice of doctors forcing treatment on patients who are wrongly suspected of refusing treatment with intent to kill themselves, the law could properly require doctors to respect *all* competent refusals of treatment, without in any way endorsing those which are suicidal'.[6]

We have spoken only of English law. What holds here, however, also holds (generally speaking) in other jurisdictions that stand in the English common law tradition – such as the USA, Canada, Australia, and New Zealand.[7] And it holds, too, in other Western legal traditions. In France, for example, the Penal Code outlaws active euthanasia as a form of murder, and considers neither the motive of the act nor the request of the victim as attenuating circumstances. Both assistance in suicide and the failure to intervene in an attempted suicide are punishable as failures to provide assistance to someone in danger. Nevertheless, the competent patient has an absolute right to refuse treatment.[8]

The Christian ethical hinterland

The thinking that lies behind the traditional legal prohibition of euthanasia and suicide in the Western world belongs to Christianity. Like any other long-standing tradition, the Christian one comprises a history of discussion. As such, it is neither monolithic nor static. It is internally diverse, containing differing opinions on most issues (as will be amply demonstrated in the course of this book). It is also dialectical. In the course of debate with rivals, whether within the Christian tradition or outside it, opinions and their reasons are modified and refined; some win an argument and acquire the status of common sense – perhaps even becoming enshrined in law – others lose and fade away (maybe to be revived later).

Nevertheless, a tradition cannot be simply diverse: in order to be distinct from a random collection, it must have a measure of coherence. Its diverse elements must have some things in common; its rival points of view must share some characteristic assumptions.

With regard to the morality of taking human life, then, the tradition of Christian ethics contains a range of positions. But it is a limited range, for the differing positions all share some common assumptions and therefore have more or less reasonable claim to belong to the same, Christian tradition. What is more, some of these common assumptions are very widely shared. Among them is the belief that bodily human life is of exceptional value.

The exceptional value of human life

Indeed, this is one of the main points on which orthodox Christianities have consistently differentiated themselves from heretical alternatives. Against those who have been wont to denigrate matter, and to think of salvation in terms of liberation into a world of pure spirit, orthodox Christians have remained faithful to their Jewish heritage – and to the classic Christian doctrines of the incarnation of God and the bodily resurrection of Jesus from the dead – in affirming the goodness of material creation and in thinking of salvation in terms of the restoration, reformation, and perfection of *this* world, not its sheer abandonment. So, for example, Augustine against the Manichees in the late fourth and early fifth centuries AD;[9] and Catholic theologians against the Cathars or Albigenses in the late twelfth and early thirteenth centuries AD.[10]

Christianity has also followed its Jewish and incarnational foundations in rating human life most highly among the manifold forms of bodily life. Sometimes this superior esteem has been justified in terms of the peculiar qualities of specifically human being – most obviously, its rationality and its moral freedom. But, beyond this, there has also been the belief that, because of these qualities, human beings have the power, the privilege, and the dignity of cooperating in the divine work of restoring and fulfilling the world (including free, rational persons like themselves); and that what humans (help to) build is both intrinsically valuable and, by the grace of God, everlasting. Each human being, then, is seen as having a unique part to play in the drama of the salvation of the world. Each has a unique vocation. According to one twentieth-century theologian, Karl Barth, this is precisely what constitutes the dignity of the human *individual*: no one else in all of history can play the part that is given me to play at this time, in this place, and in this manner.[11] My role may not be glamorous, but it is special, and the good success of the salvific operation as a whole depends upon my little performance.

For reasons like these, Christians have been wont to speak of the sanctity or sacredness of human life. By this they have meant to express, on the one hand, its priceless value and, on the other hand, the correlatively extreme stringency of rules that prohibit its injury.

The sanctity of life is usually invoked with respect to the treatment of an individual's life by others. With respect to such treatment by the individual himself, human life is often described (analogously) as a 'gift' or a 'loan' from God. The implication here is that, with regard to her life, the individual is not simply master, but beneficiary; indeed, she is beneficiary *before* she is master. In the case of life as a gift, the beneficiary is obliged by gratitude to treat it with due care and it is often assumed that 'due care' here excludes harm and destruction. The exclusion of harm and destruction follows more directly in the case of life as a loan; for whereas it is arguable that a beneficiary may (legally, at least) do as she pleases with a gift (provided it was given without conditions attached), it is clear that a beneficiary is more restricted in what she may do with a loan, since she ought to be ready to return it in good shape.

Talk of human life as sacred, or as a gift or loan, all implies that life deserves a certain care or respect, and that this excludes harm and destruction. But it does not tell us whether such harm and destruction are prohibited only as a rule, to which there may be exceptions, or in all cases. On this matter, the history of Christian discussion has given rise to divergent voices.

The justification of taking human life

One voice belongs to Christian pacifists, such as the Mennonites,[12] who regard as immoral any use (at least by Christians)[13] of violence against fellow humans. The immediate
reason for this position is the example of Jesus, who suffered
injury without offering physical resistance. Beyond this lies
a deeper rationale; namely, that following the forgiving way
of peace by not fending off an aggressor will ultimately, by
the providence of God, be more effective in curtailing the
recurring cycle of injury and retaliation than mounting
self-defence.

Christian pacifism, of course, eschews the taking of
human life in the context of a political community's
response to malicious aggression; that is, it eschews the wag-
ing of 'just' war and the infliction of capital punishment.
What it would have to say outside of this context about the
non-retaliatory taking of life – say, in a medical setting – is
not so clear.

The dominant voice in the Christian tradition, however, is
not the pacifist one. This belongs to the proponents of the
doctrine of justified war or, more broadly, justified (lethal)
harm. Again, this point of view assumes a political or civil
context, and addresses the question of what one should do
in the face of injury threatened or inflicted by a hostile military force or by a criminal. Its answer is that one may fend
off or retaliate against such injury by killing under certain
conditions.

For Augustine, the most influential of the early proponents of a Christian doctrine of justified war, the most basic
condition of the justification of the use of force is that it be
motivated by love for the neighbour – as enjoined by the
second part of Jesus' summary of the Law[14] – and not by any
'private passion', such as the lust for vengeance or for material gain.[15] Augustine had two kinds of neighbour in mind:
first, the innocent individual or political community whose
injury constitutes a just cause for retaliation,[16] but also the

enemy, who might benefit from punishment.[17] What Augustine expressly excluded is the use of force to defend oneself
against a lethal threat, on the ground that it is wrong to love
perishable life excessively.[18]

Thomas Aquinas, on the other hand, is less guarded in
affirming responsible self-love, arguing that all things 'naturally' seek their own preservation.[19] Behind this opaque and
questionable appeal to the 'natural' lies a covert and more
intelligible invocation of the Judaeo-Christian understanding of the goodness of creation:[20] all God's creatures are
intrinsically valuable; I am a creature; therefore I am valuable, therefore I should show due care for myself – including
that of self-defence against unjust aggression.

So far the conditions of the justified use of force concern
motive: love for a neighbour or proper love for oneself. These
motives then define what kinds of *intention* are appropriate,
what the ends of justified force may be. These include stopping unjust aggression and achieving a just peace; they
exclude wreaking vengeance on the enemy. So defined, right
intention generates two further conditions: discrimination
and proportionality. The first precludes the intentional
killing of 'innocents'. The second requires the damage
caused by the belligerent means to be 'proportionate' to its
end. If our intention is right, we will only cause such damage as may reasonably be thought necessary to curb aggression and achieve a just peace. Disproportionate damage,
deliberately inflicted, indicates that our intention is otherwise.[21] Accordingly, and more specifically, we may only target those who are responsible for the aggression and who
offer resistance to the establishment of a just peace. The
deliberate killing of anyone other than these – that is, of the
innocent – indicates that the taking of revenge, rather than
the doing of justice, is our actual end.

In the course of Christian thought about these matters,
the definition of 'innocent' has been tightened. For Augustine, the 'innocent' were those not guilty of unjust aggression. The problem with this moral concept of innocence,

however, is that it is difficult enough to discriminate between moral guilt and innocence in a peacetime law court: in the midst of battle it is virtually impossible. In practice, then, Augustine's concept tends to amount to the collective guilt of the enemy population (excepting the two categories of women and children, whose innocence he, along with his classical Roman inheritance, presumed).[22] Although adumbrations of a significant qualification of this 'Augustinian' position are discernible in the medieval period,[23] it was not until the sixteenth century that this became explicit. It was then that Francisco de Vitoria argued for a distinction between an objective violation of right and subjective guilt – that the one does not necessarily imply the other[24] – and effectively equated guilt and innocence with, respectively, the bearing or non-bearing of arms.[25] Here, 'innocence' exchanges its moral sense for a behavioural one: the innocent are those who are *innocens* – that is, 'non-harming' or 'non-combatant'.

The Christian doctrine of the just use of force, then, came to restrict the rule against the taking of human life to cases where the potential object of violence is 'innocent' – that is, not himself threatening harm. Where he is posing a lethal threat, his life may be taken.

What could be the rationale for such killing? One candidate is that, by posing an injurious threat, the aggressor has forfeited his right not to have his life taken away. But this does not settle the matter, because one can reasonably enquire after the rationale behind the notion of forfeiture: *why* does the aggressor forfeit his right? One somewhat plausible answer proceeds along the following lines. In posing a threat to the life of an innocent fellow human, the aggressor creates a tragic situation where the would-be victim or onlooking third parties are faced with a moral dilemma: either to respect the life of the aggressor and to fail in care for the life of the victim, by offering no (lethal) defence; or to care for the would-be victim and to fail in respect for the life of the aggressor, by offering (lethal)

defence. Since it is impossible in this case to care equally for
both lives, the due care of human life in general would be
better served by taking the life of the one who is currently
threatening an instance of it, might be disposed to do so
again, and whose unpunished example might encourage
others.

Christian just war doctrine, therefore, has come to permit
the killing of those who are actively engaged in perpetrating
unjust aggression, and to presume the innocence of all who
are not. It has also come, however, to admit that the killing
of innocents is not always morally wrong. Such killing has
been deemed permissible, provided that it is 'unintended'.
This brings us to the controversial doctrine of double effect,
famously adumbrated by Aquinas in his treatise on self-
defence.[26] Here he distinguishes between the intended effect
of a single act, and its unintentional or accidental effect,
arguing that only the first determines its moral quality. He
then proceeds to argue that it is morally permissible to kill
an aggressor provided that one's intention is to save one's
own life, and that the aggressor's death is necessary for –
'proportionate' to – this end.[27] Vitoria was the first to apply
the Thomistic principle of double effect to the killing of
innocents in warfare, holding that this may be permissible so
long as it is not by 'primary intent', and only if it is therefore
necessary for triumph over the aggressor.[28]

Christian theory of justified force enjoins respect for the
exceptional value of human life, and prohibits its taking
except under these conditions: that it is motivated, not by
vengeance, but by love both for the victim of unjust aggression and for the aggressor; that it intends an end to aggression and the establishment of a just peace; that the taking of
life be proportionate to these ends; that only those actively
engaged in aggression or resisting a just peace may be tar-
geted; but that even innocents may be killed as the unintended side-effect of a use of force necessary to achieve just
ends.

Suicide

So far our exposition of the theory of the justified use of
(lethal) force has focused on cases where one person uses it
against another. Obviously, this bears on euthanasia of all
kinds, where killer and killed are not the same person. Now
we turn to self-killing or suicide. This is relevant to voluntary
euthanasia, in that the person to be killed seeks death and so
adopts a suicidal intention. And it obviously applies to
physician-assisted suicide, where killer and killed are one
and the same, and which involves not only suicidal intent
but also a suicidal act.

Here, too, Augustine turns out to be the dominant
influence on Christian thought.[29] Arguing that the only
morally permissible taking of human life is the publicly
authorised killing of the guilty, he judges suicide, as the
unauthorised killing of the innocent, to be murder.[30] Against
pagan Romans and Donatist Christians who were wont to
regard it as morally exemplary, Augustine contended that,
whether to avoid rape, persecution, disgrace, punishment, or
future sin, suicide is variously a sign of moral weakness,[31] an
evasion of God's providential probation or reformation,[32] a
cutting off of the opportunity for repentance,[33] an act in
despair of God's mercy,[34] or an expression of (typically
Roman) excessive eagerness for honour.[35] What of biblical
cases, such as that of Samson, where self-killing is not con-
demned, or of suicides venerated by the Church as martyrs?
While Augustine suggests that these do not amount to the
force of a moral rule, since they were authorised by 'an
express command [of God] to a particular person at a particular time',[36] he is prepared to infer from them that there
might be cases of suicide that, being commanded by God,
are morally right. Moreover, while he tries to narrow this
loophole in practice by warning anyone tempted to use it 'to
take care that there is no uncertainty about the divine command', lest he incur God's punishment, his admission of the
possibility of divinely authorised suicide appears to be more

than just theoretical: 'We have only a hearsay acquaintance with any man's conscience; we do not claim to judge the secrets of the heart. "No one knows what goes on inside a man except the man's spirit which is in him" [I Cor. 2.11]'.[37]

Aquinas opens his own treatment of suicide in the *Summa* by quoting Augustine, whose judgement he follows. At certain points, however, his reasoning differs. For Aquinas, suicide is an offence against nature, against charity and against justice. It offends against nature, because it goes against the natural inclination of all things to love themselves; and it offends against charity, which includes this natural self-love. Its offence against justice is twofold: first, in that it injures the community of which the self-killer is a part; and second, in that it usurps the power that God alone has to authorise the taking of life that he has given.[38] Like Augustine, Aquinas denies that suicide is justifiable as an escape from other afflictions (rape, for example) but the reason he gives is borrowed from Aristotle, namely, that since death is the ultimate evil in this life, suicide can never be justified as the lesser of two evils.[39]

The strength of the influence upon subsequent Christian thinking of this Thomistic development of Augustine's view is evident 700 years later in the Sacred Congregation for the Doctrine of the Faith's *Declaration on Euthanasia* in 1980. Here, suicide is described in familiar terms as 'a rejection of God's supreme authority . . . [and] often a rejection of love for oneself, a denial of the natural instinct to live, and a flight from the duties of justice and charity one owes one's neighbours or various communities or human society as a whole'.[40] Nevertheless, the Declaration does introduce one relatively novel consideration, when it represents suicide as a rejection of God's 'loving plan', in accordance with which all human beings should live their lives.[41] This goes beyond asserting God's monopoly on authorising the taking of life to hint at a further objection to suicide; namely, that it is a repudiation of the individual's vocation to play his or her role in God's strategy for the redemption of the world.

Christian ethics, assisted suicide, and voluntary euthanasia

In the light of this tradition of thinking about the taking of human life, assisted suicide and voluntary euthanasia are judged immoral. Both involve suicidal intent on the part of the patient and since both also involve the intentional taking of the life of an 'innocent' – that is, of someone who threatens no harm – the person taking the life or helping it to be taken is deemed, respectively, guilty of perpetrating murder or of being an accomplice in it.

Nevertheless, the doctrine of double effect gives the traditional position a certain room for manoeuvre. It permits patients to refuse life-prolonging treatment, provided that they do so with the intention of relieving their final days of an excessive burden, and not with that of killing themselves. It also permits health-care staff to 'let die' (as distinct from 'kill') a patient by withholding or withdrawing treatment, so long as they do so because the treatment is 'futile' and not because they want the patient dead. Moreover, the doctrine permits the taking of measures to relieve pain that are foreseen to have the unavoidable side-effect of hastening the patient's death.

The cultural pressures for change

Historically, then, the intentional taking of human life in peacetime by anyone other than a public executioner has been deemed to be murder in the Western world. Since the last decades of the twentieth century, however, significant voices have been claiming a measure of moral respectability for suicide, and urging that it be made legal – under certain circumstances – for doctors to assist patients to commit suicide and even to kill consenting patients directly (that is, to perform voluntary euthanasia). In some countries, these voices have recently succeeded in gaining sufficient public

support to change the law. Since 1984 doctors in the Netherlands who practise voluntary euthanasia and physician-
assisted suicide under certain conditions have been able to
defend themselves by invoking 'necessity'. In 1995 the Right
of the Terminally Ill Bill was enacted in the Northern Territory of Australia, which permitted physician-assisted suicide
and voluntary euthanasia (until it was overturned by the
Federal Parliament in 1997). In November 1997 physician-
assisted suicide became legal in the American state of Oregon
with the coming into effect of the Death with Dignity Act.[42]
And since May 2002 Belgium has permitted voluntary
euthanasia.

What has provoked such a challenge to the Western legal
tradition and to the moral principles that have informed it?
The most basic stimulus has come, ironically, from success in
developing medical technology so as to make it possible to
prolong life to an unprecedented extent. Sometimes, however, the resultant life is of very poor quality, and there is
little prospect of significant recovery; in which case what has
been achieved is perhaps better described as the prolongation of the process of dying.

One reason why this technological prolongation is often a
very mixed blessing is that it is usually only possible in the
alien, impersonal environment of a hospital, where the
dying patient is distanced from his family, friends, and
neighbours.[43] Such isolation is deepened by intensive care, in
which a patient 'finds himself isolated, distanced from his
family and those close to him, bristling with tubes, sur-
rounded by machines, practically incapable of personal relations with the staff (violent lights, mechanical noise, the
bustle of medical personnel, drips, transfusions, electroen-
cephalograms, radiographs, tracheotomies . . .) .'[44]

Then there are political demands upon hospitals to
achieve ever greater 'efficiency', measured in terms of the
swift delivery of treatments to large numbers of patients.
This kind of efficiency requires speed and standardisation.
Accordingly, even if the apparatus of intensive care does not

stand in their way, medical and nursing staff in such a regimented environment are left with precious little time to spend by the bedside of dying individuals who suffer, as much anything else, from a deep sense of loneliness.[45]

Finally, there is the fact that their training often inclines hospital doctors to think of their vocation more in terms of prosecuting a technical war against disease and death than in terms of enabling patients to enjoy the best life possible, not only on the road to recovery but also in the process of dying. Of British doctors it has been said that they 'still find death difficult to handle and retreat from it at the slightest opportunity'.[46] This, of course, is a natural human reaction. However, it seems that medical education does little to help doctors resist this self-protective instinct in order to let them attend to care for the dying. Writing in an American context, Daniel Callahan observes that

> [d]eath is what happens when medicine fails, and is thus outside its proper scientific scope. That is why . . . a great medical classic, *Cecil Textbook of Medicine*, a primary guide for physicians, refers directly in fewer than twenty-five of its twenty-three hundred pages to death . . . This book, filled with accounts of lethal diseases and ways to treat them, is strikingly silent on treating patients in the terminal phase of those diseases, giving only three pages to the topic . . . This slighting is a stark example of the way death is kept beyond the borders of medicine, an unwelcome, unwanted, unexpected, and ultimately accidental intruder.[47]

As a consequence, their 'therapeutic zeal'[48] in fending off death can often lead doctors to ignore the real needs of patients, for whom success in prolonging survival might actually entail a kind of life that is unbearable.[49]

Faced with the prospect of continuing life under these conditions, many people have not unreasonably concluded that they would prefer to die – and sooner rather than later.[50]

To some extent, it is this fear of being at the mercy of a domi-
nating and insensitive medical expertise that has fuelled the
claim of a patient's right to autonomy over life-and-death
decisions concerning himself. However, autonomy currently
enjoys the high status of an unconditional value in contemporary Western culture, and it therefore nourishes the aspiration for the individual's control over the time and manner
of his own death quite independently of any particular fear
of medical tyranny. That this is so, is made clear in two arti-
cles on euthanasia that appeared in *The Economist* in the
1990s, where the right to individual autonomy is advanced
on its own merits: 'In a secular society it should be a man's
right to take his own life';[51] 'Individuals have a right to self-
determination, and this includes – perhaps, naturally culmi-
nates in – the right to cut short one's own life'.[52]

These various technological, institutional, and cultural
developments have raised philosophical (and some theological) critiques of elements of two fundamental aspects of the
traditional rationale for prohibiting assisted suicide and voluntary euthanasia: the concept of the value of human life as
a gift or loan from God, and the rule that the intentional
killing of innocent humans is always morally wrong. In addition, these developments have also issued in denials of contemporary apologies for the traditional position that argue
against the possibility of limiting any permission to kill the
innocent, and that therefore any relaxation of the absolute
prohibition is bound to propel society down a slippery slope
toward a state where widespread murder is casually
condoned.

In the three chapters that now follow, I will consider the critiques of the traditional concept of the value of human life
(Chapter Two), the traditional rule that the intentional
killing of the innocent is always immoral (Chapter Three),
and contemporary 'slippery slope' arguments (Chapter
Four). Each chapter will open with a presentation of the

critiques, culminating in their distillation into a set of main objections. Responses to these objections will then be made. Finally, a general conclusion will assess whether and to what extent the critiques are cogent, and the traditional position still tenable.

The Value of Human Life

The critics

I N CHRISTIAN thought – and no doubt in that of other theistic religions – it is common to appeal to the notions of human life as a 'gift' or 'loan' from God as reasons for forbidding suicide. Adopted by eminent theologians and philosophers such as Thomas Aquinas, John Locke, and Immanuel Kant, the argument runs thus: because human life is not simply our property, but a gift or loan from God, we have no right to damage or destroy it. Such a line of thinking attracts the exhaustive criticism of Margaret Pabst Battin.[1]

Battin argues that if a gift is genuine, then the donor has relinquished her rights of control: 'if life is really a *gift* from God to the individual, it is that . . . person's to do with as he or she chooses'.[2] She then observes that it would nevertheless be wrong to destroy a gift, if it were useful to someone else or if it were of intrinsic value – although what is significant here is actually not its status as something donated, but the fact that it is useful or valuable. She does acknowledge, however, that one's handling of a gift should be qualified by the virtue of gratitude – provided that the gift is a benefit. 'But if the life one is given is an unsatisfactory one – involving a diseased or deformed body, severe poverty, desperate political repression, terrifying insanity, unbearable grief or deprivation – we would be very much less likely . . . to claim that one is obliged to be *grateful* for it'.[3] Sometimes, however, we recognise the duty to be grateful even for an unsatisfactory gift, because of the benevolent intentions of the donor. This, however, only holds where the giver is subject to limitations: three acorns and a rock glued together as a birthday present may be taken to express benevolence in the case of a child, but in the case of an accomplished artist more likely lack of care or ill will. Accordingly, 'the individual who receives from [an omnipotent, omniscient] God a life disfigured by pain or deformity cannot excuse the donor on grounds of limitations, and may begin to suspect that the donor's intentions are not the best'.[4] This, of course, is to specify the question of theodicy: Is the fact of a human life of chronic suffering compatible with the existence of a God who is at once well-intentioned, all-knowing, and all-powerful? Battin briefly considers and dismisses three affirmative responses. First, while 'Jones' ought to be grateful to God for the opportunity to perfect his soul that suffering presents, this does not entail that he also has a duty to exercise it. Second, if there must be evil in the world for good to be appreciated, Jones has no reason to be grateful that it was assigned to him. And third, if human suffering is attributable to the misuse of free will, why should Jones be grateful to God for giving him something that He knew he would abuse and for which he would thus suffer?[5]

Many of Battin's arguments against life as a divine gift also apply to it as a divine loan. One argument that bears specifically on the latter is that there are a variety of circumstances where we recognise that a loan may or should be returned early – for example, when we cannot care for it properly. Therefore, by analogy, '[i]f life is construed as a loan, . . . suicide may seem appropriate in those cases in which the condition of the loaned life is threatened: the beginnings of deteriorative illness, the onset of insanity, the symptoms of degenerating character'.[6]

Christian opposition to suicide appeals, not only to a

regard for human life as a divine gift or loan, but also to a view of human beings as servants of God. This finds classic expression in Locke, and also in Kant who specifies the service as that of a sentinel. In both cases, the argument is that we may not take our own lives – we may not desert our posts – without the express command of God, our master. To this, Battin replies that servants who are severely mistreated have no obligation to remain loyal, and sentinels who have been rendered incompetent by wounds or even pathological fear should yield their post to someone else.[7] To the related notion that human beings are obliged to use their lives to do some kind of good, she replies that there are some circumstances where this is impossible:

> People in severe and unremitting pain or subject to severe mental disturbance . . . may be unable to reason or think in any coherent way. Patients who have suffered an aphasia-producing stroke or find themselves in a medical situation involving continuous intubation may be unable to communicate. And some persons may be unable to do good for others, either because of physical disability or because of . . . permanent defect of character.[8]

In addition to its various theological groundings of the notion of the 'sanctity' of human life, another important feature of the traditional prohibition of euthanasia and suicide is its refusal to distinguish between human lives that are valuable and those that are not. This entails that one may not kill a human being because he has ceased to be valuable, but only because he is threatening a grave injustice to someone else and must be stopped – in other words, he has ceased to be 'innocent' or 'non-harming'. Battin challenges this by arguing, in effect, that some human lives cease through suffering or damage to be valuable, and that this is a sufficient reason for taking them. Implicit in her position lies something like James Rachels' distinction between the 'biographical' dimension of human life, where its special value lies, and the merely 'biological' – between 'having a life' and 'merely being alive'. According to Rachels, biographical life is something that only conscious subjects can have, because only conscious subjects can have interests.[9] To have a biographical life is to have desires and aspirations, to enjoy pleasures and suffer pains, to want to understand things, to form friendships, to make decisions and to engage in projects.[10] Apart from these, such life as remains will have little value for its subject.

Rachels provides two examples of living human beings who do not 'have' lives in the biographical sense. One is Mrs Florian, a victim of Alzheimer's disease whose brain deteriorated to the stage where she lost 'all semblance of human personality', became incapable of taking care of herself in basic ways, such as feeding and washing, suffered from abnormal fears, and had her speech reduced to screaming intermittently the words 'fire' and 'pain'. By the time her husband shot her dead, 'her life', writes Rachels, 'was already over'.[11]

The second example is that of the famous Baby Jane Doe, who was born suffering from multiple defects including microencephaly (an abnormally small brain) and the complete absence of part of her cerebral cortex. Without surgery, she would die within two years and with surgery, she would have a fifty-fifty chance of surviving into her twenties. But, Rachels asks, if she were to have surgery, would she have 'a recognisably human life'? His own answer is clearly, no; for 'she would lack the mental and physical abilities to engage in even simple human activities; she would not be capable of normal associations with other people, of being curious about the world and having that curiosity satisfied, of enjoying the things that people enjoy . . .'.[12]

It is noteworthy that a certain ambiguity attends Rachels' account of the value of human life. Most of the time, it appears to consist in the possession of certain capacities for understanding, appreciating, intending, and engaging in personal relationships. On some occasions, however, it takes a more subjective turn, and amounts to an individual having whatever capacities that individual happens to find valuable. For example, Rachels writes that '[a] person's life is, quite literally, all he has, and so the value of his life, *to him*, is beyond calculation';[13] and, having described a 'subnormal' human life 'from which the various valuable elements have been removed', he adds the following significant qualification: 'Such a life will not have the value which it otherwise might have had. This judgement is not an attempt to impose some "outside" perspective on the person's situation. The point is that such a "life" will not have as much value *for the subject of that life*.'[14]

It is this subjective sense of the 'value' of human life that John Harris stresses. Human beings are more valuable than other beings, Harris argues, insofar as they are capable of valuing their own existence, and so have the self-consciousness and intelligence requisite for this.[15] 'The value of our lives', he tells us, 'is the value we give to our lives'; and this we do by shaping our lives 'for ourselves', by confirming and modifying and developing our character through our own choices and preferences. 'So autonomy, as the ability and the freedom to make the choices that shape our lives, is quite crucial in giving to each life its own special and peculiar value';[16] indeed, it is autonomy that gives a human life its 'intrinsic, cosmic importance'.[17] In the case of someone who wants to live, therefore, taking human life is wrong because it deprives her of something that she values, and frustrates her wishes. But it would not be wrong to take the life of someone who did not want to live, because such killing would not involve a violation of that individual's autonomy.[18] Nevertheless, Harris' account also involves a measure of ambiguity. The very language of 'value' connotes something that transcends the arbitrary choices of human individuals – for to 'value' something is not simply to 'like' or 'prefer' it; and this connotation of transcendence is confirmed by Harris' identification of the value of human life with its 'intrinsic, cosmic importance'.[19]

This last phrase actually belongs to Ronald Dworkin, whose engagement with the traditional position is more eirenic, more discriminate, and more subtle than any of the critics we have considered so far. Dworkin begins by accepting that the notion of the sanctity of human life is one that is widely held by people on both sides of the debate, whether religious or not. By 'sanctity' he understands an 'intrinsic, cosmic importance' that underlies the common sense of responsibility that people have for making something worthwhile out of their lives.[20] So far, so conciliatory. Where Dworkin differs from the traditional position is in its inference that respect for the sanctity of life necessarily means that one may never take action to bring it to an end. Whether or not it means that depends on how one interprets life's sanctity. According to Dworkin, this is commonly understood to consist in the 'creative enterprise' or 'investment' that a life represents. Some attribute this investment to God, others to nature conceived as a purposive, 'mysterious, inexorable force unifying all life in Life itself'.[21] Still others speak of nature as creative 'only as a metaphorical way of reporting their primitive but strong conviction that nature and art are both processes whose products are, in principle, inviolable'.[22] There are also differences in what a good life, and so a worthwhile enterprise, is taken to be. However, Dworkin implies, everyone agrees that one of the formal features of any good life will be its integrity, its coherence, its narrative wholeness.[23] It follows that we all have a genuine (morally) 'critical interest' in seeing 'that death keeps faith with the way we want to have lived'.[24] It also follows that dying – rather than staying alive – might be the best way to respect certain specific conceptions of the sanctity of life;[25] and that '[m]aking someone die in a way that others approve, but he believes a horrifying contradiction of his life, is a devastating, odious form of tyranny'.[26] For example, '[a]dding decades of immobility to a life formerly organised around action will for [the patient] leave a narrative wreck, with no structure or sense, a life far worse than one that ends when its activity ends'.[27]

One common implication of the accounts of the value of human life offered by Battin, Rachels, Harris, and Dworkin is that suffering is only worth bearing so long as it is compatible with 'biographical life' – or, at least, so long as there is the prospect of recovering it. This militates against a belief that sometimes underlies the absolute prohibition of suicide and voluntary euthanasia, and which derives from the Christian understanding that Jesus' crucifixion is crucial to the achievement of human salvation; namely, the assumption that suffering is intrinsically redemptive.

The objections

Before we set about making a response to the critics, we must first distil their several critiques into a set of main objections. As we discern them, these are as follows:

- if life is a gift, then the beneficiary may do with it as she pleases;
- we are not obliged to be grateful for an unsatisfactory gift;
- all the more are we not obliged to be grateful for an unsatisfactory gift from an omnipotent God, whose intentions must be malevolent;
- we are not obliged to avail ourselves of the opportunity to perfect our souls that suffering presents;
- we are not obliged to be grateful that we have been chosen to suffer evil, so that good might be appreciated;
- we are not obliged to be grateful to God for giving us free will that he knew we would abuse, with the result that we would suffer;
- we may return a loan when we cannot care for it properly;
- sentinels rendered incompetent should yield their posts;
- when it is impossible to use one's life for good, suicide is permissible;

- the special value of human life lies in its 'biographical' dimension, not its 'biological' one;
- the special value of human life lies in the individual's autobiography;
- suffering is only worth bearing so long as it is compatible with the exercise – or at least the recovery – of 'biographical' life.

To each of these we now respond in turn.

Responses

First objection: if life is a gift, then the beneficiary may do with it as she pleases

Even in the case of a gift that comes without strings formally attached, its sheer preciousness may oblige the beneficiary to do with it as it deserves, and not just as she pleases. Let us suppose that what is given is a painting by Rembrandt or a family heirloom. The fact that the benefactor has relinquished legal rights of control over such a gift does not mean that it ceases to carry moral obligations, both because of its intrinsic value and because of its status as a gift. Should the beneficiary handle it carelessly, should she squander it wantonly, then that would both reflect badly on her moral character and actually contribute to its malformation. Further, it would demonstrate a poor regard for her benefactor, cause the latter justified offence, and damage their relationship. Therefore, insofar as life is an intrinsically precious gift from God, we may not do with it just as we please.

Second objection: we are not obliged to be grateful for an unsatisfactory gift

Suppose, however, that the gift is 'unsatisfactory', involving considerable hardship. Would we still be obliged to care for it, whether out of respect for its value or gratitude to our benefactor? Yes, if the substantial benefits that the gift continues to confer are not outweighed by the attendant adversities. And if we understand the benefits of the gift of life primarily in terms, not of ephemeral 'satisfactions' or the crude predominance of pleasure over pain,[28] but rather of humanly fulfilling opportunities to behold what is true and good and beautiful, to identify ourselves with them, and to testify to them, then life can remain worthwhile – indeed, precious – even in the midst of terrible suffering.

Third objection: all the more are we not obliged to be grateful for an unsatisfactory gift from an omnipotent God, whose intentions must be malevolent

This objection is a specification of the classic formulation of the problem that evil poses to orthodox Christian belief: given the fact of evil in the world, either God does not have the power to prevent or stop it, or he does not have the will – either he is not omnipotent or he is not benevolent. Battin's version is this: since God is (supposed to be) omnipotent, and since he has given the gift of an 'unsatisfactory' life, therefore he is not benevolent and we are not obliged to be grateful out of regard for him. Because Battin's criticism here is only cursory,[29] a comprehensive philosophical rebuttal is unnecessary. The following answer should suffice.

What is important in a Christian vision of things is the belief that God is 'omnipotent' in the specific sense of having sufficient power finally to overcome every evil. Christians have no stake in asserting that God has the power to perform what is logically or ontically impossible. So if the development of mature moral character in responsible human agents is a result of the deliberate identification of the self with what is good, and if that identification can only occur through acts of voluntary choice, and if the voluntary nature of these choices requires the real possibility of choosing what is evil, then once God has freely committed himself to creating a world where the moral fulfilment of human beings is possible, he must also have committed himself to creating a world where evil might be freely chosen. Not even God can have one without the other.

A similar argument has been made to justify faith in God's benevolence in spite of the fact of natural or physical – as distinct from moral – evil. The emergence of organic and therefore conscious, morally responsible, human life requires a world of interacting physical systems that are composed of certain basic particles, energies, and forces, and which operate according to certain basic laws. At the same time, because these laws operate impersonally (as they must), subsystems come into chance conflict with each other and suffer consequent frustration and damage. One of these subsystems is organic human life. God cannot intervene to prevent particular frustrations and afflictions of human life, since each intervention would produce a new chain of causal effects requiring further compensatory interventions. This, of course, would undermine the very regularity of the physical world – its law-like nature – that is the precondition of human life in the first place.[30] Therefore, not even God can create human life that is invulnerable to physical suffering.

In sum, then, these theodicies argue that the fact that an 'omnipotent' God gives us the gift of an 'unsatisfactory' life need not imply that his intentions are malevolent – so long as the possibility of human fulfilment can reasonably be considered worth the risk of moral evil and the inevitable suffering of natural evil.

The truth is, however, that faith in a benevolent God powerful enough finally to overcome the evils of the world rarely stands on the simple ground of a reasoned theodicy. Usually, it will be sustained by a complex of experiences, convictions, and reflective reasoning. One of the most powerful of the founding experiences is that of being arrested by the charismatic beauty of the face of someone who, inspired by faith in God and therefore hope for a future that is beyond the ravages of time and is built by more-than-human hands, perseveres in appreciating the value of a life much hindered – a beauty that is heightened when set against the darkness that engulfs the features of someone who has allowed adversity to open the door to bitter despair. The cynic would say, of course, that beauty deceives. But this is not a naïve or sentimental beauty, for it has been tested by suffering. And if one is quite as convinced of its value as of anything else in the world, then that is one reason for owning the faith and hope that sustain it. It may not be a sufficient reason; but, then, it may not be the only one.[31]

This argument has in mind that most religious – perhaps Christian – of films, Terrence Malick's *The Thin Red Line*.[32] Its story is set in the battle between the Americans and the Japanese for the Pacific island of Guadalcanal in 1942. Its subject is not really war, however, but rather the question of what sense we should make of a world that contains at one and the same time breathtaking beauty and heart-stopping horror. On the one hand, the story presents us with those who, concluding that horror has the last word, have calloused themselves, shutting themselves off from finer and human feeling. On the other hand lies Private Witt, who, possessed by the hope that there is an ultimate 'glory' beyond the ambiguities of this world, has the power to remain vulnerable and to hold his dying and agonising comrades in a gaze of compassion. Between these two poles stands Sergeant Welsh, who leans toward the refuge of cynicism, but remains fascinated by Witt. In the end, Witt himself is killed, and the film poses to Welsh – and to the rest of us – the question, was Witt's shining face the face of a fool – noble perhaps, but nonetheless foolish? Or was it a sign of the 'glory' beyond? To its credit, *The Thin Red Line* offers no facile answer to this question, but it does nudge us obliquely toward the second option. Right toward the film's end, as he marches past the graves of a fresh cemetery, Welsh is heard to say in the privacy of his own mind, 'If I never see you in this life, let me know the lack. A glance from your eye, and my life will be yours.' At first, it seems that he must be addressing the dead Witt in his imagination, but on reflection that makes no sense – for Witt he certainly has seen 'in this life'. Then it becomes clear: Welsh is praying to God. The film wisely gives no didactic account of what it is that has moved Welsh from doubt to faith; but one thing it shows unequivocally – the compelling beauty of Witt's face, shining with vulnerability and compassion, lit up by faith.

Fourth objection: we are not obliged to avail ourselves of the opportunity to perfect our souls that suffering presents

Battin herself admits that we 'clearly [have] a duty of grati-tude for this opportunity'. What she denies is that this entails a duty to use it.[33] It is true that we are not obliged to avail ourselves of every opportunity that comes our way, partly because many are unimportant, and partly because there are always more opportunities than we have time and energy to exploit. It is also true that we may withhold our-selves from one important opportunity in order to use another that makes a stronger moral claim upon us. How-ever, there can be no claim more cogent than that of the opportunity to perfect our souls. Let 'soul' be understood here as the morally and spiritually formed self. A person's primary moral duty is to take care that his soul is well formed, that it grows more mature or perfect in its (virtuous) love for what is valuable and in its (virtuous) wisdom about how to act accordingly. Why? One reason is that virtuous personhood is itself intrinsically valuable, and the failure to achieve it is therefore an irreparable loss – a loss intensified if that achievement would have been met with the gift of life beyond death. Another reason is that, whereas we do not always have the power to shape the world outside for good, almost invariably we do have the power so to shape our-selves. A third reason is that only if we shape ourselves well, will we become the kind of people who are capable of treat-ing others as they deserve.

Fifth objection: we are not obliged to be grateful that
we have been chosen to suffer evil, so that good
might be appreciated

While orthodox Christians do not regard evil as an ontic or
moral necessity, they do recognise that, in the condition of
sin where moral sensibilities are dulled, the presence of evil
often serves to highlight the good. Moreover, since they see
the fulfilment of human life partly in the calling to bear witness to what is good, Christians place great value on opportunities to do so and affirm an obligation to be grateful for
these, even if they involve great suffering.

One example of such a view can be found in Helmuth
James von Moltke. Immediately after he had been con-
demned to death in 1944 for opposing the Nazi regime, he
wrote a letter to his wife that was almost euphoric. In it he
spoke of what had befallen him as the climax, not the nadir
of his life. It felt to him that everything had been leading to
this point; that all his life's work was about to find its
fulfilment, its final integrity, in the moment of his execu-
tion. Echoing and paraphrasing the last words of Jesus on the
cross, he wrote, 'My life is finished and I can say of myself:
He died in the fullness of years and life's experience . . . The
task for which God has made me is done.'[34] For Christians,
martyrdom is ultimately more gain than loss, and is therefore a proper occasion for gratitude.

Sixth objection: we are not obliged to be grateful to
God for giving us free will that he knew we would
abuse, with the result that we would suffer

Battin presses this point by way of an analogy: 'Just as the
donor of a pen-knife is culpable for giving it to a three-year-
old child who [sic] he knows will cut herself with it, so a God
who bestows life on a being who [sic] He knows will misuse
and thus suffer for it is not to be praised.'[35] The implication
here is that in giving us something that he knows we will
abuse, and through which abuse we will suffer, God shows
himself to be other than benevolent. However, the fact that

God foresees that we will abuse his gift and suffer for it does not mean that he intends or wants either. Moreover, since the gift of free will – unlike that of a pen-knife – is a necessary condition of the possibility of growth into human maturity and fulfilment; since it is possible that we might learn and grow even through the suffering entailed by our abuse; and since that is indeed what God wants, his giving of the gift of free will is quite compatible with benevolent motives and deserves our gratitude.

Seventh objection: we may return a loan when we cannot care for it properly

Eighth objection: sentinels rendered incompetent should yield their posts

Ninth objection: when it is impossible to use one's life for good, suicide is permissible

Each of these objections makes essentially the same point. However we conceive of the value of human life – as a loan that we are obliged to treat with care, or as a commission that we are bound to carry out, or as an opportunity for doing good that we ought to exercise – should there come a time when we are unable to treat or use life as we ought, and when it therefore loses its specific value, then we may commit suicide. As will become clear in the course of our response to the next objection, we agree with Battin that there are forms of human life that we are not obliged to sustain; although we define those forms more strictly than she. Whether we then agree with her that such life may be intentionally taken – as distinct from being allowed to die – is a question that must wait for an answer in Chapter Three.

Tenth objection: the special value of human life lies in its 'biographical' dimension, not its 'biological' one

Our response to this objection comes in two parts. The first considers whether to endorse the distinction that Rachels,

Harris, and Battin make between biographical forms of
human life that are worth sustaining and merely biological
forms that are not, and it reaches an affirmative conclusion.
The second part then proceeds to consider how we should
conceive of worthwhile, 'biographical' life.

We begin, then, with the distinct'on itself. Partly out of
resistance to the crude utilitarian reduction of the value of
human life to the predominance of pleasure over pain, and
partly because of what they fear to be its degrading implications for the treatment of severely defective human beings,
some Christian philosophers and theologians have argued
vigorously against drawing any distinction between the
value of biological and biographical forms of human life.
Foremost among them is the Roman Catholic moral theologian, Germain Grisez, who writes that:

> [b]ecause most contemporary secular humanists regard
> consciousness as the source and bearer of all intrinsic
> values, they tend to identify the human person with
> the conscious human subject, and to regard the body as
> something other than the person himself or herself.[36]

Since the body is seen as the material substratum and instrument of consciousness,

> if a living human individual is not yet conscious or
> never again will be conscious, it is not a person . . . but
> a potential person or vegetable. Moreover, if bodily life
> is not intrinsically good but is valuable only as a neces-
> sary condition for preferred conscious states, when suf-
> fering prevails over satisfaction in a person's
> experience, his or her quality of life is poor; and if there
> is no prospect of improving, he or she is better off
> dead.[37]

Over and against such mind-body dualism, Grisez denies
that bodily life is extrinsic to human persons and valuable
only as a means to other human goods. On the contrary, it
is 'a good instrinsic to human persons', 'a constitutive part'

of their very reality.[38] Indeed, it 'is the very reality of the person'.[39] Human beings are 'organisms, not spirits temporarily encased in flesh';[40] they are living human bodies informed by the soul.[41]

In support of this organic concept of the human person, with its high esteem for the human body as an intrinsic good, Grisez appeals to three theological topics. First comes the incarnation, which he identifies as 'the ultimate basis for the human body's sacredness'.[42] Then there is the resurrection of Jesus, which promises that those persons united with him will also rise from the dead and live forever in their own bodies.[43] And finally there is sin which, entailing the bodily destruction of humans, implies that 'their concrete reality as bodily beings can hardly be incidental to their relationship with God'.[44] The ethical upshot of this theology of the human body is that 'no bad [physical] condition can lessen the goodness and sanctity of human life'. Disease, disability, mutilation, or extreme poverty do not qualify life's intrinsic goodness; they only 'reduce participation' in it.[45]

What are we to make of this argument? First, we should note that Grisez conflates two significantly different versions of his typical antagonist's position. One is hedonistic and says that bodily life is good only insofar as it conduces to a preferred balance of satisfaction over suffering in a person's experience. But the other is more morally serious and less easily dismissable, holding that bodily life is a good instrumental to the pursuit of intrinsic, specifically human, goods – such as friendship or knowledge of the truth. This latter is a fair representation of Rachels' position.

Second, to say that bodily life is 'a constitutive part' of the reality of human persons is one thing. It is to say that human persons are organisms, not spirits provisionally housed in bodies that are essentially extraneous to them. It is to say that, without bodies, there can be no persons. And that, it seems to me, must be said by a Christian anthropology that is duly informed by the doctrine of the goodness of created, historical life, and by the doctrine of Jesus' bodily

resurrection from the dead as the ground of hope for historical life in the face of death.

But Grisez says more than this. Not only is bodily life a
constitutive *part* of the reality of human persons; it '*is* the
very reality of the person'.[46] This assertion implies more than
the necessity of bodies for persons. Not only can there not be
a person where there is no body, but wherever there is a living human body, there is necessarily a person. That is a different claim. For it implies that human beings whose bodily
functions are operating normally, but who through accident
or disease lack the physiological conditions of the possibility
of personal functions, are nevertheless persons and are to be
respected and treated as such. Where there is a living human
body, there is a person.[47]

What, then, of a human being who not only does not currently exhibit signs of personhood, but who lacks even the
physiological preconditions for such exercise? Can it really
be true to say that bodily life *is* the very reality of the person?
And is such a position really required by Christian theology?

Let us consider Grisez's theological warrants in logical
sequence. First comes sin, which because it entails the bodily destruction of humans, is held to imply that bodily life is
important to relationship with God. This is fair enough, but
it only establishes that living bodies are *necessary* for living
persons, not that they are sufficient.

Next, the incarnation: is it the ultimate basis for the
sacredness of the human body? Certainly, it implies that
physical reality is not alien to God, and that it is good; but
Jewish and Christian tradition have never regarded *all* forms
of physical reality as equally valuable and worthy of the
same kind of respect and treatment. Physical being of a
human kind that gives rise to, and sustains, personal being
has been uniquely accorded such value as to prohibit its
killing. And this is the kind of being whose flesh God in
Christ assumed. Therefore the incarnation certainly confirms
the sacredness of the bodily human being that gives rise to
and sustains personal life. Whether it affirms the sacredness

of a living human body that does not and cannot support such life, remains a moot point.

Finally, what about the resurrection? On the assumption that Jesus was raised bodily from the dead, and that his resurrection is a token of the destiny that awaits those who follow him, we can say the following. Bodily resurrection certainly signifies continuity and identity between the deceased and the raised. It signifies the transformation, not the abandonment, of historical life. The one raised was the one crucified. Bodiliness is therefore important for the eternal life of persons. Maybe the bodily resurrection of Jesus also betokens eschatological hope for corporeal being that is not personal. Maybe. But what it does *not* do is tell us that bodily life *is* the very reality of persons. Our conclusion, then, is that Grisez does not succeed in making his theological case against drawing a distinction between bodily or biological human life on the one hand, and conscious or biographical life on the other.

The position that Grisez holds is also maintained by his ally, John Finnis, although in philosophical rather than theological terms. Finnis denies that a human being's life is a vegetable life supplemented by an animal life supplemented by an intellectual life; rather, it is the one life of a unitary human being. Human life is human through and through, a capacity for *human* metabolism, *human* awareness, feelings, imagination, memory, responsiveness and sexuality, and *human* wondering, relating and communicating, deliberating, choosing and acting; which radically human capacity is 'more or less actualised in various states of existence such as waking, sleeping, infancy, traumatic unconsciousness, decrepitude, etc'.[48] The important point to note here is that, although the dignity of human life is 'most fully manifested' in rational thinking, choosing, and acting, these are only *some* actualisations of 'that *one* radical, dynamic capacity' which is *also* actualised in other human activities, including the metabolic.[49] Therefore it is not only human beings actually capable of intellectual activity who are persons, but 'every living being which results from human conception and has the epigenetic primordia . . . of a human body normal enough to be the bodily basis of some intellectual act'.[50] To be a person is to belong to a kind of being characterised by rational nature.[51] Living members of the human species whose brains have been so damaged as to impair or destroy their capacity for intellectual acts remain persons, albeit damaged; for they retain the 'radical human capacity' for participating according to the manner of a person – intelligently and freely – in human goods.[52] Humans in irreversible coma or in irreversible persistent vegetative state continue to instantiate the good of human life, although 'very inadequately'.[53] Tony Bland,[54] for example, though he had lost the capacity to think and feel, nevertheless retained the human life which went on 'shaping, informing, and organising his existence *towards* the feeling and thinking which are natural to human life (i.e. which human life is radically capable of and orientated towards)'.[55]

Such is Finnis' case *for* the intrinsic good of human life, at once biographical and biological. His case *against* dualism is partly that

> it sets out to be a theory of something [i.e. personal identity as a unitary and subsisting self] but ends up unable to pick out any unified something of which to be the theory . . . Dualistic accounts . . . fail to explain *me*; they tell me about two things, other and other, one a nonbodily person and the other a nonpersonal body, neither of which I can recognise as myself, and neither of which can be recognised as me by the people with whom I communicate.[56]

His other objection to dualism is the arbitrariness with which it draws a line in the spectrum of human beings in different states of flourishing and impairment of capacity, between those who qualify as persons and those who do not.[57]

Finnis is surely right to describe the life of a human being as radically human – human 'through and through'; and to insist that, no matter how badly impaired, a living human being is never simply an animal, far less a vegetable, always a damaged *human being*. Nevertheless, it is odd to say of human beings whose brains are so damaged as to have destroyed any actual capacity for intellectual acts, that they retain the 'radical capacity' for participating intelligibly and freely in human goods, and are therefore still *persons*. Certainly, they retain human bodily life that is naturally ordered to develop and sustain an intellectual capacity, but either this natural development has been irrevocably frustrated, or its product has been irreparably destroyed. So what possible sense can it make to say that they retain a capacity, radical or otherwise, for intellectual activity? What sense can it make to say of someone like Tony Bland, whose capacity to feel and to think had been irrevocably lost,[58] that his persisting human life went on 'shaping his existence towards' feeling and thinking?[59] None that is obvious.

Another theological attempt to resist the distinction between biographical and biological life has been made by Oliver O'Donovan. O'Donovan argues that individual identity is given to a human being by a definite vocation from God to play a particular role in his providential ordering of history.[60] This vocation gives individual identity to a human being 'from before his first act or thought', and it constitutes him as a person.[61] A person is therefore not to be identified with the exhibition of certain qualities or capacities (most notably, consciousness) or with possession of a certain (rational) nature; because neither qualities or capacities, nor generic nature, can give us the *individual*.[62] A person is an individual substance, lying beneath or behind its appearance in the phenomena of 'personality' (a complex of behavioural and relational capacities) or rational agency and subjectivity.[63] Therefore, biological and neurological functions can only be correlated with personality, but not with personhood and to read lack of brain-function as indicative of the presence or absence of personhood is to confuse two

logically distinct categories.[64] Personal presence cannot be
captured by detached, empirical observation; it can only be
awaited and discerned by loving commitment.[65] We must,
therefore, treat the human body with love, recognising it as
the only place of personal epiphany, and trusting the person
to reveal herself, sooner or later. We must stop opposing 'per-
sonalist' (biographical) and 'biologistic' (biological) conceptions of human being, and stop 'treating the bodily
manifestations of humanity, its genetic and physiological
structures, as though we . . . *knew* that there was nothing [or
no one] there'.[66] O'Donovan's point here seems to be that
where we meet ambiguous cases of living human bodies
whose personhood is not manifest, we must give benefit of
doubt. Among these cases he explicitly includes the severely
handicapped[67] and the deeply, even irrecoverably comatose.[68]
At one point he recognises the possibility that what initially
appears to be the human bodily phenomenon of a person
might turn out not to be so, in which case it would be inappropriate for us to maintain a committed humane response;
but the only example he gives us of this is that of mistaking
a rotted corpse for a living human body.[69] Anything less
*un*ambiguous than this, it seems, deserves our good faith:

> Personal presence emerges out of hiddenness, through
> ambiguous signs, to the point of clear disclosure, and
> then retreats into ambiguity and hiddenness at the end.
> There is no sign of behaviour of which we can say,
> 'There he is present! There he has gone!' – short of
> death itself, of course, and even then there are ambigui-
> ties too obvious to be mentioned. All we can do is *act
> personally*, as person or as friend.[70]

It is to O'Donovan's credit that he presses for a conception
of the human person that recognises his individuality. He is
right to insist that this must transcend the generic terms of
qualities and capacities. And his resort to the theological
concept of a vocation from God addressed to each unique
human being does succeed in giving us the individual

(whereas Finnis' definition of a person as a member of the human species yields only a specimen). Nevertheless, O'Donovan is wrong to imply that I am constituted as an individual simply by my vocation. How can I have a vocation if I am not – and cannot again become – a subject, a centre of free agency, a bearer of responsibility, capable of hearing and responding? A person is constituted *both* by his vocation *and* by his capacity for response to it. Hidden subjects (suffering from 'locked-in' syndrome) or dormant subjects (in a reversible coma) may be considered persons, because they either do make or might yet make responses. But this is not so with someone whose brain is so damaged that he has irrevocably and altogether lost the capacity to act responsibly. The current absence of the actualisation of responsive capacities is one thing; the absence of the very possibility of such actualisation is quite another. Therefore, while current lack of brain function need not indicate the absence of a person, the irreparable lack of an upper brain certainly does.

It is our judgement, then, that neither O'Donovan nor Finnis nor Grisez succeed in arguing away, either theologically or philosophically, the good sense of drawing a distinction between biological and biographical human life. So the conclusion to our first set of considerations is that we should endorse it.

To endorse the distinction is one thing, however; to accept the definition of its terms is another. The second part of our response to the tenth objection, therefore, will consider whether we should accept the understanding of biographical life offered us by Rachels and Harris, and if not, how else we should conceive it.

We have already noted how Rachels and Harris equivocate in their accounts of the value of biographical life – how they shift from grounding it objectively in the individual's possession of a certain set of capabilities, to grounding it subjectively in the individual's autonomous deciding for herself what she shall deem valuable. This is most pronounced in Harris.

On the one hand, Harris' talk about 'value' connotes something that transcends the choices of human individuals, since to 'value' something is more than simply to 'like' or 'prefer' it; and this connotation of transcendence is reinforced by the attribution to human life of 'intrinsic, cosmic importance'.[71] But here, as Alasdair Macintyre should have taught us to expect,[72] the language of moral realism is being (ab)used to lend credibility to a form of moral subjectivism; for the centre of gravity of Harris' account clearly lies, not in *the value* that we give our lives, but in *the act of our giving* value. Value resides not in *what* we decide, but in *that* we decide. And this deciding is not responsible to anything outside of itself – it is strictly 'for ourselves';[73] its only reason lies in the *arbitrium* of the individual, her arbitrary assertion.

One major problem with this location of the value of human life in the exercise of absolute autonomy is that it subverts common moral deliberation, responsible respect, and therefore human community itself. Suppose that a popular, bright graduate in his mid-twenties (let's call him Tom) is deeply troubled by some aspect of his sexuality, loathes himself for it, comes to regard himself as worthless, and so commits suicide. Suppose that he was quite mistaken to think that no one would stand by him if he were to admit what shamed him, that no effective help was available. Suppose that he was so self-absorbed as to be oblivious to the impact of his violent self-dispatch on others. Suppose that his suicide blights the rest of his parents' lives with a turbulent mixture of guilt ('We should have done something more or something different'), hurt ('How could he have thought of unilaterally tearing himself out of our lives?'), anger ('How dare he ruin our lives in this way!'), and mutual recrimination ('You should have given him more attention!' '*You* should have given him more space!'). Suppose that his parents' marriage consequently collapses. Harris gives us no grounds for judging Tom's suicide to have been wrong. He allows us no common moral points of reference (values, rules) by which to conduct a discussion. The individual's decision, like his morality, is immured in an absolutely private world, beyond the reach of assessment or criticism by others. Common moral deliberation is therefore impossible, as is mutual accountability and responsibility. Presumably, Harris would enjoin us to respect the absolutely autonomous decisions that others make. But what could 'respect' amount to here? It could not be approval of a morally right act. Nor could it be the more hesitant acceptance of what might be a morally permissible act. It is not born of any kind of moral comprehension at all. Rather, respect here is the uncomprehending letting-be of something that is utterly alien. It amounts to little more than a recognition of sheer fact, a shrugging of the shoulders, and a walking on. What more could it be? In this way, Harris' radically subjectivist concept of autonomy subverts human community; for in such a state of essential moral alienation how long can it be before sheer incomprehension grows bored and relaxes into utter indifference?[74]

A second major problem raised by Harris' identification of the value of human life with the exercise of absolute autonomy is this: it only makes limited and insufficient sense to talk of the fact of our deciding, rather than the content of our decision, being 'valuable'. Certainly, an act of free human self-shaping is significant – indeed, cosmically significant – if one supposes (as John Harris presumably does not) that what is at stake here is a choice between becoming really (and so freely) virtuous or becoming really (and so freely) vicious, and thereby becoming more or less fit for eternal life. But the very act of self-shaping is valuable only as a condition of the possibility of the virtuous nature of the shaping. Its value is merely instrumental, not intrinsic. But instruments have no value – indeed, they have no meaning – without ends.

Harris' account of the value of biographical human life exclusively in terms of sheer autonomy is therefore not adequate. In order for their value to make sufficient sense, human choices have to be able to refer to ends that transcend them. In this sense, they have to be located in a given, 'cosmic' moral context. John Finnis captures the point well:

> If nothing else about human existence and its forms and conditions be of objective importance, there are no grounds for thinking that the sheer fact of having an opinion or preference *is* of such importance and does call for . . . respect . . . Harris . . . fails to see that if the values themselves lack 'cosmic importance', so too must people's opinions about them. For if a human person's very being, self and flourishing or ruin are of no cosmic importance, it is mere baseless conceit to attribute that kind of importance (as Harris does) to people's self-assessments or self-disposition.[75]

The same thesis is asserted by another Roman Catholic philosopher, Charles Taylor, albeit in less irritated tones:

> Even the sense that the significance of my life comes from its being chosen . . . depends on the understanding that *independent of my will* there is something noble, courageous, and hence significant in giving shape to my own life. There is a picture here of what human beings are like, placed between this option for self-creation, and easier modes of copping out, going with the flow, conforming to the masses, and so on, which picture is seen as true, discovered, not decided. Horizons are given.[76]

The instrumental value of the freedom to choose makes full sense only if human beings are *responsible* in their freedom to a moral horizon or context that is given – created – prior to their choosing. This horizon comprises values or goods, through whose realisation human beings flourish, and a set of moral rules or laws that indicates the kinds of behaviour that promotes or diminishes those goods.

However, according to Christian theology, the respon-

sibility of human beings is not simply about obeying general
rules in pursuit of general values; it is also about responding
to a unique vocation. Human beings are responsible not
only as specimens but also as individuals. Within the space
regulated by the generic requirements of maintaining and
promoting human goods ('Don't do this sort of thing; do
that sort of thing') fall the particular requirements of a vocation ('Don't do this particular morally permissible thing,
here and now; do that one instead'). It is integral to the
achievement of my own flourishing that I should commit
myself to promoting that of others. But my powers are so
limited and my contributions so tiny and frail, that I am
tempted first to despair and then to callousness. Faith in
God, however, liberates me from this temptation by remind-
ing me that I am not the only beneficent agent in the cos-
mos, and that it is my job, not to save the world
single-handedly, but only to play my own particular part –
alongside others – in God's redemptive strategy. My vocation
will probably not be glamorous, nor my achievement
famous, and in that sense it will not be special; but it will be
special in the sense that my part is important to the success
of the whole enterprise and that no one else can carry it out
but me. It is through my vocation, then, that the value of my
individuality is established, not through an act of sheer self-
assertion in a cosmic moral vacuum. The substance of this
point is Karl Barth's, although he makes it primarily in terms
of 'command' rather than 'vocation':

> The time in which we live is our place. It may be a
> modest place, but it is ours. As such, it is our place in
> the cosmos and in history, but also in relation . . . to
> the calling, covenant, and salvation of God . . . The will
> and command of God mean very generally that we are
> simply to recognise, take seriously and occupy this
> place as our own, as the place allotted to us . . . The
> command of God summons [man] to be wholly and
> exclusively the man he can be in this place and this

place alone. It thus lifts him out of the stalls and sets him, not behind the stage, but on it, to appear at once and well or badly to say his little piece as appointed.[77]

As God addresses man, He acknowledges and reveals him as someone, a particular individual, this man . . . [T]he Word of God, spoken by the divine I to the human Thou, claims the supremely particular hearing and obedience of this specific man, and thus reveals the individuality of his being and life.[78]

This concept of the genesis and value of individuality gives rise to a different understanding of the respect that we owe one another than that proposed by John Harris. As Harris has it, I should respect another's decision because each individual is the absolute arbiter of his own value. I cannot question or criticise his decision, because it is not accountable to any reasons outside of itself. There is, in fact, nothing to discuss. This kind of respect presupposes that human beings are essentially cut off from each another, isolated monads operating in private moral worlds of their own conjuring.

Barth's theological vision is different. As he puts it:

The honour of two men is disclosed and will be apparent to both when they meet each other in the knowledge that they are both claimed, not by and for something of their own and therefore incidental and non-essential, but for and by the service which God has laid upon them. This claim is the school of true self-estimation and mutual respect.[79]

Barth has it that I should respect the special vocation of another individual, and the peculiar dignity with which it endows him. But an individual's vocation is not his own arbitrary invention. It is issued by the one God, benevolent Creator of the universal human good, into which he strives to bring his creatures. What this means is that a vocation is not *amoral*; it occurs *within* the bounds set by the moral law.

There are some things, therefore, that God would never call us to do – for example, to kill ourselves out of shame, self-hatred, and ultimate despair. So my perception of my own vocation is accountable to moral criteria. It is open to critical discussion and if I am truly concerned to hear it correctly, I will gladly enter into dialogue with others, joining them in the common task of trying to discern the Word of the one God, and thereby constituting human community.

In the light of Christian theology, then, the peculiar value of human life lies not in the freedom to *decide* value, but in the freedom to *acknowledge* and *serve* the value that is given by God, both by observing the moral law and by heeding one's vocation as an individual. It lies, not in sheer autonomy, but in responsibility first to God and therefore to one's human fellows.[80]

This understanding of the nature of the special value of human life presses for a broader definition of biographical life than Rachels gives. For responsible life can take passive as well as active forms; or, more exactly, it can take active forms that are more receptive and appreciative than assertive. We are still responsible subjects even when we are not asserting ourselves by trying to fulfil a desire (whether for knowledge or friendship), make a decision, or engage in a project. We are still responsible subjects even when we are *not* in control, when we are helpless, when life is less something we 'have' than something that happens to us. We still affirm and promote the good of human friendship when we receive the love and care of others, and even when we have no choice but to receive. And, besides, in receiving another's love we affirm it, and in affirming it we ourselves give love.[81]

One poignant illustration of this truth is to be found in the remarkable case of Jean-Dominique Bauby. Bauby, a forty-two-year-old father of two and magazine editor in Paris, suffered a massive stroke and fell into a coma on 8 December 1995. When he regained consciousness three weeks later, he was paralysed, speechless, and only able to move his left eyelid. He remained in this 'locked-in'

condition until he died on 9 March 1997; but in the course
of the intervening 14 months he managed to dictate a book
about his experience of his condition by signalling with his
eyelid. It contains the following passage:

> Hunched in my wheelchair, I surreptitiously watch my
> children as their mother pushes me down the hospital
> corridor. While I have become something of a zombie
> father, Théophile and Céleste are very much flesh and
> blood, energetic and noisy. I will never tire of seeing
> them walk alongside me, just walking, their confident
> expressions masking the unease weighing on their
> small shoulders. As he walks, Théophile dabs with a
> Kleenex at the thread of saliva escaping my closed lips.
> His movements are tentative, at once tender and fear-
> ful, as if he were dealing with an unpredictable animal.
> As soon as we slow down, Céleste cradles my head in
> her bare arms, covers my forehead with noisy kisses and
> says over and over, 'You're my dad, you're my dad', as
> if in an incantation. Today is Father's Day. Until my
> stroke we had felt no need to fit this made-up holiday
> into our emotional calendar. But this time we spent the
> whole of this symbolic day together, affirming that
> even a rough sketch, a shadow, a tiny fragment of a dad
> is still a dad.[82]

The receiving and giving of love is not the only form of
responsibility that hindered human beings can exercise.
They can also acknowledge and appreciate other values and
thereby bear witness to important truths. For example take
Arthur, Frances Young's severely handicapped child. While
on the one hand his life 'lacks event' and 'so there is hardly
a biography to be written',[83] on the other hand he displays 'a
marvellous sense of humour . . . loves music of any kind . . .
[and] wants company'.[84] Young notes how salutary and
prophetic Arthur's implicit witness is: 'Society needs handicap . . . Handicapped people remind us that life is not all go-
getting and individual achievement . . . The handicapped

often show us what true beauty and true humanity is . . . [They] present an uncomfortable challenge to the illusion of human greatness, perfection, and progress.'[85] This point is echoed by David Pailin when he writes that the handicapped person's 'delight in simple things' provides 'an exemplary contrast to the ambition-driven and strife-ridden experiences of discontented life known by many people'.[86]

We have now reached the end of our response to the tenth objection. Our conclusion, in sum, is this. We endorse the distinction between biographical or personal human life on the one hand and biological human life on the other. We deny, however, that the value of biographical life lies in the individual's sheer autonomous choice. Instead, we hold that it lies in the individual's obedient response to God's vocation to play an inimitable part in upholding and promoting created goods; and that this theological concept of responsibility pushes the boundaries of worthwhile, biographical, personal human life out from active and assertive forms to embrace passive, receptive and appreciative ones too. We believe that this theological account of the value of the life of the human individual has two advantages over Harris' (and Rachels') atheistic philosophical alternative: it is coherent, and it fosters human community.[87]

Eleventh objection: the special value of human life lies in the individual's autobiography

Dworkin's argument is both like and unlike Harris'. Like Harris, he argues for the individual's right to autonomy over when and how to die. However, he appears to endorse the view that human life has an objective sanctity because of its 'intrinsic, cosmic importance', which derives from a certain 'creative investment' in human life. Some, he tells us, attribute this investment to God; others attribute it to purposive nature; and still others speak of nature's investment only as a metaphorical way of expressing their conviction that life is inviolable. (Intriguingly, the centre of gravity of these explanations actually lies in the first one. For what is 'purposive

nature' – or 'Nature' – except another term for God?[88] And
since we choose metaphors not merely to give arbitrary
expression to our convictions, but to render them somewhat
intelligible, the fact that non-religious people find themselves reaching for an essentially theological metaphor to
make sense of a deep conviction amounts to an oblique
statement of theistic belief.) Whatever the attribution,
human life is understood to draw its value from its realisation of purposes or ends that are objective in the sense of
being given prior to human choosing – that is the import of
appeals, direct or oblique, to God or Nature. This affirmation
of the objective value of human life, however, does not
entail the equal value of all human life. Life that can no
longer realise worthwhile purposes – mere biological or 'vegetable' life – is not worth the same as that which can.[89] Thus
far, Dworkin's argument runs roughly parallel to our own.

It begins to diverge, however, where he argues (in Harris'
direction) that individuals should be autonomous with
respect to decisions about when and how they should die.
While people generally agree that life has intrinsic value,
they differ in their interpretations of this.[90] Nevertheless,
Dworkin tells us, everyone recognises the value of dying in a
manner that fits with one's own vision of a worthwhile life –
the value of writing the final chapter in one's autobiography.
Accordingly, we suffer a grave injury when we are forced to
endure a kind of life that we regard as worthless, and to
forego a kind of death that we regard as fitting. Therefore, for
liberal political (rather than meta-ethical) reasons, the individual should have a right to autonomy in these matters.

Insofar as Dworkin is arguing against a medical ethos that
takes medicine's *raison d'être* to be that of preserving human
life at all costs – for example, that of condemning someone
to linger near death 'on a dozen machines for weeks' for no
good reason – we agree. Awareness of the creaturely nature
of human being, together with hope for resurrection to eternal
life, means that part of living human life well is knowing
when it is appropriate to bow to the oncoming of death and

to let go of life.[91] While there may be certain rules that help to identify such appropriateness – for example, 'Yield to death only when you are incapable of carrying out important obligations to other people' – the interpretation of a particular case in the light of these rules will involve the weighing up of a variety of factors – for example, what kind of obligations an individual is under, and to whom, and how able he is to meet them. Since such deliberation is bound to fall a long way short of scientific precision, and since it could probably reach different conclusions with more or less equal reason, it is right that it be left to the individual concerned. While this is certainly a concession of autonomy, it is important to note how limited is its sphere. It does not set the individual free to 'decide' arbitrarily what is valuable. Rather, it leaves him free to exercise his own conscience in making a judgement about what certain common moral rules – and his vocation – amount to in a particular case. This autonomy is relative and responsible, not absolute and arbitrary.

The same cannot be said of Dworkin's version. His autonomy is completely unchecked by any duty to respect universally valuable forms of human life or by any other moral obligation. In effect, the objective, 'cosmic' sanctity of human life appears to reduce itself to the sanctity of each individual's absolute autonomy over the composition of the final chapter of his life, and over when to conclude it. In the end, then, Dworkin's position turns out to be the same as Harris' and it suffers from the same flaws.

Twelfth objection: suffering is only worth bearing so long as it is compatible with the exercise – or at least the recovery – of 'biographical' life

So far, our discussion has proceeded mainly with reference to human lives whose value is more or less doubtful because of severe brain damage. But there is another class of cases where the value of human life is in doubt; namely, where there is intense suffering that is beyond relief.

Let us suppose the case of a patient who is suffering from

physical pain so relentless that it permits her to do nothing else but struggle with it; and let us also suppose that this pain cannot be suppressed, either because the patient is languishing in a part of the world where palliative care is not available, or because hers is one of those rare cases that are not susceptible to effective palliative treatment. Does a Christian ethic require such a person simply to endure her suffering? If so, what could the point of endurance be? What could be the value of such a life?

One influential answer has been given by Pope John Paul II in *The Declaration on Euthanasia of the Sacred Congregation for the Faith* (1980). There we read that suffering

> especially in the final moments of life, has a special place in God's plan of salvation. It is a sharing in the passion of Christ and unites the person with the redemptive sacrifice which Christ offered in obedience to the Father's will.
>
> It is not surprising, then, that some Christians desire to use painkillers only in moderation so that they can deliberately accept at least a part of their suffering and thus consciously unite themselves with the crucified Christ.[92]

The theology of suffering that informs this point of view has been more fully presented in John Paul's *Apostolic Letter on the Christian Meaning of Human Suffering* (*Salvifici Doloris*, 11 February 1984). Here suffering is attributed several meanings, including those of the moral and spiritual edification of the subject of suffering[93] and of the moral and spiritual inspiration of those who witness it.[94] But as its Latin title indicates, the focus of the letter lies elsewhere, on the notion of the suffering of the faithful Christian as 'sharing' in the redemptive suffering of Christ and 'completing' it. Indeed, *Salvifici Doloris* opens with the quotation of the Epistle to the Colossians, 4:1, where the Apostle Paul writes: 'in my flesh I complete what is lacking in Christ's afflictions for the sake of his body, that is, the Church'.[95]

How does the Pope explain this notion? The short answer
is: at some length and with considerable difficulty – as is sig-
nalled by the frequency with which he qualifies his state-
ments by the phrase 'in a certain sense', without stopping to
specify which one. John Paul's grasp of the role of Christ's
suffering in bringing about human salvation from sin is less
than exact. In a single sentence he writes of the operation of
Christ's suffering in terms that allude to scapegoating, to the
making of satisfaction, and to the power of love:

> In His [Jesus'] suffering, sins are cancelled out precisely
> because He alone as the only-begotten Son could take
> them upon Himself, accept them *with that love for the
> Father which overcomes* the evil of every sin; in a certain
> sense He annihilates this evil in the spiritual space of
> the relationship between God and humanity, and fills
> this space with good.[96]

The questions begged here are all standard in the theology of
the atonement: How does the suffering of one 'cancel out'
the sins of many? If by the vicarious payment of debt, what
is the connexion between this 'debt' and sin as a subjective
condition? And in what sense is Jesus' suffering an expression of love, and how exactly does love annihilate sin?

Elsewhere in the letter John Paul writes that Christ as Son
of God comprehends 'the measure of evil contained in the
sin of man: in every sin and in "total" sin . . . Through the
divine depth of His filial union with the Father, [He] perceives in a humanly inexpressible way this suffering which is
the separation, the rejection by the Father, the estrangement
from God.'[97] In Christ's Passion, then, human suffering
reaches its culmination:

> and at the same time it has entered into a completely
> new dimension and a new order: *it has been linked to
> love* . . . to that love which creates good . . .[98]

> In bringing about the redemption through suffering,
> Christ has also *raised human suffering to the level of*

Redemption. Thus each man, in his suffering, can also become a sharer in the redemptive suffering of Christ.[99]

Does this mean that the Redemption achieved by Christ is not complete? No. It only means that . . . [in] the dimension of love . . . the Redemption which has already been accomplished is, in a certain sense, constantly being accomplished. Christ achieved the Redemption completely and to the very limit; but at the same time He did not bring it to a close.[100]

The unanswered questions pile up: What exactly is the relation between human sin and suffering? How much sense does it make to treat the condition of suffering as a universal entity, existing independently of actual sinful subjects? What does it mean to 'link' human suffering to love? In what sense is suffering thereby made redemptive? And how can Christ's redemptive work of suffering be both complete and in the process of being completed?

Something of what John Paul is trying to say in *Salvifici Doloris* can be salvaged, I think, but only in a way that severely restricts the applicability of the notion of redemptive suffering. It would also require the adoption of an account of Christ's redemptive work that moves along basically Abelardian lines, with significant developments by René Girard and Paul Fiddes.[101] According to this story, what Jesus of Nazareth exposed himself to was three-fold: first the injustice of being put to death as an innocent man; second, physical pain; and third, the pain of absorbing injury, restraining the instinct to retaliate, and responding instead with compassion and forgiveness. Insofar as we have reasons to believe that Jesus was also God Incarnate, what is true of the former is also true of the latter. Therefore, as Jesus responded to those who wronged him with compassion and forgiveness, so does God. Jesus' passion and crucifixion, then, is decisive in achieving human salvation in two respects: as a revelation of something hitherto largely unknown about the nature of God's dealings with human sin; but not just as a revelation, also as a realisation of that nature.

Is this not a recipe for cheap grace? Our sin is overcome simply and completely by God's work; we, it seems, have to do nothing except enjoy the benefits. Not so. No reconciliation can be established unilaterally. The injured party's forgiveness is necessary but not sufficient. The injurer must also accept the forgiveness offered and in order to do that, he must own and confess his guilt.

But does this not imply that reconciliation between God and human beings depends on human work? Yes, but only in part and only in response to God's grace. No reconciliation is unilateral: the guilty party's repentance is necessary but not sufficient. And besides, the work of repentance is preceded, and to some extent evoked, by the grace of forgiveness-as-compassion. Imagine that you have done wrong to a friend. Now he encounters you for the first time since his injury. Immediately you become defensive, loading your excuses and unsheathing your self-justification. Now imagine that you find your friend responding to you, not with recrimination, but with forgiving compassion. Straightaway, your defences dissolve; and before you can resist it, you are awash with regret and find your lips offering abject apology. Forgiveness is gracious, both because it is not deserved and so cannot be demanded as of right; and because it helps to create the penitent response that completes reconciliation.[102]

In these terms, what sense can we make of the notion of sharing in the redemptive sufferings of Christ, and of completing them? We can share in Christ's suffering by imitating it, by enduring his kind of suffering, by absorbing injury and meeting it with compassion, by forgiving others. Thereby we help to complete God's work of redemption in two ways: First, we take God's forgiveness of ourselves seriously – we forgive as we have been forgiven – and so play our part in God's work of reconciliation with us. But at the same time we also help to complete God's redemption by mediating His compassion and forgiveness to other sinners. It is possible, therefore, to regard human suffering as redemptive, but only of a certain kind; namely, the compassionate and forgiving suffering of injury.[103] Other, physical kinds of human suffering cannot be regarded as redemptive in the strong sense of imitating the compassion and forgiveness of God in Christ.

But could these be 'redemptive' in another, weaker sense? I believe so. Physical suffering often provokes us to review the values and priorities by which we structure our lives, and to see more clearly what is *really* worthwhile. It can help to expose our idolatry of false gods by draining their promises of savour. What is more, physical suffering often slows us down, and frees us to stop mortgaging the present in order to buy an ever-receding future and to appreciate the goods (and the people) to hand that we were far too busy, when healthy, even to notice. Suffering, then, can help to redeem *us*. But more than this, our suffering can help to redeem others, insofar as our lives, reordered and liberated by hindrance, can become a prophetic statement to them. After all, human lives are socially valuable not only for what they build, but also for what they say.

So there are some kinds of physical suffering that can be regarded as redemptive. But is that so with all kinds of such suffering? Is it true of the intense, all-consuming and unrelievable suffering of the case with which our response to the twelfth objection opened? At this point, some might ask how anyone can be sure that their part has been played out, that there remains nothing further to which God might call them? Those are fair questions, but so is this one: in a case of intense suffering, known to be permanent and unrelievable, where the patient's limited energies are entirely consumed in agony, what sense could it make to say of this person that they have a vocation to respond to?

One answer that might be plausible is this: if there is good reason to suppose that the legalisation of voluntary euthanasia might render patients more vulnerable to careless or malevolent pressure to end their lives, and undermine society's general affirmation of the exceptional value of the lives of human individuals and its concomitant commitment to support them in adversity; and if patient demand would encourage such legalisation; then a patient's choice simply to endure suffering rather than ask to be killed could be an act of love, and even of justice.

Conclusion

From our engagement with the critics of the traditional, Christian view of the value of human life we emerge with the following conclusions. The special value of individual human life lies in the opportunity it affords to hear and respond to a call from God to make a unique contribution to the maintenance and promotion of created goods in the world. The exercise of this responsibility can take dependent, receptive, and appreciative forms, as well as assertive ones. It can consist in the handicapped child's sheer delight in simple things, or the elderly patient's heartfelt gratitude for the care he receives – as much as in the thrusting public achievements of an adult in his prime.

It remains reasonable to regard human life – and the opportunity for responding to one's vocation that it affords – as a gift or loan from God that deserves gratitude and obliges care and responsible management, even when that gift involves considerable suffering. Likewise, suffering as such does not render it unreasonable to persist in viewing human beings as God's servants and sentinels, who have a duty to carry out the tasks assigned them.

On the other hand, not all physical suffering is redemptive, and some suffering can be so intense and relentless as to make responding to anything other than pain – including a vocation – inconceivable. Furthermore, severe brain damage can rob a human being even of the very capacity for consciousness that is the precondition of response.

Therefore, we think it fitting to discriminate between human biological or bodily life that is able to support biographical – or, better, responsible – life, and that which is not; and to ascribe 'sanctity' to the former but not the latter. It is important to note, however, that our concept of responsible life includes responsive as well as assertive modes. Nor is its value simply decided by the individual. That notion of absolute autonomy is both incoherent – as the equivocation of those who propose it suggests – and subversive of human community.

In addition to conclusions, our engagement with critics of the traditional view of human life and suffering has raised three important questions that we must take with us beyond this chapter: Can the will to die or an act of suicide ever be an expression of the responsible management of the gift of human life? Could this be so in a situation where someone has become permanently incapable of performing any beneficial service, however broadly and generously conceived? Or if there were sufficient reason to suppose that the social acceptance of suicide and voluntary euthanasia as 'rational' acts might undermine society's general high esteem for the lives of human individuals, and so jeopardise its members' ordinary commitment to support one another in adversity, could a patient's very refusal to adopt a suicidal intention constitute just such a beneficial service? The first two questions we shall answer in the following chapter, the third in Chapter Four.

chapter three

The Morality of Acts of Killing

The critics

CRITICISM OF the traditional position does not limit itself to basic assumptions about the value of human life and suffering. It extends to the moral analysis of acts of killing – that is to say, the explanation of what makes some acts right and others wrong. One feature of traditional analysis that attracts critical attention is that it prohibits the killing of patients, and yet permits them to be allowed to die. Critics argue that no general moral distinction can be made between active killing and passive letting die, for an agent is responsible for what he omits as well as for what he commits. Some critics go on to infer from this that to be responsible for an act of omission that issues in death is to intend to kill and that since it is permissible to let patients die, it should also be permissible to kill them.

James Rachels opens his critique with two cases for consideration:

> In the first, Smith stands to gain a large inheritance if anything should happen to his six-year-old cousin. One evening while the child is taking his bath, Smith sneaks into the bathroom and drowns the child, and then arranges things so that it will look like an accident.

In the second, Jones also stands to gain if any
thing should happen to his six-year-old cousin. Like
Smith, Jones sneaks in planning to drown the child in
his bath. However, just as he enters the bathroom Jones
sees the child slip and hit his head, and fall face down
in the water. Jones is delighted; he stands by, ready to
push the child's head back under if it is necessary, but
it is not necessary. With only a little thrashing about,
the child drowns all by himself, 'accidentally', as Jones
watches and does nothing.[1]

Rachels then denies that Jones' behaviour was less reprehensible than Smith's, for 'both had exactly the same motive,
personal gain, and both had exactly the same end in view
when they acted'; and he concludes from this that the bare
difference between killing and letting die makes no moral
difference.[2] Indeed, sometimes letting die rather than killing
can be 'patently cruel', insofar as it prolongs suffering.[3]

Michael Tooley makes the same point, arguing that 'it is
just as wrong intentionally to refrain from administering an
antidote to someone who is dying of poisoning as it is to
administer the poison, provided that the same motive is
operative in both cases', and concluding that the distinction
between killing and intentionally letting die has no moral
significance *in itself*.[4] Tooley proceeds to suggest that the
reason why we tend to view killing someone as more
seriously wrong than intentionally letting them die is attributable to *other* factors: that the motive in the first kind of
case is generally more evil than in the second kind; that the
alternative to letting someone die – saving their life – might
involve considerable risk and expenditure; and that refraining from saving someone's life is unlike killing them, in that
it does not necessarily close down other routes to survival.[5]
This line of thinking also appears in Peter Singer, who holds
that 'there is no *intrinsic* moral difference between killing
and allowing to die', although a significant difference can be

introduced by factors other than the mere distinction between an act and an omission.[6]

R. G. Frey brings to the surface the main practical point of criticism of the moral distinction between killing and letting die, when he argues that a patient's refusal of what he knows to be life-sustaining or life-saving treatment is an act of suicide; that a physician who acquiesces in it intends his patient's death; and that since the refusal of treatment is permitted, so should physician-assisted suicide be.[7] Others would extend this conclusion to voluntary euthanasia.

Another major feature of the traditional position that attracts criticism is the doctrine of double effect. While this doctrine finds its roots in the thought of Aquinas, it has been elaborated over the centuries and has assumed a variety of forms.[8] Nowadays it is commonly articulated in terms of four conditions that render morally permissible an act that causes an evil effect that is foreseen. One oft quoted version is Joseph Mangan's:

> A person may licitly perform an action that he foresees will produce a good and a bad effect provided that four conditions are verified at one and the same time: 1) that the action in itself from its very object be good or at least indifferent; 2) that the good effect and not the evil effect be intended; 3) that the good effect be not produced by means of the evil effect; 4) that there be a proportionately grave reason for permitting the evil effect.[9]

Jonathan Glover conveys the standard utilitarian complaint against this doctrine that it makes a moral distinction between cases where the outcome is exactly the same[10] – as where one patient refuses life-sustaining treatment and another is assisted in committing suicide. Rachels, claiming Pascal's mantle,[11] develops the point's theoretical hinterland by asserting that purity of intention belongs strictly to the moral evaluation of character, which is 'another thing entirely' from that of acts.[12] 'A pure heart cannot make a wrong act right; neither can an impure heart make a right act wrong' – because the rightness and wrongness of acts is determined only by their effects.[13]

Glover, pressing home the attack on the practical front, points out that there are cases where the doctrine of double effect actually prefers the act that results in the worse of two outcomes. For example, it typically

> allows that a pregnant woman with cancer of the womb may have her life saved by removal of the womb, with the foreseen consequence that the foetus dies. But, if the doctor could save only the mother's life by changing the composition of the amniotic fluid and so killing the foetus while still attached to the womb, this would not be permitted. In the second case the death of the foetus would be an intended means; in the first case it would be merely a foreseen consequence.

Arguably, however, the death of the mother (upon whom others depend) is a worse outcome than the death of the foetus.[14]

Taking a different tack, albeit still with utilitarian wind in his sails, Glover observes that the fourth condition laid down by the doctrine of double effect forbids an act that intends to achieve a small benefit at the expense of disproportionately damaging foreseen consequences – 'I may not tell the truth about an innocent fugitive's whereabouts to an assassin, with the foreseen consequence that he is murdered.' Since this involves an estimation of the costs and benefits of consequences, Glover reads it as a concession to utilitarian calculation and asks, rhetorically, 'Where is a line to be drawn, and why?'[15]

Next, he casts doubt upon the doctrine's assumption that there is such a thing as an intrinsically bad act – in particular, the intentional killing of the innocent (for example, through euthanasia or physician-assisted suicide) – that may never be justified in terms of consequences. He implies that this rests on a blind – and, to atheists, deeply unimpressive –

appeal to divine authority. He proceeds, however, to entertain the possibility that an absolute prohibition of intentional killing might find a rationale in the argument that it is 'in general better' that people do not do it – that is, in the beneficial consequences of keeping a rule. However, he says, '[t]his raises the problem: why should I obey the rule in cases where to do so does not have the best overall consequences'. Further, there are other kinds of conduct that are generally undesirable, but which are not made the subject of an absolute prohibition – lying, for example.[16]

To Glover's complaints against the doctrine's absolute prohibition of the intentional killing of the innocent, Rachels adds that a person's 'innocence' means only that certain justifications for killing him – such as self-defence – cannot be used. It does not mean that there might not be other justifications. Since the traditional doctrine wrongly supposes that the principle of 'innocence' governs the morality of killing in every context, Rachels concludes that it is 'misguided in its most fundamental approach'.[17]

Arguably the most scathing criticism of the doctrine of double effect has been reserved for the alleged arbitrariness of the moral distinction it draws between effects that are intended and those that are merely foreseen, and for the gross irresponsibility that this appears to justify. John Harris identifies the problem as one of providing good reasons for limiting the re-description of actions and he regards this as 'immense . . . and . . . insoluble'.[18] To make his point, he quotes an example of the moral distinction given in a report of Roman Catholic provenance:

> Imagine a pot-holer stuck with people behind him and water rising to drown them. And suppose two cases: in one he can be blown up; in the other a rock can be moved to open another escape route, but it will crush him to death . . . There might be people among them who, seeing the consequence, would move the rock, though they would not blow up the man because that

would be choosing his death as the means of escape. This is a far from meaningless stance, for they thus show themselves as people who will absolutely reject any policy making the death of innocent people a means or end.[19]

The way that this case is described, argues Harris, is calculated to make plausible the notion that blowing up the pot-holer is directly bound up with killing him, whereas moving the rock is not – that the first is an intended means, whereas the second is only a foreseen side-effect. A change in description removes the plausibility:

> ... suppose two cases: in one he is crushed leaving room to escape; in the other a hole can be blown in the rock at its weakest point, but this will dismember the pot-holer ...

Here it is moving the rock that appears to involve direct killing, whereas blowing a hole in it does not. From this exercise Harris infers that 'it is a feature of any action that its description is almost infinitely expandable or contractable', that there is no way of defining what counts as a legitimate description, and that therefore no distinction of any moral significance should be made to hang upon it. His conclusion is that reasoning in terms of double effect amounts to 'comprehensive sophistry'.[20]

Similarly, Mary Warnock finds 'something artificial and indeed Jesuitical' (echoes of Pascal, again) about the distinction between intended and unintended effects,[21] and she presents cases where it seems 'not only absurdly pedantic but morally reprehensible'[22] to try to separate the intention from the foreseen consequence of the act:

> For instance, a man has been hired to take responsibility for keeping the drinking-water tank full for a family, in the house they have rented for the holidays. He fully intends to carry out the duty for which he is being paid. Someone warns him that the water-supply has become

seriously polluted. Nevertheless, he continues to carry out his obligation to fill the tank, and the family is poisoned.[23]

Assuming that the doctrine of double effect would absolve the man of blame on condition that he bore the family no ill will and simply intended to fulfil the terms of his contract, Warnock comments: 'The separation here between intention and foreseen consequence, even though it may be made in theory, seems in practice to be ethically positively monstrous.'[24] A point implicit here is rendered explicit by Peter Singer: 'We cannot avoid responsibility simply by directing our intention to one effect rather than another. If we foresee both effects, we must take responsibility for the foreseen effects of what we do.'[25] Another point that Warnock states is one that we have already met in Harris: 'an action, or plan of action, can be truthfully presented under so many descriptions, some narrower than others (e.g. "What are you doing?" "I'm putting a fork to the left of a mat", or "I'm getting ready for my dinner-party"), that no one description can be the only true description, and so no one intention can be the only real intention'. Double effect thinking, then, operates with 'a fake exactitude'.[26]

Jonathan Glover raises the same objections against the distinction between intended means and foreseen side-effects, but he analyses the issue somewhat further and in terms of a different case:

> If, as a political protest, I throw a bomb into a football crowd, causing an explosion and killing several people, are their deaths intended means to my protest or inevitable consequences of it? On what principles do we decide whether the explosion alone is included in the means or whether we must count both explosion and deaths as part of the means?

Glover denies that the principle can be that of 'virtual inevitability' – that is, whether the deaths were the virtually inevitable result of the explosion – because, he tells us, the doctrine of double effect holds that there can be consequences foreseen to be inevitable, but which do not count as intended means. But if not this kind of 'closeness' between cause and effect, then what kind? 'Is it closeness in time? If so,' he says with sarcasm, 'having someone poisoned in order to prevent them catching and killing me will turn out not to be forbidden if the poison used is *very* slow-acting', More fundamentally, what moral importance could such 'closeness' have except in terms of establishing the extent to which the effect is inevitable or desired?[27] 'A lot of explaining seems called for', Glover comments in a tone replete with confidence that no satisfactory explanations will be forthcoming.[28]

The objections

Again, before responding to the critics, let us first isolate their main complaints. These are:

- a patient who refuses life-saving treatment, and a doctor who acquiesces in this refusal, are both responsible for – and so intend – the death that ensues. To let a patient die, therefore, is morally equivalent to deliberately killing him and since the former is permitted, so should the latter be;
- where the outcome of two acts is the same, there is no moral distinction between them;
- purity of intention is a criterion of the morality of character, not of acts;
- the doctrine of double effect sometimes prefers the act whose outcome is worse;
- the doctrine contradicts itself by engaging in utilitarian calculation;
- there is no reasonable, non-arbitrary way of distinguishing between intended and unintended effects, because the definition of what is intended shifts according to which

description of an act is selected from a variety of legitimate accounts. Besides, the doctrine of double effect's separation of what is intended from what is foreseen can render gross irresponsibility morally permissible;
• the intentional killing of the innocent is not intrinsically bad, and so should not be subject to an absolute prohibition.

Our responses now follow.

Responses

First objection: a patient who refuses life-saving treatment, and a doctor who acquiesces in this refusal, are both responsible for – and so intend – the death that ensues. To let a patient die, therefore, is morally equivalent to deliberately killing him and since the former is permitted, so should the latter be Rachels and Tooley are quite correct to assert that the distinction between killing and letting die has no moral significance in itself. We are morally responsible for what we choose not to do, as well as for what we choose to do, and we do not necessarily make ourselves less culpable by not acting than by acting. Indeed, there may be cases where our failing to act to save someone is as immoral as our acting to kill them – namely, where we have the opportunity and ability to save them, where our so doing would not be forbidden by another more binding moral duty (e.g. to save someone else instead), and where the risks and costs incurred by us would not be unreasonable.

Accordingly, Tom Beauchamp and James Childress are correct to gainsay those who argue that, when life-sustaining treatment is deliberately withheld or withdrawn – omitted – and death results, the underlying disease or injury is the cause and is 'responsible'.[29] One who holds this is Daniel

Callahan: 'With "letting die", it is the disease that causes the patient's death, not the doctor . . .'.[30] Another is Arthur Dyck:

> it is misleading simply to describe physicians as causing death when, through increasing pain relief or withdrawing some type of life support, they foresee and tolerate the death of their patients. Physicians cannot, by willing it to be so, assure [sic] that a given disease will or will not be fatal. Patients properly diagnosed as terminal will die because of the effects of their disease upon their bodies . . .[31]

Both Callahan and Dyck fail to distinguish clearly between causality, responsibility, intentionality, and culpability. If a doctor withdraws life-sustaining treatment – that is, treatment that is actually effective in sustaining life[32] – he does help to cause the resultant death, and he causes it to occur earlier than would otherwise have been the case. If he withdraws the treatment deliberately, then he is *responsible* for helping to *cause* the death. Still, this does not settle the questions of whether he *intends* to cause the death, and whether he is *culpable* for doing so. Their answers are determined by other considerations. (We explain the distinctions between physical causality, responsibility, intentionality, and culpability in our responses to the sixth and seventh objections.)

Rachels and Tooley are mistaken, however, in their assumption that all proponents of a conservative position on euthanasia affirm a significant moral distinction between killing and letting die, between acts and omissions, *as such*. Germain Grisez, for one, makes it perfectly clear that he does not[33] and, according to Werner Wolbert, the official teaching of the Roman Catholic church makes it sufficiently clear that neither does it.[34] Rachels is also mistaken (here with Frey, not Tooley)[35] to infer from the agent's responsibility for letting die a general moral equivalence with active killing. While a physician is responsible for a choice to let die, as for a choice to kill, he may be morally justified in making the former but not the latter. On the one hand, to choose to let a patient die could be primarily a morally admirable choice to cease futile efforts to stave off death in order to begin to support the patient in the process of dying by, for example, providing effective palliative care. Paul Ramsey makes the point eloquently: 'we cease doing what was once called for and begin to do precisely what is called for now. We attend and company [the patient] in this, his very own dying, rendering it as comfortable and dignified as possible.'[36] On the other hand, to choose to kill a patient when effective palliative care is available could be a morally culpable act of impatient abandonment. As we shall argue below in response to the sixth objection, there can be a morally significant difference between what one intends and what one foresees and chooses to accept. To choose an action that will probably or certainly result in death is not necessarily to intend it, provided that one does not *want it*, and that there are sufficiently good reasons for accepting the unwanted.

Second objection: where the outcome of two acts is the same, there is no moral distinction between them

This criticism denies an act's intention the crucial moral significance that the doctrine of double effect accords it, and transfers that significance entirely onto its effects. The point of so doing is to subvert the fine moral distinction that traditional analysis draws between on the one hand, a morally permissible case where an analgesic drug is administered with the intention of relieving pain and causes a death that was foreseen and accepted as the unavoidable result of the necessary dosage; and on the other hand, a morally impermissible case where a lethal dosage of a drug is administered with the intention of killing as the only available means of relieving pain.

That this objection suffers from a major flaw is indicated straightaway by its implicit denial of any moral difference between involuntary homicide and murder, the outcome – death – being the same in both cases. The nature of its flaw is that it attends to only one kind of outcome, namely, the immediate, objective effects of an act upon the world external to the agent. What it ignores is the subjective, reflexive impact upon the agent himself of his will's commitment, through intention, to a right or wrong act. When we intend something that is wrong, we identify ourselves with moral evil. Thereby we corrupt ourselves. In addition, by becoming familiar and comfortable with evil, we increase our inclination to do it – and thus to multiply evil effects – in the future. If today I act out of malice or undue carelessness and intend an injustice in one situation, then tomorrow I will be more inclined to do so in others. Norvin Richards, a rare consequentialist who appreciates this point, puts it thus: 'As causes actions affect the likelihood of various consequences. As symptoms of personality, they do the same, but in a different way: by making it more likely the person will act in ways which have those consequences.'[37] Therefore, the fact that the objective outcomes of two acts are the same does not mean that those acts are morally indistinguishable. They may yet be differentiated by the different subjective outcomes caused by their different intentions. Against this second objection, therefore, two major assertions are being made: first, that through his intending an agent shapes himself for good or ill; and second, that it is ultimately the intention of an act, not its outcome simply, that decides its moral quality.

Third objection: purity of intention is a criterion of the morality of character, not of acts

Certainly, purity of intention is a criterion of the morality of character. To commit oneself to an evil intention is to make one's character (in a certain respect) bad. Insofar as an evil intention is discernible, it is a mark of bad character, and if it is a mark, then it is a criterion.

Nevertheless, purity of intention is also a criterion of the morality of acts. An act is not made morally evil merely by producing harmful effects, for some harmful acts are blamelessly accidental or involuntary. Among the things that may make a harmful act morally wrong is that the harm is intended, whereby the malevolence or culpable carelessness of the agent converts the mere fact of harm into an injustice.

In the light of this, we both agree and disagree with Rachels' assertion that '[a] pure heart cannot make a wrong act right; neither can an impure heart make a right act wrong'.[38] To the first clause we say that it is true that a pure heart – or intention – cannot make a wrong act right, because once its enactment has been shown to be morally wrong, either the declared purity of intention becomes doubtful or its genuine purity is outweighed by an irresponsible acceptance of unintended harm. We shall explain this in response to the sixth objection below.

To the second clause we say that if an impure intention shapes an act by ordering it to achieve some harm, then it *cannot* be right in the first place. The only acts that impure intentions do not render wrong are ones upon which they have no bearing. It is true that there may be acts that realise evil intentions, but which nevertheless *appear* to be right because their outcomes *appear* to be wholly good. Suppose that you and I shared an elderly grandmother whom we visited, separately, every week. You did it because you love her; I did it because I was hoping for a healthy bequest from her estate. Being a master of deception, I was successful in hiding my real intention, and my grandmother was just as much cheered by my visits as by yours. To her dying day, she supposed herself to be loved by us both. Were our acts then, morally speaking, the same, notwithstanding our different intentions? Did my impure intention fail to make my beneficial act wrong? No, because my act was not simply beneficial. My grandmother may have been cheered by my visits, but she was also actually cheated by my deceit into making a bequest to someone who despised her. And even if we grant that my act was simply beneficial in regard to my grandmother, it was not so in regard to myself and others. For, in realising my malevolent intention what I did confirmed my identification with evil and advanced the

corruption of my character, to the detriment both of myself
and of all those with whom I have interacted since.

Fourth objection: the doctrine of double effect
sometimes prefers the act whose outcome is worse

In responding to this question we must be careful, again, to
consider the full range of outcomes. The objection itself is
narrowly focussed only on one of these: the effect upon a
certain patient. It may be that the doctrine does sometimes
prefer an outcome that involves greater suffering for this
patient than other outcomes would; but if this is so, it could
be because it judges that breaching the prohibition of all
killing of the innocent has a morally corrupting effect upon
medical agents, thereby upon medical institutions, and
thereby upon all those who serve in and are served by them,
and that this justifies the ruling out of other less painful outcomes in this particular case. The immediate impact of an act
upon the patient in question is not the only effect that
deserves consideration.

Now, of course, whether the decision not to relieve the
patient's suffering is indeed justified by wider considerations
is a question yet to be settled. That will involve determining
whether the act in question can reasonably be held to corrupt its medical agents and if so, whether such corruption is
likely to infect medical institutions and thereby to render
other patients and members of society vulnerable to abuse.
These are matters that we will treat in Chapter Four.

Fifth objection: the doctrine contradicts itself by
engaging in utilitarian calculation

Not all deliberation about the 'proportion' between costs
and benefits is utilitarian. According to utilitarianism, such
deliberation *alone* decides the moral quality of an act.
According to the doctrine of double effect, however, what
decides the rightness or wrongness of an act is the quality of
the agent's will, and it is only as a means of determining this

that the estimation of the proportion or disproportion between costs and benefits is significant.

Moreover, estimating proportion need not be the same as pretending to aggregate so-called 'quantities' of pleasure or happiness, and of pain or unhappiness, and to 'calculate' which 'outweighs' the other. Whether the cost of a benefit is disproportionate can be determined, not at all by its comparative 'weight', but by whether or not it is unavoidable or whether it undermines the benefit that is supposed to justify it. So, for example, it would be disproportionate to relieve someone's chronic and excruciating pain by lethal means when non-lethal ones are available, because the cost of pain relief – death – would not be necessary. So, too, it would be disproportionate to defend liberal democracy in a manner that risked global devastation by nuclear weapons, because the cost of defence would result in the obliteration of what is being defended.

Sixth objection: there is no reasonable, non-arbitrary way of distinguishing between intended and unintended effects, because the definition of what is intended shifts according to which description of an act is selected from a variety of legitimate accounts. Besides, the doctrine of double effect's separation of what is intended from what is foreseen can render gross irresponsibility morally permissible

The doctrine of double effect makes a crucial moral distinction between the effects of my action that I 'intend' and those that I 'accept'. Good effects (e.g. pain relief) I may 'intend' as ends or means, but evil effects (e.g. death) I may 'accept' only as side-effects. The result of this is to permit some actions whose effects are ambiguous – for example, the administration of a drug that is at once palliative and lethal. The rationale is that, by merely 'accepting' rather than 'intending' the evil that his act causes, the agent avoids identifying himself with it. In attributing crucial importance to this distinction, the doctrine assumes that it is possible to define what is and is not intended in a way that is rationally defensible. Some of its critics disagree, however. They doubt that such a distinction can be cogently drawn. Moreover, even if it were possible, it would be morally undesirable since it serves to absolve agents of responsibility for the evil that they cause.

It might be thought obvious that what defines an evil effect as an intended means – rather than an unintended side-effect – is that it is immediately prior in time to, and therefore 'directly' causes, the good effect. This is what some proponents of the doctrine of double effect have argued.[39] If I shoot you in an act of self-defence against the lethal threat that you pose, and you die straightaway from my shooting, then the good effect of my security against harm will be the immediate result of the prior bad effect of your death. According to this version of the doctrine of double effect, your death would then be the intended means of my self-preservation and as such it would be ruled illicit.[40] On the other hand, the same version would permit a doctor to perform a therapeutic hysterectomy, in which a cancerous womb containing an unborn child is removed, with the consequence that the child dies. Here the child dies *after* being removed from the mother's body, because it is not viable. The child's death, then, is not intended as the means of removing the mother's womb and so of preserving her life, and it is therefore morally permissible.[41]

This line of reasoning, however, has rightly been challenged by another proponent of the doctrine of double effect, Germain Grisez, who denies that the temporal sequence and immediacy of effects are morally significant. As he sees it, our agency – and our responsibility – extend equally to every effect that we expect to follow naturally and inevitably from what we do: 'all of the events in the indivisible performance of a unitary human act are equally immediate to the agent; none is prior (a means) to another'.[42] Moreover, the order of intention is strictly distinct from the orders of 'outward performance' and objective causality.[43]

The fact that my security follows immediately upon your death at my hands does not necessarily mean that I intended your death as the means to my self-preservation. I am responsible for your death, but I need not have intended it, and I need not therefore be culpable for it.[44] In a panic, I might not have had the presence of mind to aim my gun accurately, with the result that, while intending merely to incapacitate you, I had the effect of killing you. The temporal sequence and the causal immediacy or directness of effects is no determinant of what is intended.[45]

How then *should* we pick out the effects that we intend from all those that we cause? Henry Sidgwick proposes that we 'include under the term "intention" all the consequences of an act that are foreseen as certain or probable'.[46] Against this, Alan Donagan raises the valid objection that it extends the boundaries of responsibility too far, so as to encompass the voluntary actions of other people.[47] This would entail that 'a Christian who, given a choice between apostasy and martyrdom, refuses apostasy, intends his own death and persecution'. 'Such a result,' comments Donagan, 'seems to me intolerable.'[48] Rightly so: the fact that I do something that I foresee will very probably incline you to do something else, does not necessarily mean that I intend you to do it.

However, it is not just the intervening voluntary action of another person that distinguishes foresight from intention. I can foresee that it is highly probable that a certain state of affairs will result from what I do, directly and without the intervention of anyone else, and still not intend it. If this were not the case, and if what is foreseen as highly probable is equated with what is intended, then, should a patient die under high-risk surgery, the surgeon must be thought to have intended the death.[49] Another example is furnished by J. L. Austin:

> By exacting the payment of a debt, a creditor foresees that he will cause the ruin of his debtor. He does not desire to ruin him; but, on the other hand, he has

calculated that, if he is not repaid, he himself will suffer severely. So, with a heavy heart, he exacts repayment.[50]

Donagan comments that, while it is true that the creditor voluntarily ruins his debtor – his action causes the ruin, and he *knows* that it will – it is not true that he intentionally does so, because it is not part of the plan according to which he acts.[51] It seems, then, that for Donagan – as for Grisez[52] – what distinguishes an intended from an unintended effect is that it falls within the agent's 'plan'.

One possible problem with this restriction of what is intended to what is contained within a 'plan' is that it could be taken to absolve the agent from responsibility for effects that he causes, but which are not strictly – theoretically – instrumental in achieving his aim. So, even though I foresee a very high probability that the bombs I drop will slaughter civilians, the fact that my 'plan' is to destroy a munitions factory, and that civilian deaths in no way cause that destruction, would be sufficient to establish the purity of my intention. Against this version of the doctrine of double effect, G. E. M. Anscombe has argued that an intention is not 'an interior act of the mind which [can] be produced at will . . . It is nonsense to pretend that you do not intend to do what is the means you take to your chosen end'.[53] Or, to be more precise: it is nonsense to pretend that we do not intend to cause *all* of the foreseen effects – even the non-instrumental ones – of our chosen means.

Initially, Donagan does not quite agree. Withholding himself from identifying what one intends with whatever one chooses to do, he merely concedes that we are responsible for all the effects that we voluntarily cause:

> In choosing to act according to a certain plan, a man chooses thereby to bring about *all* the causal consequences of doing so, whether or not they fall within the plan. He cannot escape responsibility for his choice by pleading that he did not desire or intend to do what he voluntarily did.[54]

That is to say, we are responsible – and may be culpable – for effects that we choose, even if we do not intend them. Later, however, Donagan makes the mistake of going beyond this to join Anscombe in equating what we choose to do and are responsible for with what we intend, and he extends intention to cover all the foreseen, naturally consequent effects of our voluntary action: 'whatever is done voluntarily is also . . . done intentionally'.[55] From this he infers that '[t]he distinction drawn by some post-Reformation Roman Catholic casuists between the directly and the indirectly voluntary, corresponding to what is intended as opposed to what is brought about voluntarily but unintentionally, is therefore untenable';[56] and he subsequently broadens his target when he attributes the notion that 'what lies outside the scope of a man's intentions in acting does not belong to his action, and so is not subject to moral judgement' to 'all forms of the theory of the double effect', Grisez's implicitly included.[57]

Grisez, of course, demurs. On the one hand, he agrees that '[w]e are responsible for more than just what we aim at and choose' and that 'one can bear responsibility for foreseen consequences which are no part of one's proposal [or plan]':[58]

> Since they are foreseen, these effects are voluntary. One could avoid them by not choosing what one chooses. One might not want them, but one does accept them. Thus, while primarily responsible for choices, which directly determine oneself and shape one's character, one is secondarily responsible for the foreseen consequences of carrying out one's choices.[59]

By admitting that moral responsibility extends to foreseen consequences that lie outside of one's chosen 'proposal' or 'plan', Grisez implies that what one 'accepts' as well as what one 'intends' – the foreseen effects of one's action that lie outside the 'plan' as well as within it – is relevant to the determination of the moral quality of the act in question. He implies that both require justification. This implication is then confirmed when he admits that right intention alone is not sufficient to secure the rightness of an act – it does not justify the acceptance of any foreseen side-effect. My intention to listen to music does not absolve me from responsibility for the foreseen side-effect of disturbing my neighbours in the middle of the night. Whether an act is right depends also on whether its side-effects are morally acceptable; and that depends on whether it observes 'the modes of responsibility' that forbid acting out of hostility toward or carelessness for human goods, and therefore unfairly or in dereliction of duty.[60] Thus far, Grisez concurs with Anscombe and Donagan: we are responsible, not only for the end we aim at (e.g. the destruction of a wicked enemy's munitions factory) and the effects we cause that are instrumental in realizing that aim (e.g. its collapse through bomb-blasts) – that is, for our 'plan' – but also for all the other foreseen effects that we cause at the same time (e.g. the deaths of civilians). *All* of these determine the moral quality of our act.

Grisez diverges, however, where he insists on maintaining a distinction between the responsibility we bear for the plan we choose and the responsibility we bear for the foreseen side-effects that we accept. 'Moral responsibility', he writes, 'is to be found first and foremost in one's choosing [of a plan]', because it is primarily in such choosing that one determines oneself.[61] This asymmetry of responsibilities is reflected in Grisez's consistent reservation of the vocabulary of choice to describe how we relate to our 'plan' – to describe our intending. Indeed, his use of language here serves to exaggerate the asymmetry by implying that we *only* attach our selves through our wills to what we intend, and that *only* through what we intend do we determine ourselves. The truth is, however, that we choose what we accept as well as what we intend; and that therefore we determine ourselves, not only in choosing a plan, but also in choosing to cause whatever non-instrumental effects are the inevitable concomitants of that plan. To shape ourselves well, it is not enough that our chosen end is good. Our acceptance of the evil effects of our chosen means must also be proportionate, fair, and faithful to our obligations.

Nevertheless, while Grisez is wrong to suggest that what we intend or plan is always more morally determinative than what we accept – and even that what we intend is the only determinant – he is correct to maintain a conceptual distinction between them. This is because sometimes our wills do relate differently to different foreseen effects that we cause. We want some; we do not want others. What we want and choose, we 'intend'. What we do not want but choose nevertheless, because we cannot have what we want without it, we merely 'accept' as a 'side-effect' – that is, as an effect beside our intention or *outside* our plan. Grisez gives us this example:

> a man, such as Jesus, who freely accepts certain death as a side effect of continuing to carry out his upright commitments does not choose to kill himself; thus he is not guilty of the destruction of his life. But a man who chooses to kill himself is guilty of the destruction of his life, even if he is killing himself for the sake of some human good which he rightly desires to serve.[62]

The plan that Jesus chooses – to carry out his upright commitments – is what he wants; whereas the evil side-effect of his chosen means – his death – he only tolerates reluctantly for the sake of what he wants. What he wants, he 'intends'. What he tolerates, he only 'accepts'.

This conceptual distinction is morally significant. Since evil effects comprise damage to something valuable, we ought not to want them – we ought not to 'intend' them. If we do choose to act in such a way that causes them, at very least we should choose with reluctance – we should only 'accept' them. If our reluctance is genuine, then it will not remain an interior phenomenon but will find expression, first in attempts to avoid the evil effects, then in enquiry about whether or not they are proportionate (for example, whether they undermine the instrumental effects), and finally in steps to minimise them. Our not wanting evil to result from our action is an important and necessary element of its possible rightness. It is not, however, sufficient. For our action to be morally justified, not only must the foreseen evil side-effects be 'accepted' with genuine reluctance; they must also be fair and faithful to existing obligations. Suppose, for example, a professor not long in his current post is offered a more attractive position in another university. Suppose that on balance he wants to move, and has sufficiently good reasons for doing so. Suppose also, however, that his current department will suffer damage, should he leave at this point. If his decision to take the new post is to be morally justified, it is certainly important that he should not want to cause damage, and that he should take steps to avoid or minimise it. But that is not enough; for it is also important that he should not be bound by any clear moral obligation to stay – for example, a promise made to see his department through a particular set of difficulties.

Sometimes, then, the distinction between what we intend and what we accept is morally significant and a necessary, if not sufficient, determinant of the moral quality of what we do. Or, to be more exact, sometimes there is good reason to mark a moral distinction between different effects that we cause by labelling some as 'intended' and others as 'accepted'. This is not always the case, however; for sometimes the effects of our action are too 'close', morally speaking, to be told apart.[63] When is that so?

Jonathan Bennett presents several possibilities. One is logical entailment. However, as Bennett points out, if this is what it takes to collapse morally significant distinctions, then some distinctions would survive intact that nobody wants. For example, a terrorist bomber would be able to argue that he intended only a state of affairs in which people's bodies are in such a condition as will cause a general belief that they are dead – which is all that is logically required by his aim of lowering enemy morale – and that the *actual* death of civilians was merely an unintended side-effect.[64] The latter is not logically entailed by the former.

Instead of this, Bennett himself argues that different outcomes of our action are too 'close' to be distinguished into intended and unintended effects when the distinction between them is 'inconceivable' or 'sheer fantasy'. The logical distinction between the appearance and the actuality of civilian deaths would seem to be one such; whereas a distinction between the destruction of a factory by a tactical (as distinct from a terrorist) bomber and the concomitant deaths of nearby civilians is not, since '[w]e can fairly easily imagine getting technology that would allow bombs to be aimed much more precisely'.[65] This is unsatisfactory, however, because Bennett lays down no clear boundary between what is 'fanciful' and what is 'imaginable'. After all, are not 'fantasies' 'imaginable'? In which case, surely the terrorist could sensibly be said to 'fairly easily imagine' an elaborate deception whereby civilians appear to be dead, but are not?

Later on, however, Bennett changes his terms. Instead of talking about inconceivability or fantasy, he talks of practical impossibility. On the one hand, there is the case where a bomber knows that he cannot destroy a factory without killing civilians. Here, Bennett implies, to describe such a bombing as not intending civilian deaths would be 'indefensible', because the practical impossibility of destroying the factory without killing civilians renders any moral distinction between intended and accepted effects specious. On the other hand, if those deaths are at all less than certain, and there is reasonable scope for trying to avoid or minimise them, or at least scope for hoping 'unfancifully' that they will not occur, then the bomber has 'a certain moral advantage which is possessed by *many* of those who foresee bad as a by-product of their means'.[66] What Bennett appears to be saying is that there are *some* cases where a moral distinction between intended means and foreseen side-effects makes sense – namely, where it seems that the occurrence of the latter is not actually inevitable – but that this fails to confirm the 'means principle' in the doctrine of double effect, which

> [i]n general . . . aims to contrast bad effects that are intended means to one's end with bad effects that are *inevitable* by-products of one's means. It is common ground throughout all this literature that one may intend M and only foresee B without intending it, even if it is (known to be) causally impossible to have M without B.[67]

The problem with Bennett's proposal is that there are cases where the evil side-effect is, to all practical intents and purposes, inevitable, and yet where it still seems inappropriate to describe it as 'intended'. Take a woman who interposes herself between her child and an attacking animal.[68] Her being mauled (if we suppose an animal large and fierce) is virtually inevitable, as she would foresee; but it would be odd to say that that is what she *intended*. Why? Because the word 'intend' connotes a certain positive willing, a desire for what is intended. To say that the woman intends to be mauled implies that that is what she wants; whereas presumably she hopes against hope (fancifully?) that it will not happen. Certainly, she is resolved to suffer mauling – to 'accept' it – if that is what it takes to protect her child, but she does not 'intend' it. Therefore it seems, *pace* Bennett, that a distinction between 'intended' and 'accepted' effects does make sense, even when the latter may be foreseen to be (virtually) inevitable; because it differentiates different dispositions of the will.

That this is so receives confirmation from the failure of Bennett's attempt to show that the distinction between intended and accepted effects is not supported by a distinction between dispositions of the will. He makes the attempt in terms of a comparison of two cases. In the first, there is a terrorist attack in which civilians are killed, in order to lower enemy morale and thereby to increase the likelihood of the enemy's capitulation.[69] In the second, there is a tactical attack in which a munitions factory is destroyed, in order to reduce the enemy's military capacity and thereby to increase the likelihood of the enemy's capitulation; but in which civilians living close to the factory are inevitably killed.[70] According to traditional double effect analysis, the terror and tactical bombers differ in what they 'hope for', what they would 'welcome', what they 'want': '[o]ne wants civilian deaths, though not for themselves, whereas the other does not want them at all'.[71] In other words, the terror bomber 'intends' civilian deaths as a means to his end, whereas the tactical bomber merely 'accepts' them as a foreseen-but-unintended side effect of what he intends. Although Bennett admits, without explaining, that 'there is truth in [this analysis]', he proceeds to try to subvert it. He argues that *both* bombers would 'welcome' – be 'glad' at – news of civilian deaths, the terror bomber because he needs this for his end, but the tactical bomber too because

> that is evidence that something has happened that he needs for his ultimate aim. Because the raid on the factory will inevitably kill many civilians if it succeeds in its purpose, it would be bad news for the tactical bomber if he heard that few civilians had died, for that would show that something had gone wrong – his bombs had not exploded, or had fallen in open countryside.[72]

The two bombers, according to Bennett, do not differ in 'how greatly glad they will be, or, therefore how greatly they will hope for and want civilian deaths'. Nor (oddly)[73] do they differ in their reluctance:

> The tactical bomber's wish for the [these] deaths is a reluctant one: if he could, he would destroy the factory without killing civilians. But the terror bomber too, if he could, would drop his bombs in such a way as to lower enemy morale without killing civilians.[74]

The tactical bomber is just as committed as the terror

bomber to pursuing a path that will inevitably lead to civilian deaths, so long as that is necessary to achieve his aim.[75] In sum, Bennett sees no moral difference in the quality of character – of willing – of the two bombers, such that it would make sense to say of one that he 'intended' the deaths of civilians, but of the other that he only 'accepted' them.

I think that Bennett is wrong here. His account does not do justice to the qualities of reluctance and regret that uniquely attach to the tactical bomber's willing, and which make it quite unfitting to talk of his 'wanting', 'hoping for', or 'gladness at' the news of civilian deaths. Those deaths gain him nothing. Even as evidence of the factory's destruction they are otiose; for presumably the primary evidence of that will be the rubble, not the corpses buried beneath it. Since they gain him nothing, this bomber does not 'want' civilian deaths. Indeed, before concluding that they are practically inevitable (and the certainty of practical inevitability is always less than that of logical necessity), he will have striven to find ways of avoiding them. Then when convinced of their inevitability, he will have thought again about whether the good he hopes to achieve would be worthy of their price, and about the likelihood of their being able to purchase it. Finally, having decided that civilian deaths are not too high a price to pay, he will have taken steps to minimise them. In contrast, it is not unfitting to say of the terrorist bomber that he 'wants', 'hopes for', and would 'be glad at' news of, civilians deaths, because they are *essential* to the success of his project in a way that is not so with that of his tactical counterpart. That this is so is shown by the fact that, far from trying to avoid or minimise civilian casualties, the terrorist will have striven to ensure and maximise them. In the light of this, the 'reluctance' that Bennett implicitly attributes to him must be of a highly theoretical kind, since it is nowhere evident in his actual behaviour.

The difference between the two bombers in the quality of their willing can be brought out by a counter-factual question, but this needs to be carefully phrased. 'If you could achieve your aim without killing civilians, would you?' will not do the job, because it allows the terror bomber to join the tactical bomber in giving an affirmative answer by appealing to a fantasy world where it is possible to lower enemy morale by producing the appearance of mass civilian deaths without the reality. Such a response expresses no commitment to strive to avoid and minimise those deaths *under current conditions*. Like his reluctance, the sincerity of the terror-bomber's answer is idle. A more effective question would therefore be, 'Suppose that your bombing fails to kill civilians, would you repeat it?' To this the terror bomber would give an unequivocal 'Yes!' The tactical bomber's response, on the other hand, would be tellingly qualified: 'Only if the factory had not been sufficiently destroyed.'[76]

Contrary to Bennett's analysis, then, we judge that the terror bomber is committed to kill civilians – he wills their deaths – in a way that the tactical bomber does not; that there is reason to say of the first that he 'intends' those deaths, but of the second that he only 'accepts' them; and that this indicates a difference of moral significance between the characters of the two agents. It follows, then, that we do not accept that the drawing of a moral distinction between an intended good effect and an unintended evil one is rendered invalid by the practical impossibility of separating them, any more than by their logical entailment or by the fanciful nature of their separation. None of these forms of 'closeness' collapses the moral distinction between what one intends and what one accepts. What does collapse the distinction, however, is the acceptance of evil that could have been avoided or minimised or that could have been foreseen to undermine the good end that is supposed to justify it; for this implies that the will of the one who accepts is not as pure as it purports to be. The relevant 'closeness', then, is that of an approximation between the evil effect and the agent's will – either because (notwithstanding his declaration to the contrary) the agent actually wants or intends it, or because it does not repel him sufficiently to take active steps to avoid or minimise it.[77]

Our response so far to the sixth objection has brought us to the following general conclusions. It is morally important to make a distinction between intended effects and unintended ones, insofar as this marks a difference in the disposition of the agent's will – insofar as it indicates that the agent wants the former, but only accepts the latter reluctantly. It matters that an agent should not want to cause evil. It matters for the moral integrity of his character, and this matters partly because damage to that integrity is damage to something of intrinsic value – an individual person who has the possibility of growing in virtue and thereby becoming fit for life beyond death – and partly because what an agent commits himself to want today shapes how he will be disposed to treat others tomorrow. It is, of course, important that the agent's reluctance to cause evil should be genuine. This means that he will not cause it needlessly, in the sense that it could have been avoided; nor will he cause it in vain, in the sense that it undermines the good effect for whose sake it is being tolerated. It also means that he will not cause more of it than he has to. What these considerations imply is that we are equally responsible for *all* the foreseen effects of the acts that we choose to perform, whether intended or accepted, because *both* kinds determine the moral quality of those acts and the moral quality of our character through them. If I accept needless, vain, or excessive evil, then at very least I have been culpably careless; at very worst I have actually wanted the evil that I have only pretended to accept. Either way, my irresponsible acceptance of evil could be such as to render my act immoral. However, even if there is a genuine moral distinction between my intending a good effect and my reluctantly accepting a concomitant evil effect, and even if my acceptance is necessary and proportionate, that alone is not sufficient to make my act morally permissible. For I must also ask whether it is fair to other people that I accept this evil and whether my doing so is in accord with my existing obligations. In other words, while a genuine moral distinction between what is intended and what is accepted is an important factor in deciding the moral quality of an act, it is still not a sufficient one.

Now let us bring these conclusions to bear directly on the two questions that originally provoked it. The first of these is this: Is there a reasonable, non-arbitrary way of distinguishing between an evil effect that is intended and one that is unintended or accepted? Our answer is clearly, 'Yes'. The distinction operates in terms of the disposition of the agent's will. An intended effect is one that is wanted. An accepted effect is not wanted, but is instead tolerated with an appropriate degree of manifest reluctance. Such a distinction can be reasonably made, because while a physical act or performance can be described in a variety of more or less equally legitimate ways, its intention cannot. Take again, for example, the case of the mother who interposes herself between her child and the bear. The mother's physical performance can be accurately described in all sorts of different ways – as an act of moving her legs or arms (to position herself between her child and the bear), or of crossing the road (that separates them from her), or of casting her child into shadow (since by placing herself between the child and the bear she also comes between the child and the sun). However, the fact that a single physical performance with a variety of aspects may be variously and fairly described, does not mean that any number of conflicting or mutually alternative intentions can be attributed to it with equal reason. Certainly, a single performance may enact a series of intentions (for example, to move one's leg, to cross the road, to intervene between the child and the bear); but the elements of the series are ordered one to another as means to ends, and the last in the series completes the meaning of its predecessors. Certainly, too, a single performance may enact separate intentions (to protect the child *and* to commit suicide). Nevertheless, the attribution of intentions to a performance is not arbitrary; it is done on the basis of reasons. So, given the general solicitude of mothers for children, and in the absence of evidence of suicidal tendencies in this particular case, when the mother interposes herself between her child and a bear, it is reasonable to presume that she intends the protection of her child. It would not be equally reasonable to presume that she intended her own mauling to death. Likewise, in the case of the tactical bomber. Provided that he has taken all reasonable measures to find ways of destroying the enemy's munitions factory without putting civilians at risk, that he has honestly and seriously considered whether the destruction of the factory is sufficiently important to warrant civilian casualties, and that he has sought to keep those casualties to minimum, it would be reasonable to attribute to him the intention of destroying the factory, while it would not be reasonable to attribute to him the intention of killing civilians.

Our response to the first part of the sixth objection, then, is that a reasonable distinction between intended and unintended effects can be made. What about the second part? Does such a distinction render gross irresponsibility morally permissible? To this we respond that it does so only if it is wrongly supposed that agents are not also responsible – accountable – for their acceptance of unintended effects, and if it is overlooked that this acceptance may sometimes be so irresponsible as to determine the act as wrong in spite of its pure intention, if not to call into question the declared purity of the intention itself.

Our discussion will not be complete until we return to the three sets of criticism from which the sixth objection was abstracted, and comment on them in the light of our responses to it. Using the illustration of the pot-holer case, John Harris argued that different descriptions of an act attribute greater causal directness to different aspects of it, and therefore warrant quite different accounts of that act's intention. His mistake here is to confuse the order of physical causality with that of intention: the fact that I act foreseeing that I shall thereby cause something directly does not

mean that I intend it. The different descriptions of the physical performance do not warrant different accounts of
intention.[78]

Mary Warnock complained against the doctrine of double
effect that one's intention cannot be separated from the foreseen effects of one's action. But the doctrine – as we now
understand it – does not separate them; it distinguishes
them. If acceptance of the evil effects of an action is culpably
negligent or malevolent (as must be so in the case of the
caretaker who continues to fill a family's drinking-water tank
despite being warned that the water supply has become
seriously polluted), then that raises doubts about the
protested purity of the agent's intention. And should the
purity of his intention withstand sceptical scrutiny, his will's
purity will not. For he is morally responsible both for what
he intends and for what he accepts.

Like Harris, Warnock also argued that the account of an
act's intention varies according to which of several legitimate descriptions of that act is selected. Certainly, a single
action may involve a series of intentions: I intend to put a
fork to the left of the mat, because I intend to get ready for
my dinner party, because I intend to foster an evening of
scintillating conviviality. In this one act, then, are enacted
several intentions that comprise a coherent series. Therefore,
while it is correct to say with Warnock that no single intention is the real (that is, the only) intention, it would be incorrect to say that no single series is the real series. Further, the
distinction between the various things that I intend and
those that I do not is clear enough. I may foresee that one of
my more sparkling guests might drink too much wine and
provoke an embarrassing quarrel, and when I invite him, I
accept that risk. Provided that my reasons for doing so are
strong enough (when he's on good form he really is the life
and soul of a party, and I reckon that I will be able to keep
control of the bottle), it would be quite incorrect, should my
worst fears be realised, to include among my intentions that
of staging a drunken brawl.

Finally, Jonathan Glover doubted that it is possible to arrive at any plausible criterion for defining an intended means, and for deciding what to include in it. In the light of our discussion above, he is right to dispute the candidacy of temporal closeness and of virtual inevitability; but he is wrong to presume that no better candidate can be found. Our proposal is that intended means can be clearly defined as whatever is strictly instrumental in relation to the wanted end – with the proviso that sometimes the acceptance of concomitant evil that is unnecessary or disproportionate will indicate that what is actually wanted is (at least) more morally ambiguous than first appeared.

Seventh objection: the intentional killing of the innocent is not intrinsically bad, and so should not be subject to an absolute prohibition

We have argued that sometimes, where it would be wrong to want someone dead, it may nevertheless be permissible to choose to act in such a way that is likely or certain to kill them – provided that one does not want their death, that one accepts it with a genuine and active reluctance, and that one's acceptance is proportionate, fair, and faithful. The question before us now is whether it is ever morally permissible to want someone dead and to intend to kill them. In order to work out a response, we must first analyse two important lines of reasoning that support the traditional prohibition of the intended killing of the innocent. We begin with the classic treatment by Thomas Aquinas, and then proceed to a contemporary one by Germain Grisez, whose discussion of the doctrine of double effect has been described even by one of his arch-opponents as '[o]ne of the most ranging and profound . . . developed with relentless consistency and subtlety'.[79]

Aquinas implies that not all intentional killing of human beings is wrong. He avers that members of a community who are 'dangerous or infectious' to other members may be killed by those with public authorisation;[80] and he makes no distinction here between killing that is intended and that which is unintended.[81] This appears to be because he does not hold it 'an evil in itself' to kill sinners, since in sinning a man 'falls away from the dignity of his manhood . . . and falls into the slavish state of the beasts'; and he implies that to kill a sinner is therefore no more evil than to kill a beast.[82] Provided that one intends the common good as one's end (and that one has public authorisation), one may intend a sinner's death as a means, because it is not 'evil in itself'.

However, when Aquinas comes to discuss whether it is permissible for a private individual to kill in self-defence, he changes his ground. Here, adumbrating the doctrine of double effect, he argues that one may kill the aggressor, but intend only self-preservation. The aggressor's death must be 'beside the intention'. The reason for this change of tack appears to be Aquinas' concern that the violence employed be strictly governed by the end of self-defence, and therefore that the motive of 'private animosity' be ruled out.[83] The implication of this is that intentional killing so involves private animosity that to exclude the latter we must prohibit the former. Yet Aquinas evidently does not regard the connection between the two as necessary; for he deems it possible for public officials to intend the deaths of sinners without being moved by animosity. Why, then, does he assume a connection in the case of self-defence? Two possible reasons present themselves. One is that the end of self-preservation provides human sinfulness with greater cover for selfishness than does the end of the common good; and so to be sure of excluding 'private animosity', we must entirely remove any ready cover. Another is that, since self-defence does not strictly require the death of the aggressor (only his incapacitation), if it is intended then it is bound to be expressive of animosity; whereas, since the death of someone who threatens the common good is necessary for its protection, to intend it is not necessarily to give animosity vent. To this latter point it could be objected that the death – as distinct from, say, the incarceration – of someone who poses a public menace is not necessary for the preservation of the public good. However, a cogent response would be that the death penalty might be necessary if a society cannot afford the expense of long-term imprisonment (or any other effective alternative), and if the menace is very grave.

It follows from Aquinas' reasoning about killing with public authorisation and in self-defence that the intentional killing of the innocent is always wrong. By definition the 'innocent' (or 'innocuous') are those who pose no threat to the common good – indeed, they preserve and forward it. Therefore there can be no good reason to kill them.[84]

This line of argument is one of those that Aquinas employs to rule out suicide: since an (innocent) member 'belongs' to his community – and presumably, therefore, owes it a duty of faithful service – his suicide would injure it. The other two arguments appeal to the duty of proper self-love and to God's monopoly of the authority to take life.[85]

Behind Aquinas' prohibition of the intentional killing of the innocent, then, lie three implicit claims: first, that intentional killing need not be motivated by an ill will; second, that it can therefore be justified as a means of serving the common good, including the defence of innocent neighbours against those threatening harm (the 'nocents'); but, third, that where killing is not strictly necessary for such an end – as in the case of the killing of innocents – to intend it is to give expression to malevolence.

Germain Grisez's line is simpler and significantly different. As he sees it, no one may ever intend to violate any basic human good, including that of life.[86] Permissible killing of any kind, therefore, must always be a proportionate side-effect of an act that intends to respect human goods. This applies equally to those acting in a public capacity and to those acting in a private one.[87]

Why does Grisez, unlike Aquinas, rule out all intentional killing? The answer lies in what Grisez means by 'intention'. As we saw in response to the previous objection, he thinks of 'intending' something as choosing a proposal or plan of action.[88] In so choosing, we commit ourselves to something, we identify ourselves with it; and in this commitment we determine ourselves.[89] In other words, through our intending we shape our character well or badly. And for Grisez, this is the crucial matter. In somewhat Kantian mode, he puts it thus:

> In morality good will – if it is genuine and persistent – is infinitely more important than good results. The reason is that choice is self-determination. In choosing to adopt one or another course of action one not only sets oneself into motion for the measurable time the action takes and one not only commits oneself to the use of a certain amount of energy and possessions. One also, and first of all, makes oneself be a certain kind of person . . .[90]

Or, in more biblical terms: '. . . the morality of actions depends more on the heart from which they flow than on the results to which they lead'.[91]

Granted, then, that to intend something is to shape one's character for good or ill, why does Grisez suppose that intending someone's death is always self-corrupting? One can intend death in two ways, either as an end or as a means. To intend it as an end is to want someone dead simply and for no ulterior reason. The motive here would be an equivalent of Aquinas' 'private animosity': some species of 'hostility' – hatred, anger, resentment, distaste, impatience – which leads the agent to regard the life of his would-be victim as an evil.[92] The paradigmatic instances of this would be murderous crimes of passion, lethal acts of vengeance, or killing out of racial hatred.

Grisez would agree with Aquinas that to intend to kill someone as a means to some good – say, the common good – rather than as an end in itself, need not involve hostile emotions at all. Nevertheless, against Aquinas, he considers it wrong. As he sees it, this is because, surrendering to a preponderant emotion or desire, one subordinates one good (say, the life of the victim) to another (say, that person's relief from pain or another person's life) when there is no reasonable basis for such a hierarchy of value.[93] Both are goods and there is no rational way of weighing them against each other, determining that one is more valuable than another, and so deciding that killing would be better (the lesser evil) than foregoing what it would achieve.[94] This is not just an intellectual error, however, it is also a moral failing. The choice to deprive someone of the intrinsic good of life as a means to some other end, is a failure to will the 'integral fulfilment' or 'complete good' either of that person[95] or of that person together with all others – a failure of 'volitional love'.[96] And this remains the case, even if killing someone is motivated by feelings of sympathy or care, and its ulterior end is to release or prevent them from suffering.[97] In this sense 'the act of a wife who reluctantly gives a lethal dose of drugs to her terminally ill husband after he has begged her repeatedly to do so' has the character of 'malice'.[98] Likewise, the act of a spy who kills himself to 'avoid torture and prevent the enemy from acquiring secret information which would cost many lives'.[99]

So, according to Grisez, to intend to take someone's life, even as means to a good end, is intrinsically wrong. This is basically because it involves a failure of volitional love or commitment to complete well-being – a failure brought on by an irresponsible capitulation to emotion, whether hostile or sympathetic, which expresses itself in an irrational subordination of the good of life to some other good. The qualification of 'love' with 'volitional' here indicates that what is decisive in making morally wrong an intentional act of killing, according to Grisez, are not the emotional motives (e.g. hatred, indifference, sympathy). These incline the will, but it is the will that decides to capitulate or not. What makes an act of killing wrong, then, is that it enacts a commitment wherein the will has turned against complete human well-being or 'integral human fulfilment', by irrationally preferring some goods to others. The validity of

Grisez's absolute prohibition of intentional killing depends, then, on the validity of his claim that a fully rational commitment to integral human fulfilment cannot permit any partiality regarding its components. This calls for closer scrutiny.

Grisez defines integral human fulfilment as 'a single system in which all the goods of human persons would contribute to the fulfilment of the whole community of persons'.[100] It is an ideal that will be realised, not in this imperfect world, but in heaven.[101] Its 'more-than-human' ground is God, who will recreate all things in Jesus.[102] Knowledge of its possibility, therefore, depends on faith – although 'a generous and reasonable love of human goods' will lead one to act in a manner consonant with it.[103] Integral human fulfilment is therefore not 'a definite goal to be pursued as a concrete objective of cooperative human effort'.[104] Rather, it is an ideal to which we ought always to 'maintain a constant disposition', a 'constant openness'.[105]

Grisez's concept of integral human fulfilment stands in judgement upon consequentialism (or utilitarianism) – the approach to moral decision-making that pretends to be able to calculate the amounts of good and evil that various options for action will produce, to weigh them against each other, and then to identify which one will achieve the overall maximal good and the minimal evil; and that holds that such deliberation is *all* that is required to determine the rightness or wrongness of an act. In the light of the ideal of the complete human good, the basic theological flaw of consequentialism is exposed: '[i]t confuses human responsibility with God's responsibility. We, however, are not responsible for the overall greater good and lesser evil – the good and evil of "generally and in the long run" – for only God knows what they are.'[106] The consequentialist is able to pretend to know what they are only either by doing violence to the complex human good by reducing it to a single category – say, sensible pleasure[107] – so that like may be weighed against like; or by claiming to employ a 'calculus' for weighing different kinds of good against each other that really amounts to nothing more than an obscure intuitionism, an uncritical conventionalism, or an arbitrary wilfulness.[108]

Much of what Grisez says here is correct and important. It is surely true that the fulfilment of each human person together with all others – and let us not forget the dead – is something well beyond human achieving. It is also true that consequentialism's closest approximation to such fulfilment amounts to an arbitrary privileging of some goods or persons over others; and that, from a theological point of view, this looks very much like an atheistic attempt – as reckless as it is impatient – to seize the Kingdom of God and drag it into history. Faith in the God who raised Jesus from the dead, however, fosters the hope that fulfilment that is beyond human engineering might yet be possible. Thus it renders rational an acceptance of the constraints upon human beneficence, which acceptance, being hopeful rather than merely disillusioned, is nevertheless eager to achieve whatever it may. In this way Grisez makes a thoroughly appropriate Christian theological impression on the understanding of moral life. So far, so unobjectionable.

The objectionable part comes when Grisez proceeds to argue that the virtue of faithful openness to the divine possibility of integral human fulfilment requires us to avoid choosing against any good.[109] To choose against a good, he tells us, is to treat it as 'nongood (or as less good than it seemed)', to deafen oneself 'to an appeal to which no one can possibly be deaf, because it comes from within oneself', to 'set up an idol' by asserting that the good is limited to what humans actually attain, to fail to be open to God.[110] So, for example, to choose to attack human life is to treat it only as an instrumental rather than an intrinsic good and also (he implies) to turn against the hope that the doctrine of the resurrection inspires.[111]

There are two problems with this. The first is the ambiguity of the notion of 'choosing to act against' something. As we have argued above in response to the previous objection,

I choose to act against something both when I intend or want to do it damage, *and also* when I accept the unwanted damage that will probably or inevitably occur as a side-effect of my intended means. The former is always wrong; the latter might be permissible. In his discussion of what faithful openness precludes, Grisez muddies the waters by failing to distinguish clearly between these two kinds of 'choosing against', and by offering a permissible instance as an example of the immoral kind. This is the case of the spy who kills himself to 'avoid torture and prevent the enemy from acquiring secret information which would cost many lives'.[112] *Pace* Grisez, in choosing to end his life the spy does not necessarily regard it as a 'nongood' and deafen himself to its appeal. On the contrary, he might value it highly and wish that he could hold onto it. It is just that, in the circumstances, he feels that his obligation to other people tragically requires him to lay it down. In other words, he does not want his own death – he does not intend it – but he does accept it reluctantly (he has searched desperately for viable alternatives) as the inevitable side-effect of rendering himself incapable of betraying others and putting them at serious risk; and his acceptance is proportionate, not because his one life is 'worth' less than many others (perhaps God has dignified him with a vocation far more important than those of all the others put together), but because he is bound by a duty – by faithfulness – not to betray even one other person.

So much for the wrong turning. Let us return to the main road. Instead of telling us that the virtue of openness requires us to avoid choosing against any good, Grisez should have said that it requires us either to avoid intending damage to a good (whether as an end or as a means), or to avoid accepting it without due reluctance, disproportionately, or in derogation of an obligation. Then the question becomes: does faithful openness imply that it can never be rational – proportionate – to accept damage to one good for the sake of another? Our answer to this will expose the second problem with Grisez's interpretation of the implications of integral human fulfilment.

Grisez does not actually deny that there is a hierarchy of value. 'Instrumental' goods (such as money and property) are extrinsic to human fulfilment; they can be obstacles as well as means. The 'sentient' goods of sensible satisfaction (such as the pleasure of eating) are intrinsic, but less valuable than 'substantive' goods (that is, life and health, knowledge of truth and appreciation of beauty, and skilful performance at work or play).[113] Likewise, these substantive goods are less valuable than 'existential' or 'spiritual' goods (that is, self-integration, practical reasonableness, justice and friendship, and religion);[114] and among these existential goods, the religious dimension is 'most important'.[115]

Nor does Grisez say that difference in status may never be a reason to prefer the higher to the lower. When a choice must be made between them, both substantive and existential goods should be preferred to instrumental ones,[116] to sensible ones, or to the avoidance of sensible evils – so the good of healthy teeth should 'override' an aversion to painful dental treatment.[117]

However, since both substantive and existential goods are equally 'essential and closely related aspects'[118] of human fulfilment 'as a whole'[119] – that is, since they are both 'intelligible' goods – one can never have a good reason to choose to destroy, damage, or impede any one of *them* for the sake of another.[120] What, then, do we do when faced with a tragic situation where we cannot maintain one without, in effect, damaging another – when we cannot avoid choosing between them? Grisez denies, of course, that we can make the choice by any kind of quasi-quantitative comparative 'weighing'. Take, for example, the case of the pregnant mother who cannot save her own life except by aborting her child. There is no sufficiently rational way of comparing the value of the two lives so as to warrant the conclusion that one 'outweighs' the other. Such a case should be decided, Grisez tells us, not by any pseudo-calculus, but by reference to absolute moral norms – for example, to the Golden Rule of fairness ('treat others as you would have them treat you') or to 'faithfulness'.[121] Accordingly, it would not be unreasonable for the mother to prefer to die with her child rather than abort it, on the ground that unfaithfulness is 'a greater evil' than accepting the risk of a natural disaster in which she and the baby will both die.[122] In choices between intelligible goods, then, decisions should be made by appeal to the decisive authority of norms drawn from existential goods. Fairness is the virtue that corresponds to a specification of the existential good of practical reasonableness (the so-called 'fifth mode of responsibility': 'One should not, in response to different feelings toward different persons, willingly proceed with a preference for anyone unless the preference is required by intelligible goods themselves').[123] 'Faithfulness' in general is a constitutive feature of the existential goods of interpersonal friendship and of religion (that is, friendship with God); and more particularly it is also the virtue that corresponds to another specification of practical reasonableness (the 'fourth mode of responsibility': 'One should not choose to act out of an emotional aversion except as part of one's avoidance of some intelligible evil other than the inner tension experienced in enduring that aversion')[124] as this has been transformed by Christian faith ('[One should] endure fearlessly whatever is necessary or useful for the fulfilment of one's personal vocation').[125]

Grisez's account of intelligible goods and his prohibition of any preference among them provoke a number of objections. First, while we should not intend damage to any intrinsic good as a means to any other – we should not *want* to do harm – we may accept damage, *if* it is proportionate. Such acceptance would be proportionate where the good to be damaged is less intrinsically valuable than the good to be served. Grisez denies that we can ever say such a thing of an intelligible good, for all intelligible goods are *equally* basic. We dispute this, however. It seems reasonable to us to prefer at least one of Grisez's intrinsic, intelligible goods – human

life – to one other – skilful performance at play. Jean Porter
provides the illustration:

> During the Superbowl, the police in Dallas are told that
> a bomb has been planted in the stadium, and it will go
> off at half-time. Imagine further that the police have
> every reason to believe that this is no hoax; there really
> is a bomb, a big bomb, and if it goes off there will be a
> tremendous loss of life. Can the police stop the game
> and evacuate the stadium? If we apply the logic of the
> Grisez/Finnis analysis of morality, they cannot. The
> football game in progress is an instantiation of the basic
> good of a skilled performance, and as such, it cannot be
> destroyed or impeded, even to avert a threat to the
> basic good of life.[126]

Surely the difference in value between human life and a
game of sports should be sufficiently clear to justify a
straightforward preference of one over the other?

Second, in Chapter Two we disputed Grisez's claim that
human bodily life is an intrinsic good, while we agree that it
is a basic one. It is true that it is not instrumental in the sense
of being a purely extrinsic means. Unlike money or property,
bodily life is the *conditio sine qua non* of the intrinsic goods
that grow from it, and such a one that whatever grows from
it must continue to participate in it. That is why it makes
sense to say that human fulfilment is bodily, but not to say
that it is monetary. Nevertheless, human bodily life is instrumental, albeit in a unique fashion. It does not continue to
have an intrinsic value when, through severe brain damage
or intense and relentless pain, it lacks irremediably the
power to enable other forms of human flourishing such as
friendship. Therefore, when bodily life has become permanently incapable of sustaining someone's capacity for participating in intrinsic goods – her capacity for responsible life –
it would be proportionate to choose to end it, whether in
order to release relatives from emotional limbo or scarce

health-care resources for the service of other, responsible human beings.

Finally, Grisez takes the view that the avoidance of pain, or relief from it, can never be a sufficient reason for acting against an intelligible good. Presumably, what he has in mind here are cases of taking life, whether in suicide or euthanasia, in order to avoid or end suffering. One reason for his stance is his belief that faithfulness to one's vocation as a Christian entails the duty to endure *all* suffering as a sharing in the redemptive suffering of Christ:

> [t]he Christian must be utterly carefree . . . with joy in suffering because it is a way of sharing here and now in everlasting fulfilment. Hence, the law of the cross links self-denial and the taking up of one's cross in the fulfilment of each Christian's personal vocation.[127]

We have already explained in Chapter Two why we dissent from this view.[128] The second argument that Grisez offers for denying that the avoidance of pain can ever be a sufficient justification for taking life begins with the valid statement that '*in general* the experience of pain . . . belongs to a healthy organism as part of its survival equipment'; but then it leaps to the highly dubious one, '*Thus* pain does not have the character of privation, and so it is not intelligibly bad.'[129] While it is true that pain does not always involve the deprivation of substantive and existential goods and so is not always 'intelligibly bad', there are nevertheless occasions when it does involve such deprivation, weakening or virtually eliminating one's capacity for friendship or intellectual activity or aesthetic appreciation. Timothy Chappell puts the point well:

> it is surely true that pain of any considerable intensity, while it lasts, deprives humans of any chance of integral human fulfilment. . . . It is not, as Grisez seems to think, that there is something self-centred about being prepared to attend to pain. On the contrary, the

impossibility of attending to anything else during
severe pain is – partly – what makes pain such a bad
thing.[130]

What this implies is that where intense pain is so exhausting
and all-absorbing as to render someone incapable of responsible life, and where there is no prospect of recovery, suffering has ceased to have a point; in which case there remains
no good reason not to end it.

From our critical analysis of Aquinas' and Grisez's reasoning about the taking of human life, we now move immediately to a brief summary of the rationales that they offer for
the prohibition of the intentional killing of the innocent,
and subsequently to an evaluation. For Aquinas the reason
for the rule is that those who are not a threat to a community (the 'innocent') are a support to it ('the life of righteous
men preserves and forwards the common good')[131] and
underneath this may well lie the Christian eudaimonist
assumption that individuals fulfil themselves in the service
of others. For Grisez, one may not intend to kill the innocent
because to do so would corrupt one's own character by
enacting and confirming either hostility or a failure of volitional love; nor may one accept their death for the sake of
some other good without arbitrarily degrading the value of
their lives.

How cogent are these reasons, when brought to bear on
the kinds of case that concern us – cases where patients
intend to kill themselves or have themselves killed, or where
doctors help patients to commit suicide or kill them with
their consent? No one, whether health-care professional or
relative, should intend to kill a patient out of animosity or
hostility or resentment or contempt or impatience. Nor
should patients commit suicide out of a self-hatred born of
shame and despair, since (at least from a Christian point of
view) nothing that can be repented of is beyond forgiveness,
and the pride that prevents repentance is a destructive vice.

In sum, no one should intend – want – the death of a (responsible) person as an end in itself.

Nor should one intend it as a means. No good end can justify wanting a responsible human being dead – not the relief of relatives' or nurses' or doctors' distress, nor efficiency in the use of scarce health-care resources. Valuable though such relief or efficiency are, they are not commensurable with the life of a responsible human individual; and the decision to sacrifice the latter for the former would be arbitrary in content and reckless in form.

On the other hand, it might be proportionate to accept the risk of a patient's death – and should the gamble fail, the fact of it – in order to relieve her pain and thereby restore her to some form of responsible life. One condition of this is that the level of pain be so severe as to require the administration of a risky dose of analgesic drugs. Another would be the unavailability of any other means of pain-relief that is at once equally effective and less risky.

There remain, however, cases of patients whose continuing biological life can no longer sustain responsible life and its participation in intrinsic goods. This might be because of severe brain damage, or because of pain so severe as to overwhelm responsible life and to require analgesic palliation no less overwhelming. Unless biological life and the sheer enduring of pain have intrinsic value, which we doubt, there do not appear to be reasons why, in such cases and all other considerations apart, patients should not intend their own deaths and doctors should not assist in their suicide or kill them.

To permit this, of course, would offend against Aquinas' prohibition of the intentional killing of the innocent. Like all moral rules, this one has in mind certain exemplary situations – paradigmatic cases – where it clearly applies.[132] It presupposes a case where a malevolent aggressor deliberately does lethal harm to a responsible member of society, who is posing no threat to others. But the cases where we think that the intention to kill could be right are ones where the human being to be killed is permanently incapable of responsibility. These are not cases to which the rule against killing the innocent clearly applies, since they differ in a morally crucial respect from the paradigm.[133]

To permit the intentional killing of patients permanently incapable of responsible life would also offend against Grisez's absolute prohibition of the intention to take human life. In the cases that we envisage, killing is not an expression of hostility in any of its forms. It is, however, the expression of a preference among goods, that is, of a choice to promote the health of some, responsible human beings (by relieving their considerable emotional distress or by channelling health-care resources in their direction) at the expense of other, non-responsible ones. Unlike Grisez, we do not regard it as irrational to prefer the health of responsible humans to the survival of those who have been permanently reduced to a biological level of existence.

Our critical analysis of two major rationales for the prohibition of the intentional killing of the innocent, therefore, leads us to the provisional conclusion that it is untenable as a universal rule applicable to all cases. Our conclusion is provisional, because there may yet be other, wider social considerations that will cause us to retreat from it. For the time being, however, we hold that it can be morally permissible to intend to kill human beings who pose no threat to anyone else, on condition that they are irreparably bereft of the capacity to engage in responsible life. Perhaps at this point it would be salutary to recall that we conceive such life in terms less stereotypically male and self-assertive than those of Rachels' 'biographical' life, and as encompassing participation in friendship and the performance of any good service, even in the passive forms of appreciating what is good and beautiful and of being a sign of truth and hope.

The position at which we have provisionally arrived, then, does amount to a concession to the critics of the doctrine of double effect, insofar as that presupposes the ruling out of all intentional taking of human life. Notwithstanding this, our stance meets with a significant measure of corroboration from a wide range of contemporary Christian ethicists. In order to demonstrate this support, as well as to illuminate our position by comparative light, we will now proceed to locate it on the map of contemporary Christian ethics.

It is least surprising that support should be forthcoming from Protestant circles, where, with the egregious exception of Paul Ramsey, the doctrine of double effect has found little favour. This has much to do with the post-Kantian Protestant suspicion of the eudaimonist structure of Thomist moral theology, according to which the ultimate rationale for moral action is that it promotes, or is at least consonant with, the achievement of the individual's *eudaimonia* or well-being. Protestants are wont to suspect this partly because of its non-biblical, ancient philosophical provenance; but also because it gives moral endorsement to a certain kind of self-love, and even accords it priority over love for one's neighbour.[134] Hence James Gustafson, considering the case of suicide as self-sacrifice for the sake of others, writes:

> The principle of double effect would require . . . that . . . suicide not be a means in an extended sequence of causality for the desired effect. This, like the intention sincerely not to desire the evil effect, only the good, is a distinction made for the sake of preserving the moral rectitude of the agent. . . . I believe this is a questionable consideration in the circumstances one can imagine here; the morally proper concern is not for the self but for the other.[135]

It should be clear from the initial sections of this chapter that this is not a point of view that we share. We do not regard a concern for the agent's moral rectitude – the purity of his intention – and a concern for other people to be alternatives: as I intend today, so will I be disposed to act – and affect others – tomorrow. Putting this aside, however, Gustafson's position approximates our own in three important respects. First, he denies that the preservation of life is an end in itself, arguing that '[i]ts almost absolute value stems from the fact that it is the condition sine qua non for the individual to value anything else and to make contributions as a participant in life'.[136] Second, he denies that there is an obligation to endure unbearable and irremediable suffering.[137] And third, he contends that 'for all too many persons there are good and realistic grounds for the deepest despair',[138] and that where someone faces suffering that is 'reasonably perceived' to be unbearable and beyond relief, and has 'no other reasonable choice', (intentional) suicide can be 'morally proper'.[139]

To this our own position would add two qualifications. The first is that while of course there is no obligation to bear what cannot be borne – we cannot be obliged to do the impossible – we ought not to take what purports to be 'unbearable suffering' at face value. This is because often what makes suffering intolerable is not physical pain pure and simple, but the social isolation of the sufferer, which renders his pain pointless. Sometimes, therefore, to be reminded of a social obligation can render bearable what would otherwise not be. The moral demands of obligation do not tie merely by constraining. They also tie by (re)connecting to society, thereby conferring social significance upon the one who is bound. In binding, then, obligation can also save. Our second qualification is that despair of relief short of death should be distinguished from despair in God. That this is not an idle, academic distinction is shown by the example of Henning von Tresckow, who took part in the July 1944 plot to assassinate Hitler. When news came through that the attack had failed, von Tresckow decided to take his own life because he had no confidence in his capacity to withhold the names of his accomplices under torture.[140] As he took his final leave of a friend, before driving out into no-man's land to blow himself up with a hand-grenade, he said this:

> When, in a few hours' time, I go before God to account

for what I have done and left undone, I know I will be able to justify in good conscience what I did in the struggle against Hitler. God promised Abraham that He would not destroy Sodom if just ten righteous men could be found in the city, and so I hope that for our sake God will not destroy Germany. None of us can bewail his own death; those who consented to join our circle put on the robe of Nessus. A human being's moral integrity begins when he is prepared to sacrifice his life for his convictions.[141]

There are different kinds of despair, and sometimes their differences are morally significant. Presumably despair of God (and especially of his will and power to revive good things that have perished) is one kind that Christians could not with integrity regard as morally right, no matter how sympathetically they might view those who succumb to it. However, other kinds of despair – say, of one's own natural capacity to withstand torture and resist the temptation to betray one's friends – they might well deem realistic, not lacking in faith, and therefore morally responsible.[142]

It is to Karl Barth that Gustafson appeals when he denies that human life is an ultimate value.[143] '[H]uman life has no absolute greatness or supreme value,' says Barth, '. . . it is not a kind of second god . . . [L]ife is a loan from God entrusted to man for His service'.[144] Initially, he infers from this only that sometimes we should not will its continuation at all costs, we may be ordered to risk and expose it, and we should earnestly will the termination of our temporal existence but without 'actually encompassing or effecting it'.[145] This affirmation of a readiness for self-sacrifice falls significantly short of sanctioning a form of suicide, which he explicitly refers to as 'self-murder',[146] associates with a rebellious self-sovereignty or autonomy, and describes as 'frivolous', 'arbitrary'[147] and motivated by despair at our failure 'to make something significant of ourselves'.[148] Nevertheless, before Barth finishes his treatment of this topic, he admits that '[n]ot every act of self-destruction is as such suicide in this sense'.[149] There is the (rare) possibility of suicide that is faithful to God – that God might command someone to *'cause that he should possibly or even certainly die or be put to death'*.[150] This could never be motivated by 'negligence or arrogance, or imprudent or unnecessary readiness for risk'[151] and would intend 'self-offering' rather than 'the taking of one's own life'.[152] In support, Barth observes that 'in the Bible suicide [as such] is nowhere explicitly forbidden';[153] and that even Augustine, while rightly wanting to exclude the taking of one's own life 'merely to escape from temporal troubles, or for fear of the threat of others' sins, or in despair at his own sins, or out of longing for death', nevertheless kept ranks with Eusebius of Caesarea, Jerome, and Chrysostom in allowing the possibility of obedient suicide.[154] With regard to voluntary euthanasia, in contrast, Barth's denial of moral legitimacy is absolute. The reasons he gives are that 'it is for God and God alone to make an end of human life',[155] the impossibility of knowing that 'even the life afflicted with the severest suffering has ceased to be the blessing which God intends for this person',[156] the questionable motivation of relatives, and the compromising of the medical profession's vocation to be 'the unconditional and indefatigable servant of life'.[157]

Clearly, Barth's position on euthanasia differs in certain respects from our own. Against him, we point out the ambiguity of the assertion that it is for God alone to make an end of human life. On the one hand, this could mean that God alone can *authorise* killing. That is true, but it does not support Barth's stance here, since it does not answer the question, Might God ever authorise voluntary euthanasia? On the other hand, Barth's assertion could mean that God alone *has the right actually to take* human life. That would support his absolute prohibition of euthanasia, but it is not consistent with his admission elsewhere of cases where the deliberate taking of life by some human beings from others might be commanded by God and therefore be morally legitimate.

Further, if by 'the blessing that God intends for a person' we understand some form of specifically human flourishing, then we have explained why we think that there are in fact good reasons for supposing that human being permanently bereft of the capacity for responsible life has ceased to be such a blessing. With regard to Barth's discussion of suicide, we believe that it would have benefited from the making of distinctions between what one intends, what one accepts, and what one causes. We also think that the explication of the conditions of morally responsible self-killing could have gone beyond the statement of impermissible motives to the presentation of examples of the proportionate acceptance of one's own death. Notwithstanding these differences, however, Barth's thinking tends to agree with ours on two major points: that human life – at least in its merely biological form – is not an absolute, intrinsic value that may never be deliberately harmed; and that there might be morally responsible cases of self-killing.

Although it can hardly be characterised as Protestant, Alan Donagan's analysis of the issue of suicide is certainly Kantian. As his basic moral principle, he holds that respect for human beings as rational ends-in-themselves is preferable to Grisez's Thomistic principle of respect for basic human goods (including life) as inviolable – partly because the latter can permit the use of deadly violence in defence of the innocent only by invoking the (as he judges it) flawed doctrine of double effect, which he supposes (wrongly) to assert 'that what lies outside the scope of a man's intentions in acting does not belong to his action, and so is not subject to moral judgment'.[158] Applied to the issue of homicide, Donagan's Kantian principle of respect issues in the rule that one may not kill in such a fashion as to degrade the killed to the status of 'a mere manipulated means'[159] – which does not exclude suicide as such, since that can hardly be against the will of the person killed.[160] The principle itself, however, does prohibit those forms of suicide that 'hold one's life cheap, as something to be taken at will'.[161] Nevertheless, the possibility of morally permissible suicide remains, Donagan suggests, in cases where it is necessary to ensure the lives or fundamental well-being of others, to spare them excessive burdens, and to save oneself from a life that has become 'not merely hard to bear, but utterly dehumanised' – that is, from a condition where 'a genuinely human life will cease before biological death'.[162]

About Donagan's conclusions we have only one reservation: we doubt the proportionality of accepting the death of a *responsible* human being in order to spare others 'excessive burdens' that amount to something less than a threat to their lives. We have further reservations, however, both about the content of the basic, Kantian principle underlying Donagan's reasoning, and about one direction in which that reasoning could be extended. To take the second point first, the principle of respect for human being as a rational end-in-itself places the value of 'autonomy' at centre-stage.[163] This could be read as implying that the human good consists more in individual self-determination than in relationships of love, and that a condition of dependence on other people is 'dehumanising' and therefore a sufficient ground for suicide. While this might be true of some such conditions, it is not true of all. Certain forms of dependence are perfectly natural to human creatures, and learning to live with them and in them is part of growing into human maturity. The second, more fundamental problem is that whereas Donagan presents the principle of respect for human beings as ends-in-themselves as a superior alternative to that of respect for human goods, he is unable to explicate the former without covertly appealing to – and ordering – the latter. The object of the respect that he enjoins equivocates between someone's well-being *as that person subjectively sees it*, and his well-being *as it objectively is and as others may judge it*. The first conception limits respect's proper object to the autonomy of others; the second broadens its scope to encompass other goods – and transforms the principle of respect into one of beneficence. This surreptitious move away from Kant and back to Aquinas is confirmed by Donagan's explicit acknowledgement that the human good is richer and more complex than simple autonomy: 'human well-being is a matter of human flourishing: that is, of the development and exercise of human *potentialities*'.[164]

The ambiguity and indeterminacy of Donagan's principle of respect – in particular, what it means to treat someone as a 'means' – is the subject of a complaint by Richard McCormick.[165] McCormick prefers to take an openly Thomist route, and thinks of what is moral explicitly in terms of maintaining and promoting human goods. Unlike Grisez, however, he is a 'proportionalist', holding that there is nothing morally wrong as such with intending non-moral evil (e.g. someone's death) as a means, since it does not necessarily involve turning one's heart against a basic good.[166] It is only wrong – it only expresses an evil will – if it lacks 'proportionate reason', that is, if it is not the only way of protecting a higher good, if it is not strictly ordered or proportioned to that end, and if it undermines that protection in the long term.[167] McCormick claims, *pace* Grisez, that estimating proportion or 'commensurating' need not amount to the weighing of rival quantities of good and evil, but can take the form of measuring the relation of means to the end[168] – say, by testing whether the means produces more evil than achieving the end strictly requires, or whether the evil effect subverts that achievement. Nevertheless, he evidently does believe that there are cases where it is reasonable or proportionate to choose some goods as 'outweighing' others. If one has to choose between saving more or saving fewer instances of the same basic good – say, human life – then, all other things being equal, it is reasonable or proportionate to choose to save the greater number: 'This is the instance where both mother and fetus will die without an abortion but where at least the mother can be saved with an abortion. It is also the case of the drowning swimmer where the hopeful rescuer cannot be of help because he cannot swim.'[169] McCormick also believes in a hierarchy among the goods, which makes certain choices of greater over lesser reasonable. For example, 'one sacrifices the instrumental for the basic, because instrumental goods are lesser in the order of goods. Thus one prefers life to property.'[170] While on some occasions he denies that such a preference could be reasonable among 'basic goods',[171] on others he affirms that it is. So he tells us that while life is a basic good, it is still only relative in value and 'to be preserved precisely as the condition of other values'.[172] These other values, to which life is implicitly subservient, are pre-eminently relational, for 'the meaning, substance, and consummation of life are found in human *relationships*, and the qualities of justice, respect, concern, compassion, and support that surround them'.[173] Therefore, in cases where the struggle for survival so dehumanises people that their potential for human relationships is 'totally absent' or 'totally subordinated', there is no duty to preserve life and, McCormick implies, it could be permissible to take it (intentionally).[174] It is important to note here, however, that McCormick explicitly denies that dependence as such is dehumanising. In contrast to Rachels and to a certain development of Donagan, he deliberately affirms the 'passive virtues' of meekness, humility, and patience, and urges that dependence be seen 'as essential to our notion of human dignity'.[175] Beyond cases of choosing between more rather than fewer instances of the same basic good, or where a rational preference can be made between different basic goods, there are also those where a choice must be made between two basic goods that are equally valuable – for example, where either I save my life at your expense, or I save yours at mine – and where it therefore cannot be made in terms either of greater number or of greater value. Here McCormick advises that the dilemma be resolved in favour of my self-sacrifice, not because my life is reckoned less valuable than yours, but because that is what is required if I am to mature as a human being in a world of sin and weakness.[176] What he is invoking (although, tellingly, he does not quite call it by its proper name) is the duty of charity – which seems akin to Grisez's duty of faithfulness.

McCormick's equivocation at this point is symptomatic of a reluctance to affirm deontological elements, which we consider a weakness. Otherwise, the only point where we diverge from him is over the intending of death as a means. Insofar as to intend is to want, we hold that one should never intend the death of a responsible human being either as an end in itself (say, out of vengeance) or as a means to something else (say, out of callous ruthlessness). The blood of malevolence runs cold as well as hot. One may, however, *accept* death with proportionate reason.

Lisa Sowle Cahill invokes McCormick in the course of her own argument that biological life deserves to be preserved *insofar* as it is able to ground other human values, pre-eminently 'the love of God achieved at least in part through love of other persons'.[177] She also appeals to Aquinas, or at least those parts of his corpus where he affirms the proper subordination of a human being's physical nature to his rational or spiritual one.[178] However, against Aquinas' (Aristotelian) assertion that death is 'the ultimate and most fearsome evil of this life',[179] she contends that while 'death for the Christian is never an unambiguous good . . . it is sometimes a lesser evil than the evil of suffering, and is . . . a good in a limited but positive sense'.[180] This is because physical pain, together with mental exhaustion or sedation, can sometimes be disintegrating, making it difficult 'to sustain a vital concern for the needs of loved family members and friends'.[181] Accordingly, if continued life looks set to detract from the fulfilment of a person's primary duty to love God and her neighbour, and if the active appropriation of death can be understood as an act of obedience to God and charity to others, then it is permissible actively to kill.[182] The rule against the direct or intentional killing of the innocent does not apply here, because in the cases under consideration the innocent consent to their own deaths.[183]

We doubt, however, that consent is enough to justify an

exception to the rule against killing the innocent, insofar as the bare exercise of autonomy does not establish its moral validity. Consent can be given on morally inadequate grounds. Our reason for restricting the application of the rule, therefore, differs from Cahill's: not the consent of the innocent, but their objective status as non-responsible persons. Apart from this, we would only add a plea to remember that love has passive as well as active modes, and so to entertain a generous conception of responsible life. Whether our two positions will otherwise coincide depends on how we adjudicate the disagreement between Cahill and McCormick over whether decisive weight should be accorded reservations about the long-term social effects of permitting 'active' or 'direct' (that is, intentional) killing of the sort proposed. McCormick thinks that it should; Cahill thinks not.

Paul Ramsey's position on this issue is, as ever, subtle. Like both McCormick and Cahill – and to the surprise of those who follow Rachels[184] in assuming him to be a conservative in these matters – he asserts that there may be exceptions to the rule against direct or intentional killing. These arise in cases where a dying person is 'irretrievably inaccessible to human care', either because he is permanently and deeply unconscious,[185] or because he is suffering severe and prolonged pain that cannot be relieved.[186] In either case, it is 'a matter of complete indifference whether death gains the victory over the patient in such impenetrable solitude by direct or indirect action'.[187] Nevertheless, Ramsey argues, it does not follow that medical practice should admit these exceptions, unless a negative answer can be given to the question, 'Would doctors who are the moral agents in these exceptional acts of killing the dying . . . be corrupted by them, and medicine's impulse to save be weakened?'[188] On the one hand, Ramsey affirms that a negative answer is possible, given an ethos where the limits of the exceptions are strictly observed. On the other hand, he warns against presuming too confidently upon the security of such an ethos by quoting an expert on Nazi medical abuses: 'Whatever proportion these crimes finally assumed, it became evident to all who investigated them that they had started from small beginnings . . . It started with the acceptance of the attitude . . . that there is such a thing as life not worthy to be lived . . . its impetus was the attitude toward the non-rehabilitable sick.'[189]

In his caution about the social ramifications of relaxing the rule against intentionally killing the innocent, Ramsey aligns himself with McCormick against Cahill. Whether I shall stand with or against him must await the conclusion to the next chapter.

Conclusion

Before we open that chapter, however, we pause here to summarise the main conclusions that we have reached through our discussion in this one.

The life of the human individual is precious because it is constituted and dignified by a unique vocation by God to promote what is valuable in the world, at least by bearing witness to it. No one should *want* or *intend* to damage or destroy such precious, responsible life either as an end or as a means, for to do so would be to vitiate the agent's will, to corrupt his moral character, to jeopardise his fitness for life beyond death, and to increase the likelihood of his committing further malevolent harm in the world. Nevertheless, it may be permissible to choose to act in such a way as to cause the death of a responsible individual (e.g. by means of a dose of morphine), provided that what was intended was something other than his death (e.g. pain-relief), and that the possibility of his death was accepted with an appropriate and manifest reluctance (e.g. the dosage was proportionate to the level of pain, and no effective, less risky alternative was available). Morally speaking, deliberately to cause death in this fashion is not the same as intending to kill. Therefore, to permit the former is not a ground for permitting the latter.

However, there are situations where living human beings are rendered permanently incapable of responding to a vocation, whether by severe brain damage or by intense pain that cannot be relieved so as to permit the recovery of responsible life, generously conceived. In these rare cases – and other considerations apart – it could be morally permissible to intend to take human life because, that life having lost its unique preciousness – its sacred value – the intention would not be malevolent. Nor would it involve an impatiently irrational preference for one good over another, since it would not be unreasonable to subordinate merely biological human life to the good of relieving relatives of the emotional burden of attending upon someone irretrievably beyond the reach of their care, or to the good of conserving health-care resources for use in bettering the conditions of afflicted, but still responsible humans. Certainly, even the taking of human life reduced to a biological level should be accompanied by sorrow at the fact that an individual person has died. Still, this sorrow need not amount to the reluctance demanded by the deliberate but unintentional killing of a responsible individual.

Intentional killing in such cases *could* be permissible, other considerations apart. Whether it actually *should* be permissible in a *medical context* depends on the denouement of one further consideration: can intentional killing of patients by themselves or by doctors be permitted without undermining a humane society's general commitment to the preciousness of human life, and without undermining the ordinary resolve of its members to support each other in adversity? This brings us to the issue of slippery slopes and the threshold of Chapter Four.

Chapter four

Slippery Slopes

The critics

J OHN GRIFFITHS is singularly unimpressed by 'slippery slope' arguments against the legal permission of voluntary euthanasia. 'The slippery slope', he writes, 'is . . . more a bit of suggestive rhetoric than a serious argument.'[1] Indeed, someone who appeals to it 'has no real objection to euthanasia but fears that it will lead to practices to which he does object'.[2] Griffiths presses his attack further by arguing that the conceptual or logical version of this kind of 'argument' is 'almost childishly simplistic'. This is because it holds that once one has accepted A (e.g. voluntary euthanasia in cases of terminal illness and suffering) based on principle P (e.g. personal autonomy), one is bound to accept B (e.g. voluntary euthanasia in cases where patients are not terminally or even physically ill) because it also follows from P. Since B is assumed to be repellent, it follows that P is flawed and that A must therefore be rejected. What this overlooks is that social practices may be governed by more than one principle; and that one (e.g. the principle of beneficence) may limit what can be authorised by another (e.g. the principle of autonomy).[3] In the end, Griffiths contends, 'the conceptual version of the slippery slope is actually not conceptual at all but empirical: people will not be *logically forced* to go from A to B, they *will in fact do so*'.[4]

R. G. Frey and Ronald Dworkin feel no need to distinguish sharply between the logical and the empirical versions of the argument in their critique of the 1994 report of the New York State Task Force on Life and the Law. This report argues that, were voluntary euthanasia or physician-assisted suicide to be made legal, current social inequality and bias in the provision of health care would subject minorities, the poor, and the elderly to unfair pressure to 'choose' them, in particular because the limited availability of palliative care and treatment for depression would severely limit their options, and generally because of the concern of doctors, hospitals, insurers, and governments to save money.[5] This economic concern would also threaten the effectiveness of any safeguards against abuse. It is therefore right, the report holds, to curtail the liberty of the few who would freely choose to have their lives artificially shortened, for the sake of the 'far larger group of individuals' who might choose it because of depression or coercion or untreated pain.[6]

To this argument Dworkin retorts that it also applies to allowing patients to refuse treatment: 'If a physician can manipulate the patient's request for death, he can manipulate the patient's request for termination of treatment. If the patient's death is cheaper for the system, then it is cheaper whether the patient commits suicide or is withdrawn from a life-support system.' In support, he cites data from the Van der Maas survey of 1991 that shows that by far the largest number of non-voluntary deaths in the Netherlands resulted from the withdrawing or withholding of medical or palliative treatment rather than from active euthanasia.[7] Further, provided that the option of physician-assisted suicide is restricted to competent patients suffering from terminal or incurable illness, the pool of eligible patients would be smaller than that of those eligible for the withholding or withdrawal of treatment – and so would the scope for abuse. Again he appeals to Dutch statistics, which show that patients dying as a result of non-treatment decisions far outnumber those dying from assisted suicide and euthanasia together.[8]

Both Frey and Dworkin find the Task Force's report far too

pessimistic about the capacity of safeguards to provide a firm foothold on the slippery slope.[9] Frey does not think it beyond human ingenuity to develop an effective system for safeguarding patient autonomy by monitoring requests for death, in order to identify requests motivated by undiagnosed or untreated pain and to detect abuses in the form of family or financial coercion.[10] To the argument that, once voluntary euthanasia is established as 'therapeutic', it will seem unjust to deny it to those incapable of consent and for whom it is clearly in their 'best interests', Dworkin responds that that is one reason for preferring physician-assisted suicide, since it requires the request of a competent adult.[11] He then proceeds to deny the report's assertion that 'the logic of suicide as a compassionate choice for patients who are in pain or suffering suggests no limit'.[12] He sees no serious problem with formulating a law that stipulates that physician-assisted suicide may only be performed on certain conditions – e.g. that a medical condition be present, that it not be susceptible of cure or effective palliation, and that the patient experience it as not allowing her to lead the kind of life that she regards as worthwhile. 'It is not apparent,' he writes, 'why the legal system would have a harder time dealing with these notions than with the kinds of issues that have arisen with respect to withdrawal of life support, termination of artificial hydration and nutrition, and doctrines of proxy consent and substituted judgment.'[13] Provided that assisted suicide is hedged about by these conditions, Dworkin reckons that there is no reason to suppose – as the report does – that its legalisation would 'blunt our moral sensibilities and perceptions'[14] any more than administering a potentially lethal dosage of morphine or 'terminal sedation', where patients are put into a coma and allowed to die of lack of food and water.[15]

Finally, Dworkin considers the argument that granting a right to request death diminishes a patient's welfare by putting his existence into question and requiring him to justify his choice to maintain it in the face of the costs, both financial and emotional, borne by his family and friends.[16] He concedes that for some the welfare costs of such a right will exceed the benefits; but he holds that for others the reverse will be the case. And he believes it likely that there are 'many more' of the latter, and that the magnitude of the benefit of being spared great suffering exceeds the magnitude of the harm of being made to feel guilty about going on living or of being pressured into ending 'a rather miserable existence (remember we are talking about people with terminal or incurable illness)' sooner than they would have wished.[17] His conclusion is that it is unfair that even a small number of patients should suffer greatly to save others from the possibility of pressure or abuse; because whereas the former 'certainly'[18] have a 'stringent'[19] claim to be able to avoid needless pain and misery and to shape the end of their lives in accordance with their fundamental values, the latter have no claim to be relieved of having to face pressures on their choices – especially when the likelihood and extent of those pressures is unclear.[20]

Dworkin's conclusion approximates that of Margaret Pabst Battin, who, having frankly admitted that the social and legal acceptance of the notion of rational suicide carries with it the risk of the 'large-scale' manipulation of some into 'choosing' it,[21] nevertheless holds that 'perhaps' the duty to protect vulnerable individuals is not as strong as the 'fundamental right to die'. Why does she think this? Because 'a rational person may be willing to accept the possibility of manipulation which is engendered by the notion of rational suicide, in exchange for the social freedom to control one's own dying as one wishes'. Why? Because the alternative of maintaining an absolute prohibition of suicide 'is particularly cruel to precisely those people for whom death is or may become a rational choice – that is, those persons in the most unfortunate circumstances of us all'. On these grounds Battin concludes that we should accept the notion of rational suicide, notwithstanding 'the moral quicksand into which this notion threatens to lead us'.[22]

Lisa Cahill's conclusion is similar to those reached by Dworkin and Battin, insofar as she holds that the duty to offer relief to 'grossly suffering terminal' patients, if necessary by deliberately lethal means, is stronger than the duty to spare patients whose vulnerability might be increased by the granting of that relief. Her argument does not proceed, however, by way of asserting a right to autonomy or via utilitarian pseudo-calculation. Rather, appealing to Aquinas, she holds that there is a greater responsibility to avoid a certain moral evil than an uncertain one; that the present evil of permitting the spiritual, personal, and physical degeneration of some patients is more certain than the future, possible evil of a decline in care for human life on the part of the hospital staff; and that therefore the avoidance of the latter does not amount to a proportionate reason for permitting the former.[23]

The objections

Now, for the third and final time, we pause to analyse the critics' several critiques into a list of main objections. These are:

- an appeal to slippery slopes against physician-assisted suicide or voluntary euthanasia is not a serious argument;
- the logical or conceptual version of the slippery slope argument is simplistic;
- it is possible to formulate and police effectively a law that stipulates that voluntary euthanasia or physician-assisted suicide may only be performed under certain conditions;
- physician-assisted suicide, which by definition involves the request of a competent adult, would avoid the feared slippage from voluntary into non-voluntary euthanasia;
- the effects of permitting physician-assisted suicide would be no worse than those of permitting the refusal of life-sustaining treatment, since patients can be manipulated

as easily into the latter as into the former, and since their number – and so the scope for abuse – would be smaller in the case of assisted suicide than in that of refusing treatment;

• the claim to be relieved of terrible suffering is stronger than the claim to be protected against unwanted pressure to choose to die.

Our last set of responses now follows.

Responses

First objection: an appeal to slippery slopes against physician-assisted suicide or voluntary euthanasia is not a serious argument

Griffiths seems to think that a 'serious' argument must be one that objects to assisted suicide or voluntary euthanasia *as such* – that is, one that views them as intrinsically evil and therefore morally impermissible under *all* conditions. But why does he suppose that the only objection worthy of consideration must be a crude absolutist one? Why does he dismiss as merely 'rhetorical' a more subtle, discriminate position that judges these kinds of act to be morally permissible in extraordinary circumstances (say, on the battlefield) but morally wrong in normal social ones (say, in an institution of health-care)? Is it because he assumes that such a distinction must be arbitrary? But on what ground would he do that? The distinction could be made for the reason that permission in normal social circumstances would be impossible to limit to 'extreme' cases and would therefore come to pose a grave threat to a humane society's general presumption in favour of helping its members live responsible lives in adversity – that is, it would send society down a 'slippery slope' – whereas permission outside of normal circumstances would not have the same deleterious effect. Such an argument would certainly be less simple than one that forbade voluntary euthanasia and assisted suicide unconditionally. It would depend in part on arguments about contingent social phenomena and probabilities, and those would be controversial. But why should that make it unworthy of serious consideration? Griffiths does not explain. Indeed, were he to try, it is hard to imagine what he would say.

Second objection: the logical or conceptual version of the slippery slope argument is simplistic

If an instance of the logical slippery slope argument were to take the form that Griffiths describes, neglecting the possibility that the pernicious implications (e.g. the involuntary euthanasia of those whose lives are supposed to be worthless) of one principle (e.g. beneficence) might be excluded by the requirements of another (e.g. patient autonomy), then it would indeed be simplistic. The question that remains open, however, is whether the logical version of the argument need take this form.

In order to find an answer, let us take the recent argument made by a major opponent of the legalisation of voluntary euthanasia and physician-assisted suicide, John Keown. Keown argues that the acceptance of voluntary euthanasia is bound to lead to the acceptance of non-voluntary euthanasia, because the judgement that some patients are better off dead 'can logically be made even if the patient is incapable of making a request'.[24] Griffiths would rightly object here that the possibility of extending this logic could be excluded by appeal to the principle of the patient's absolute right to autonomy.

However, Keown's argument is not as purely logical as he (Keown) seems to think. It depends on an empirical premise, which he claims is assumed by advocates of liberalisation; namely, that doctors do not behave simply as the uncritical suppliers of the demands of their patient-consumers, but as 'professionals who form their own judgement about the merits of any request for medical intervention'. If this is the case, Keown observes, then it is not really the patient's autonomous request that is decisive in justifying voluntary euthanasia, 'but the doctor's judgment that the request is justified because death would benefit the patient'.[25] Accordingly, if a doctor thinks himself qualified to judge that death would benefit a competent patient, then he will think himself equally qualified to judge that it would benefit an incompetent one.[26] Therefore if voluntary euthanasia were made available to competent people who requested it, 'it would soon be argued that it should be extended to the incompetent, either on the ground that it would be discriminatory to deny them this benefit because of their incompetence or because VAE [voluntary active euthanasia] is what they would have wanted had they been competent to ask for it'.[27]

Keown's argument is not purely logical, and it is less simplistic and more cogent for not being so. The logical element lies in consistency of judgement: if we judge that death would be a benefit in the case of this competent patient, then we must *logically* judge that it would also be a benefit in cases that are the same in every respect, except that the patient lacks the competence – or at least the good sense – to recognise and affirm it. While Griffiths would be correct to point out that our granting the benefit of death in these other cases could be forbidden by the rule that this may only be done upon the patient's request, Keown implies that the conviction that our judgement is true will incline us *psychologically* at least to lobby for a relaxation of the law in this respect, and at most to break what seems to us to be an irrational regulation – since it is hard to respect what we believe to be erroneous, and all the harder when the error results in what seems to us perfectly needless (and economically wasteful) suffering. It would therefore be incorrect to conclude, as Griffiths would, that since Keown's argument is not purely logical, it must be simply empirical. In fact, it combines elements of both into an argument about the psychological power of beliefs and of their logical implications.

The rhetorical force of this partly logical, partly empirical slippery slope argument depends, of course, on our agreeing with Keown that the relaxation of the law so as to make the patient's request no longer necessary would indeed be wrong – that what lies further down the slope is indeed abhorrent. If, however, one believes it correct to judge that in certain circumstances death would be a benefit to a competent patient, then one would also be correct to judge that in the same circumstances it would be in the 'best interests' of an incompetent patient. The argument here – and it is one that Griffiths makes[28] – is no longer that it is possible to avoid sliding down the slippery slope (by appeal to the principle of patient autonomy), but that there is actually no good reason to try to avoid it.

However, Keown's argument could be extended to the lowest reaches of the slippery slope, which Griffiths' apologia for non-voluntary euthanasia does not cover. Here, the benefit of death is accorded a patient *against his expressed wishes* – that is to say, involuntarily. If, as a doctor, I have decided that in certain conditions life would not be worth living, and that death would therefore be a benefit, I will believe that of someone in those conditions regardless of whether they believe it themselves. It is true that I might be required to 'respect' the wishes of a patient who does not believe it, but since I will judge those wishes to have been ill informed by foolishness, weakness, or selfishness, my 'respect' will tend to be grudging and formal and highly susceptible of being overridden by economic and other 'urgencies' or 'necessities'. In other words, once it is permissible for a doctor to judge that certain forms of human life are not worth living, the combined weight of logic, psychology, and social forces will press very heavily indeed upon any barrier erected against involuntary euthanasia.[29]

In addition to an argument about the 'psycho-logical' implications of the belief that there are certain kinds of human life where death would be a benefit, Keown mounts another 'logical' version of the slippery slope argument.

This is that, insofar as respect for patient autonomy is regarded as decisive in justifying voluntary euthanasia, there can be no good reason for limiting euthanasia to patients who are experiencing 'unbearable suffering' – or even to patients who are suffering physically.[30] In order for this to persuade us against embarking on the slippery slope, we must first agree with its assumption that killing patients simply on (their) demand would indeed be abhorrent. One reason that might compel our agreement is that a humane society's general esteem for the exceptional value of human life would be undermined if the law were to permit the killing of people subject to any other than the most grave and extreme suffering; and unless we subscribe to John Harris' untenable position that the value of human life consists entirely in whatever an individual chooses to make of it,[31] then this argument *should* compel our assent. It is, of course, exactly this high esteem for human life that can provide reasons for restricting the exercise of autonomy over life and death to certain cases of 'unbearable suffering', and so for halting any slide down the slippery slope. This consideration makes clear that Keown's argument only tells against those who hold the principle of autonomy to be supreme; but since some (such as Harris) actually do hold it, Keown's argument is not 'simplistic', *pace* Griffiths; it is merely limited in its application.

Third objection: it is possible to formulate and police effectively a law that stipulates that voluntary euthanasia or physician-assisted suicide may only be performed under certain conditions

Those who use slippery slope considerations to resist the liberalisation of the law that prohibits physician-assisted suicide and voluntary euthanasia often try to substantiate their argument by appeal to data from those jurisdictions where the law has been relaxed, and which show, they claim, that abuse has increased and cannot be adequately controlled. The country where liberalisation has been most developed, and about whose experience we have most data, is the Netherlands.

In outline, recent legal developments in the Netherlands are as follows.[32] In 1984 the Dutch Supreme Court held that, while it remains an offence under the Criminal Code to kill another person at his request, a doctor who ends a patient's life may justify his act by appealing to the defence of 'necessity' under certain conditions, arguing that such killing is a reasonable way of resolving the unavoidable conflict between the duty to obey the law prohibiting voluntary euthanasia and physician-assisted suicide and the duty to relieve suffering. The Court's judgement was informed by a set of guidelines for voluntary euthanasia that had just been published by the Royal Dutch Medical Association (KNMG), and which require that a patient make a voluntary request that is well considered and persistent; that she is subject to intolerable (not necessarily physical) suffering without hope of improvement; that euthanasia be the only reasonable option; that euthanasia must be performed by a doctor; and that the doctor consult first with a colleague in the same institution and then with an independent doctor (e.g. the local medical examiner or coroner).

In 1994 the Supreme Court's decision was given statutory force with the coming into effect of a new law prescribing the procedure by which doctors should report death in cases of euthanasia, assisted suicide, and life-terminating actions without an explicit request. According to this, the doctor must inform the local medical examiner, who should inspect the body of the deceased externally and take from the doctor a statement with the relevant information (the patient's history, request, possible alternatives, consultation with a second doctor, and intervention). This report, together with the examiner's evaluation, is then submitted to the public prosecutor who assesses whether the termination of the patient's life contravened the Criminal Code as interpreted by the courts.

In 1998 the legal regulation of the procedure for reporting was amended. Henceforth, the attending doctor's report and the examiner's evaluation should be sent for assessment directly, no longer to the public prosecutor, but rather to a regional euthanasia review committee. Comprising a physician, a lawyer, and an ethicist, this committee should evaluate the case in the light of the courts' relevant decisions. If it decides that the relevant criteria have not been met, it should then add its opinion to the doctor's and examiner's reports, and forward them all to the prosecutor.[33] The purpose of this change was to encourage reporting by introducing greater distance between the euthanising doctor and the legal authorities.

Most recently in April 2002 a new law became effective that gives statutory force to the 'guidelines', and renders acts of euthanasia and physician-assisted suicide legal so long as they are carried out in accordance with them.[34] Again, the purpose was to encourage doctors to report cases by removing any ambiguity about their (conditional) legal permissibility, and by shifting the burden of proof from the doctor to the prosecutor, who, in order to initiate prosecution, must prove that the physician has not met the requirements.

John Keown, one of the best informed critics of the Dutch arrangements,[35] argues that the guidelines themselves are too imprecise and loose to be capable of closely regulating the practice of voluntary euthanasia. First of all, the concept of unbearable suffering is highly elastic, and can be stretched to include non-terminal, non-physical distress. For example, one leading Dutch practitioner – Dr Herbert Cohen – interviewed by Keown in 1989 seemed to think that it could apply to a hypothetical case where an old man requests voluntary euthanasia because he feels a nuisance to relatives who want him dead so that they can get their hands on his estate.[36] Further, in 1994 the Supreme Court ruled in the actual case of Dr Chabot that it applied to the persistent grief of a fifty-year-old woman at the death of her two sons.[37] And in 2000, a court in Haarlem implied in the case of Dr Sutorius that a patient who wanted to die not because of any serious physical or mental illness, but because he felt his life to be 'pointless and empty', could be considered subject to 'unbearable suffering'.[38]

Second, Keown holds, the checks imposed on the physician are less than exacting. It is left to the doctor to call in the medical examiner and to provide the relevant information; and according to one senior Dutch prosecutor (who supports voluntary euthanasia), the medical examiner lacks the necessary investigative expertise, while the reporting procedure requires prosecutors to lower their professional standards below the 'absolute minimum'.[39]

Beyond arguing that the guidelines are too lax, Keown proceeds to analyse two major surveys of the practice of euthanasia in the Netherlands, in order to judge the extent to which it actually conforms to the law. The first of these covered the year 1990, was conducted by P. J. van der Maas at the behest of a government commission chaired by the Attorney-General, Professor J. Remmelink, and was first published in Dutch in 1991. This estimated that, out of a total of 129,000 deaths from all causes, voluntary euthanasia – defined as the intentional, active termination of life at the patient's request – occurred in about 2300 cases (1.8 per cent), and that physician-assisted suicide occurred in about 400 cases (0.3 per cent). It also estimated, however, that in an additional 1000 cases (0.8 per cent) physicians administered a drug 'with the explicit purpose of hastening the end of life without an explicit request of the patient'[40] – that is, they committed non-voluntary euthanasia.

Analysing the survey's data himself, Keown observes that in about 1350 further cases medication was administered, and in about 4000 further cases treatment was withdrawn or withheld, 'with the explicit purpose of shortening life'.[41] In approximately 450 of the first class of cases, and in all of the second class, there was no explicit request from the patient.[42] This means that in more than 60 per cent of the total of 9050 cases where it was the doctor's primary purpose to hasten death by act or omission, there was no explicit request made by the patient.[43] In addition, of the 6750 cases where medication was administered 'partly with the purpose of shortening life', 5058 (75 per cent) lacked such a request.[44]

Regarding the 1000 cases of non-voluntary euthanasia exposed by the survey, the Commission admitted that a 'few dozen' of them had involved competent patients, and resolved that such killing should be prevented in the future. The rest it justified by appeal to the patient's 'death agony' and 'unbearable suffering'.[45] Keown challenges both the factual assertion and the justification. He notes that interviews with physicians established that 14 per cent (140) of the patients were totally competent and a further 11 per cent (110) partly competent.[46] He also notes that the doctors did not list 'agony' as a reason for killing the patients:

> The reasons given by doctors were the absence of any prospect of improvement (60%); the futility of all medical therapy (39%); avoidance of 'needless prolongation' (33%); the relatives' inability to cope (32%); and 'low quality of life' (31%). Pain or suffering was mentioned by only 30%.[47]

Of the 8100 patients whose deaths were hastened by palliative drugs, either explicitly (1350) or partly (6750) on purpose, Keown observes that 59 per cent (4779) had never indicated anything about life termination[48] and of these 60 per cent (2867) were competent.[49]

On the matter of reporting, Keown notes that of the 2700 cases of voluntary euthanasia and physician-assisted suicide in 1990 recognised as such in the survey, 82 per cent were illegally certified by doctors as death by 'natural causes'[50] – mainly to avoid the 'fuss' of a legal investigation, to protect relatives from a judicial enquiry, and out of fear of prosecution.[51] Likewise, nearly all of the 1000 cases of life termination without request were certified as natural deaths – and for similar reasons.[52] Keown comments that the failure by the vast majority of doctors to report deprived the authorities of even the *opportunity* of review and control. Even in relation to those cases which were reported, it must be doubted, in view of the lax system of investigation – not least the extent to which it relies on doctors to expose their own wrong-doing – whether the authorities had any realistic hope of detecting abuse of the guidelines.[53]

From his critical analysis of the van der Maas survey, Keown concludes that the Dutch system of regulation had failed to prevent 'major non-compliance' with the guidelines for voluntary euthanasia,[54] and that within six years of their promulgation non-voluntary euthanasia 'was not uncommon'[55] and was widely condoned. The survey itself reveals that a majority of doctors either had killed without request or would be prepared to do so.[56] Commenting on the survey in their report, the Remmelink Commission defended the vast majority of the 1000 cases of killing without request as 'care for the dying' that is justifiable by appeal to the 'necessity' of providing relief from 'unbearable suffering'.[57] Shortly afterwards, a committee established by the KNMG condoned the termination in certain circumstances of incompetent patients including babies and patients in persistent coma, and canvassed opinion on the killing of patients with severe dementia.[58]

In order to show the extent of the slide from voluntary to non-voluntary euthanasia, Keown asserts that '[t]he growing condonation of NVAE [non-voluntary active euthanasia] . . . contrasts markedly with pronouncements made not so long ago by Dutch supporters of VAE [voluntary active euthanasia]'.[59] In support of this, he notes that three of the five guidelines published by the KNMG in 1984 'sought to ensure not only that there was an explicit request by the patient, but that it was free, well considered and persistent'; that a State Commission on Euthanasia concluded in 1985 that third parties should not be permitted to request euthanasia on behalf of (incompetent) minors and others incapable of expressing their opinion such as the mentally handicapped and the senile elderly; that its vice-chairman, H. J. J. Leenen, commented in 1987 that the Commission had proposed an amendment to the Criminal Code prohibiting the intentional termination of an incompetent patient's life on grounds of serious physical or mental illness, in order to underscore the importance of the patient's request; that two years later he reaffirmed that such a request was 'central' to the Dutch definition of euthanasia, adding that 'the family or other relatives, parents for their children, or the doctor cannot decide on behalf of the patient'; that in the same year Henk Rigter of the Dutch Health Council wrote that '[i]n the absence of a patient request the perpetrator renders him or herself guilty of manslaughter or murder'; and that Rigter's position 'received ringing endorsement from a galaxy of leading Dutch VAE advocates' – including the Secretary of the Dutch Society of Health Law, the Board of the Dutch Society for Voluntary Euthanasia, and the Director of the National Hospital Association.[60] Keown's conclusion is that the slide from voluntary to non-voluntary euthanasia between 1984 and 1990 was swift.[61]

The second of the major surveys of the practice of euthanasia in the Netherlands covered the year 1995, was carried out by van der Maas and G. van der Wal, and was first published in Dutch in 1996.[62] This estimated that, out of a total of 135,000 deaths from all causes, voluntary euthanasia occurred in 3200 cases (2.4 per cent), and physician-assisted suicide in 400 (0.3 per cent).[63] In 17 per cent of these, there were treatment alternatives, but in almost all the patients did not want them.[64] Keown comments that these cases contravene the judgement of the Dutch Supreme Court in 1994 that doctors should not hasten death in cases of mental suffering when a palliative alternative was available, which was then extended to cases of physical suffering by the Ministers of Justice and Health and the KNMG.[65]

This second survey recorded a slight decrease (from 1000 to 900) in the cases of non-voluntary euthanasia between 1991 and 1995.[66] In 15 per cent of cases where discussion was possible, it did not happen because the doctor reckoned that termination was clearly in the patient's best interests.[67] In 37 per cent of the 900 cases there had been a discussion with the patient about possible termination of life, and some 50 per cent of this subgroup of patients were fully competent; yet their lives were terminated without 'an explicit, contemporaneous request'.[68] In 17 per cent of the 900 cases, treatment alternatives were thought to be available by the attending physician.[69] In 40 per cent of cases physicians had not discussed their action with a colleague, and in 30 per cent not even with a close relative.[70]

Of the approximately 1000 cases of neonates who died before their first birthday, Keown estimates that doctors administered a drug in 90 of them, and withdrew or withheld treatment in 410 of them, with the explicit intention of shortening life.[71] Forty-five per cent of neonatologists and intensive care specialists and 31 per cent of general paediatricians said that they had given drugs explicitly to end the life of a neonate or infant, and 29 per cent and 49 per cent respectively who had not done so said that they could conceive of situations in which they would do so.[72]

Of all the cases of voluntary euthanasia and physician-assisted suicide, 41 per cent were reported by doctors to the local medical examiner.[73] Keown acknowledges that this represents 'an improvement' on the 1990 figure of 18 per cent, but notes that it still means that 'a clear majority of cases, almost 60%' went unreported.[74] The most important reasons given for the failure to report were the wish to avoid the inconvenience (for the doctor and/or the relatives) of an investigation by the authorities, and the wish to avoid risk of prosecution – 'though, as the consistently tiny number of prosecutions indicated, this risk was negligible'.[75] Thirty per cent of doctors stated that they did not report because they had not observed the guidelines, and 12 per cent because they considered voluntary euthanasia to be a private matter between doctor and patient.[76]

Keown evaluates the data as follows. There was 'some improvement in compliance' between 1991 and 1995. However, the high incidence of intentional life-shortening evidenced by the survey, together with the fact that the reasons given for voluntary euthanasia in many cases arguably fall short of 'unbearable suffering', suggest that voluntary euthanasia was not confined to cases of last resort and was sometimes used as an alternative to palliative care. This contradicted what was then[77] the opinion of the Supreme Court, the Ministers of Justice and Health, and the KNMG that voluntary euthanasia is impermissible when treatment alternatives are available, even if the patient refuses them. Further, notwithstanding the improvement in reporting, a clear majority of cases went unreported, removing even the opportunity for official scrutiny of the majority of cases of voluntary and non-voluntary euthanasia and physician-assisted suicide. In conclusion, Keown judges that the 1995 survey serves to reinforce doubts about Dutch claims of effective regulation, scrutiny and control.[78]

One of the most substantial and carefully considered responses to Keown's critique of Dutch developments comes from John Griffiths. Griffiths agrees that 'in the Netherlands there is far more medical behavior that intentionally shortens life than suggested by Dutch data covering only euthanasia and termination of life without an explicit request . . . and that much of this is non-voluntary'. So far he considers Keown's argument to be 'a solid one'.[79] Where he differs, however, is in refusing to make the move – 'so typical of foreign criticism'[80] – from these data to the conclusion that the legalisation of voluntary euthanasia has caused the Dutch to slide down the slippery slope into the practice of non-voluntary euthanasia. In order to substantiate that, Griffiths argues, Keown would have to show that such practice has increased after the legalisation of euthanasia – or that it is higher in Netherlands than elsewhere – and that there is a causal relationship between the two.

With regard to the first requirement, Griffiths notes that between 1990 and 1995 the number of cases of termination of life without an explicit request appears to have been stable or declining – suffering 'a small but not statistically significant decline' (from 1000 to 900); and that the number of cases of death due to pain relief administered partly with the intent to shorten life, and without an explicit request, also declined slightly.[81] (Remarkably, he makes no mention at all of the number of cases where pain relief was administered with an explicit intention to shorten life and without an explicit request,[82] which, according to Keown, stood at 450 in 1990.[83]) As for cases of death due to abstaining from medical intervention with the explicit intent to shorten life and without an explicit request, Griffiths concedes that the number rose 'somewhat' (from 8500 to 13,000 – that is, by over 50 per cent!), arguing that 'if the Dutch data exhibit a slippery slope, death due to abstinence is where it is to be found'.[84] He argues, however, that it is 'more likely' that this is attributable to a combination of developments in medical technology, which by increasing the possibilities of life-support have also increased the occasions on which decisions must be made to stop it, and of developments in medical ethics, where doctors are urged with increasing insistence to refrain from futile treatment and let patients die.[85] In other words, he denies that Keown has met the second requirement of a demonstration of a causal connexion between the legalisation of voluntary euthanasia and an increase in cases of non-voluntary euthanasia. (Keown obliquely confirms Griffiths' reading when, admitting that the data concerned are ambiguous since 'a note to the relevant question [in the survey] states that an intention to "hasten the end of life" could also be understood as an intention "not to prolong life"', he supposes that in many of these cases doctors may have intended to withhold/withdraw treatment 'not to end the patient's life, but because the

treatment was futile or too burdensome'.[86]) Griffiths avers
that '[i]n the end, a reasonable observer would have to conclude that there is no substantial evidence that the frequency of termination of life without an explicit request is
higher in the Netherlands than it used to be; and if there has
been any increase, it is probably the result of developments
also taking place in other countries which have not legalized
euthanasia.'[87]

Griffiths presses his case by pointing out that Keown
makes no comparison between the situation in the Netherlands and those in other countries.[88] Therefore Keown's
assertion that the Netherlands is the only country in which
euthanasia is officially condoned and widely practised is
tendentious. Had he made international comparisons,
Griffiths thinks that it 'would probably not have bolstered
his argument', since he would have discovered that such
data as exist suggest that much of what he regards as essentially the same as voluntary euthanasia is officially condoned and widely practised 'all over the world'.[89] In support
of this point, Griffiths cites research conducted in Australia
by Helga Kuhse,[90] which shows rates of voluntary euthanasia, assistance with suicide, and the non-voluntary shortening of life (through pain relief or abstinence from treatment)
either very similar to – or even higher than – those in the
Netherlands.[91] (In his latest work Keown disputes the value
of Kuhse's survey, arguing that in an important question it
conflated an intention not to prolong life with an intention
to hasten death.[92]) Griffiths concludes that 'to the extent
that relevant data are available, international comparisons
give no support to the idea that the Dutch, unlike countries
which have not legalized euthanasia, are sliding down a
slippery slope to non-voluntary termination of life'.[93]

On the matter of the current regimen of control in the
Netherlands, however, Griffiths agrees with Keown that 'it
leaves much to be desired',[94] and that the results of the 1991
and 1996 surveys amount to a 'pretty devastating' judgement upon its effectiveness.[95] Not only do about 60 per cent

of cases of euthanasia go unreported, but these include 'the more problematic cases'.[96] Worse, the current regimen does not require the reporting of deaths due to abstaining from life-prolonging treatment (20 per cent of all deaths) or due to pain relief (18.5 per cent), even though many of these are morally and legally indistinguishable from cases of euthanasia and assistance with suicide (3 per cent) and from cases of termination of life without request (less than 1 per cent).[97] In sum, the reporting procedure 'is a bit of a paper tiger', and little serious enforcement is undertaken in reported cases that fail to meet the legal criteria.[98] In part, the problem lies in the fact that the system is based on self-reporting and involves no pro-active control; therefore 'a doctor who wants to conceal what he has done would have to be extraordinarily careless to give them [the law-enforcement officials] reason to doubt his report of a "natural death"'[99] – and, indeed, there is evidence that in their reports doctors do 'make cases appear legally more clear-cut than they actually are'[100] and describe what happened 'in rather self-serving terms'.[101] For this reason, the authorities have almost no chance of discovering abuses.[102] Another part of the problem is that abstinence from treatment and pain relief are considered to belong to 'normal medical practice', and deaths resulting from them do not have to be reported at all. This means that doctors who do not wish to have their actions subjected to official scrutiny merely have to take care in how they describe them. Moreover, since (according to Griffiths) the distinction between euthanasia and intentional termination without explicit request on the one hand, and abstinence from treatment and pain relief (with the intention to kill?) on the other, is arbitrary and 'constructible', they can also choose to accomplish their intended end in the least legally controversial manner.[103]

However, while Griffiths concedes to Keown that 'the existing control system, depending as it does on self-reporting, cannot be regarded as adequate',[104] he nevertheless argues that

since the Dutch brought euthanasia out of the taboo
sphere, they have steadily worked on defining ever
more precisely the circumstances in which it is permissible and specifying the procedural 'requirements of
careful practice' that must be followed. The Dutch
courts have produced an extensive case law dealing in
ever more detail with the various problems that
arise . . . There is national legislation and rules, and
specific institutional facilities for their enforcement . . .
In short, there is much *more* legal control in the
Netherlands than there used to be when, as elsewhere
in the world, legal control began and ended with an
unenforced and unenforceable criminal prohibition.[105]

What Griffiths is claiming is that in jurisdictions where voluntary euthanasia and termination of life without explicit
request are simply prohibited, they are in fact widespread
but hidden; whereas in the Netherlands, notwithstanding
its imperfect regimen of control, they are subject to 'at least
some legal control' – and, step by step, that control is being
made more effective.[106]

Griffiths is confident that a sufficiently effective regimen
of control can be developed, but he does not think that it
can be built around the criminal law. The reasons for this are
both theoretical and practical. The theoretical ones consist
in incongruities between, on the one hand, legal concepts of
causality, intentionality, and omission, and on the other
hand, the medical ones used by the current control regimen.
The criminal law, according to Griffiths, regards death as
attributable to the action of a doctor and not to the pre-
existing disorder of the patient, where the doctor hastens
the moment of death at all. Doctors, on the other hand,
view causality in terms of the dominant factor in the death
of the patient, and may attribute the latter to the dying
process and report it as 'natural', even if they hasten it by
administering a drug. 'The foundation of the reporting procedure rests, thus, in the conceptual quicksand that lies

between the meaning of causality in the legal and the medical worlds.'[107] (Griffiths makes no attempt to adjudicate between the alternative interpretations, but he implies that what he presents as the doctors' view is valid enough to warrant a regulatory revolution. This is a mistake; for both the law and the doctors, as Griffiths presents them, are confused. On the one hand, doctors ought not to attribute responsibility for death simply to the natural dying process, if that death was caused in part by their act, and if it could have been foreseen or was actually intended. On the other hand, the criminal law ought to be able to tell the difference between responsibility for causing a death and responsibility for intending it.)

Regarding intentionality, Griffiths tells us, the criminal law works with an objective conception: an agent is taken to intend the natural and probable consequences of his act – hence in every case where medical conduct shortens life, the doctor is held to intend the patient's death. However, in order to escape from that conclusion, and to distinguish between death due to euthanasia and death due to pain relief, the law appeals to the doctrine of double effect. Not only is this doctrine 'philosophically untenable', but it calls for distinctions that cannot be made in actual criminal prosecution practice, and it makes enforcement impossible by defining intention subjectively, since a doctor who does not want to attract the attention of the prosecutorial authorities 'has only to describe his intention in the required way'.[108] (As we have argued in Chapter Three above, however, the doctrine of double effect is not philosophically untenable and may reasonably be used to escape from the false conclusion that in every case where medical conduct shortens life, the doctor should be held to intend the patient's death. Moreover, the doctrine does not define intention subjectively, since there is a correlation between what someone intends and accepts, on the one hand, and what they objectively do, on the other.)

As for the role of the idea of an omission, according to

Griffiths, doctors use it to distinguish the 'passive' abstaining from life-prolonging treatment, which does not violate the prohibition of intentional killing, and the 'active' termination of life, which does. The criminal law, however, views a doctor as having a general duty of care toward a patient for whom he is responsible, in which case withholding treatment is no longer the sort of omission to which criminal liability does not attach. 'In short, the circumstances of medical practice are totally different from those contemplated by classic examples of omissions often invoked in discussion of the subject (man sees baby drowning in ditch and walks by).'[109] (Here it appears that there is a discrepancy between legal and medical views. However, with respect to Griffiths, this provides no ground for emancipating medical practice from the constraints of criminal law, since the law's view is ethically correct. Doctors are morally responsible for acts of omission – for withholding treatment – and they should be legally liable for them.)

The second set of insuperable problems that, Griffiths believes, render the criminal law incapable of mounting an effective control regimen is practical. One of these is that, were the rate of reporting to be significantly improved, and were obligatory reporting extended to all 'normal medical practice' that intentionally causes death, then the prosecutorial authorities would 'completely lack the capacity and the expertise required to deal with the number and complexity of cases that would be involved'[110] – which Griffiths reckons at some 60,000 cases per annum.[111]

Another practical problem is that the criminal law offers doctors insufficient legal security. This is partly because the risk of criminal liability cannot be known in advance with a reasonable degree of certainty, since the law is in a process of development and promises to continue to be so for decades to come. It is also because prosecutorial decisions in unsettled areas of the law concerning euthanasia and the termination of life without explicit request lend themselves to political exploitation. If to these considerations are added the considerable costs of undergoing a criminal prosecution, even for someone confident in his own innocence, then it should become clear why a doctor who fears himself to be at any risk at all will be discouraged from reporting a case of non-natural death.[112]

One solution to the problem of doctors' legal insecurity would be to 'legalise' euthanasia and assistance with suicide, by adding a provision to the Criminal Code to the effect that the prohibition does not apply in cases where a doctor has observed certain stipulated 'requirements of careful practice'. Griffiths objects to this, however, because putting the rules that have been developed in case law into the Criminal Code does not change the conditions under which euthanasia can be legally performed: 'It is therefore not clear why such legalization would have the desired effect on the rate of reporting.'[113] Further, the codification of the rules will give prosecutors and judges less room for manoeuvre in applying them to 'the varying circumstances of individual cases', thus increasing the risk to be taken by a doctor who reports a case in which, maybe for good reason, he did not meet all of the procedural requirements. Further still, the definitive formulation of the requirements, which legalisation requires, would cut short the current development of practical and moral wisdom about the termination of life without an explicit request.[114]

Instead, Griffiths' recommendation for improving the system of control is that *all* medical conduct that shortens life should be 'decriminalised' by being considered to fall within an implicit exception to sections of the Criminal Code defining offences against the person, deemed therefore part of 'normal medical practice', and subjected to the control normally applied by the medical profession to the behaviour of its members.[115] This would comprise the delegation, not the abdication, of society's responsibility for control to the medical profession.[116] The professional character of such control would enable it to retain a degree of casuistic flexibility.[117] Moreover, since the illegality of euthanasia and the prospect of a criminal investigation have been the major reasons for doctors' failure to report under the current regimen,[118] decriminalisation might reasonably be expected to result in an increase in self-reporting: 'The fact that control is professional and not connected to any risk of criminal prosecution makes it embarrassing for a doctor not to be cooperative and deprives him of the main incentive for not being open about his behaviour.'[119] Griffiths admits that the chance of a doctor being caught, should he not report, would remain small, but argues that since there would be far less to gain from not reporting, even 'a very modest risk' of being apprehended would amount to a substantial incentive to do so.[120] Certainly, the risk of disciplinary proceedings will deter some from reporting, but the collegial character of the review committees, the strict confidentiality of their proceedings ('[e]ven if what a doctor reveals to the committee amounts to murder'), and the greater confidence of doctors in medical disciplinary law than in criminal law 'will cause the balance to tilt far more often than is now the case in the direction of reporting'.[121]

Our critical account of the debate over the significance of recent Dutch experience, as represented by Keown and Griffiths, is now complete. What remains, of course, is for us to evaluate it and take a position. We begin with the central question of whether the Netherlands has in fact experienced a slide down the slippery slope as a result of its 'legalisation' of voluntary euthanasia and physician-assisted suicide. Griffiths denies that the data provided by the 1991 and 1996 reports support a positive answer with regard to a slide from voluntary to non-voluntary euthanasia. M. Angell, the editor of the *New England Journal of Medicine*,[122] and Raanon Gillon[123] agree. Keown implicitly concedes this point, when he responds to Angell that 'a more plausible interpretation of the evidence is that the descent had already occurred by 1990'.[124] On the one hand, Keown's response raises the obvious question of why such an alleged slide between 1984 and 1990 should have levelled off between 1990 and 1995, and to this he gives no answer. On the other hand, Keown has convincingly demonstrated a shift from official insistence in the 1980s on the necessity of an explicit request by the patient for euthanasia, and on the impermissibility of the termination of the lives of incompetents (minors, the mentally handicapped, the comatose, the senile elderly), to substantial official condonation of non-voluntary euthanasia in the 1990s. The burden of proof surely lies with those who would claim that such official endorsement of non-voluntary euthanasia – by, for example, the Remmelink Commission and the KNMG – had *not* 'served to lessen doctors' inhibitions against it'.[125]

Moreover, the shift from euthanasia upon request to euthanasia without it is only one possibility. A second possibility is the movement from the practice of euthanasia in rare and medically definite cases of dying patients in severe physical pain that is not susceptible of relief, to its practice in a much wider range of cases – for example, where non-terminally ill patients suffer from chronic mental distress, or where they simply make it known that they want to die. On the one hand, as has been admitted by one of Keown's allies in opposing Dutch liberalisation, Henk Jochemsen, the fact that there are far fewer cases of voluntary euthanasia than there are requests makes clear that Dutch physicians in general are not terminating patients' lives on demand;[126] and there is some evidence to suggest that this is unlikely to become the case.[127] Nevertheless, on the other hand, Keown has shown that the concept of 'unbearable suffering without prospect of improvement' is so elastic in its meaning that it can be stretched to cover the condition of someone in deep and chronic grief and someone who feels a nuisance to his avaricious relatives. The fact that in the 1000 cases of non-voluntary euthanasia exposed by the 1991 survey, only 30 per cent of doctors gave pain or suffering as a reason for killing their patients, suggests that some doctors regard the concept as a restriction so loosely defined as to impose no practical limits. Of course, that figure alone cannot show any movement over time from a strict interpretation to a lax one. Still, it is surely reasonable to suppose that the modification of the law to permit hitherto forbidden killing on such a very elastic condition is bound to have encouraged the taking of patients' lives in a much wider range of circumstances than before.

It is our judgement, then, that in these two respects the Netherlands has experienced a shift in the practice of euthanasia. Moreover, there are good reasons to suppose that in both cases the movement has been caused at least in part by changes in Dutch law. One crucial question remains open, however: Have these movements involved moral degeneration? In each respect, has the 'shift' constituted a downward 'slide'?

If one regards all instances of the intentional killing of human beings without their express request as immoral, as Keown does, then there would appear to have been a morally downward slide from strictly voluntary euthanasia to non-voluntary forms. However, we have implied that there are extreme circumstances in which it would be reasonable, even from a Christian point of view, to intend to take one's own life – namely, where there is no hope of recovering responsible life and where, therefore, suffering has become pointless. A classic case would be that of being trapped in a burning vehicle without prospect of being released.[128] A closely analogous case would be that of being terminally ill without prospect of recovery, and suffering physical pain that is all-consuming and beyond adequate relief. It is not difficult to imagine that in such circumstances, were we unable to kill ourselves, we would welcome assistance, whether more or less direct. Therefore, should we find ourselves in the presence of someone else in those circumstances, who is unable either to kill themselves or to ask for assistance, a straightforward exercise of compassionate imagination – or the invocation of Jesus' Golden Rule – would give us good reason to suppose that it would be in such a person's 'best interests' that we should kill them. In the frank words of the Church of England's classic report, *On Dying Well*:

> There are bound to be cases in which any of us who is honest with himself and asks 'What do I wish that men should do to me in this particular situation?' will answer 'Kill me'. We have already mentioned such unusual cases ['men trapped in blazing gun-turrets . . . wounded who face death by torture if left on the battlefield'][129] in which many of us would wish to have our deaths hastened so that the manner of them might be less unbearable. Thus a direct application of the teaching of Jesus [about loving our neighbours as ourselves] to these cases would legitimize at least some instances of euthanasia.[130]

And of these, some could be non-voluntary. Therefore, the fact that the liberalisation of Dutch law has led to instances of non-voluntary euthanasia need not be morally objectionable, insofar as these have concerned human beings – whether newborn or adult – who are terminally ill, without prospect of recovery, and in physical agony beyond adequate pain-relief; or who, through birth-defect or injury, lack the physical preconditions of the possibility of consciousness and therefore of any kind of responsibility at all.

However, while there are some extreme cases in which there can be very good reason to presume that it is in a person's best interests that they be killed, or that a human being is incapable of having any personal interests at all, there will be many other cases where there is room for substantial doubt. And so long as we esteem the life of human persons highly, and recognise the value of its receptive and appreciative modes as well as of its assertive ones, we will deem it very important indeed to impose tight restrictions on the circumstances in which it would be acceptable to make such a fateful presumption.

In the light of these considerations, how does the evidence of the practice of non-voluntary euthanasia in the

Netherlands look? On the one hand, Griffiths points out that the category of 'termination of life without an explicit request' (1000 in 1990, 900 in 1995) is quite heterogeneous and includes 'a very small number' of severely defective neonates (15 in both years) and 'a relatively large number' of very sick or dying patients 'who are clearly suffering severely' (194 in 1990, 70 in 1995).[131] If we yield benefit of doubt here and assume that this suffering was beyond adequate relief, and that both it and the severe neonatal defects were such as to preclude even the possibility of responsible life, then we find nothing objectionable so far. On the other hand, however, Griffiths tells us that the figures also include 'a very small number' of cases of inhabitants of institutions for the mentally handicapped (1 in both years) and 'a small number' of cases of dementia (30 cases in 1990, 130 cases in 1995).[132] On the assumption that these various subcategories do not overlap, we may infer that the cases involving persons with mental handicap and dementia were neither sick nor dying and subject to severe physical suffering; and if Griffiths sees fit to describe the 70 (1995) cases of the sick and dying in severe pain as 'a relatively large number', it seems inconsistent of him to downplay the 130 (1995) cases of dementia as 'a small number'. Moreover, Griffiths' apologetic analysis of this heterogeneous category only accounts for just over 25 per cent of the cases in each of the two years.[133] This leaves 745 instances of the termination of life without explicit request in 1990, and 669 in 1995, involving persons who were neither severely defective neonates, nor long-term comatose, nor mentally handicapped, nor demented, nor sick or dying and suffering severely. Given the reasons offered by doctors for committing all of the acts of non-voluntary euthanasia in this category, we may infer that the remaining patients were killed because it was presumed that the quality of their lives was so poor as to be not worth sustaining in the absence of any hope of improvement and in face of the distress suffered by relatives. Such presumption in these cases is so much more dubious than in the extreme ones mentioned above that it trespasses on the presumptuous.

Of the additional cases of non-voluntary euthanasia in 1990 that Keown identified – the 450 cases where medication was administered, and the 4000 cases where treatment was withdrawn or withheld, with the explicit purpose of shortening life and without an explicit request by the patient – we are given no analysis. The fact that Griffiths offers no defence here – indeed, the fact that he omits any mention at all of these cases, despite their being identified in one of the works by Keown that appears in his bibliography[134] – can only serve to augment our doubt and further weaken his case.

We conclude, then, that at least many of the cases of non-voluntary euthanasia committed in the Netherlands have involved dubious presumption; and that therefore there is reason to fear that the shift from voluntary to non-voluntary euthanasia has indeed constituted a moral slide.

In our moral consideration of the first shift, we reckoned that what is morally significant is not the practice of non-voluntary euthanasia as such, but rather its practice under far too relaxed a set of conditions. This anticipates – and, indeed, depends upon – a negative conclusion to our moral assessment of the second shift: namely, the expansion of the conditions under which euthanasia may be practised, which the elasticity of 'unbearable suffering without prospect of improvement' invites. It might be argued that such elasticity is required by respect for a certain patient autonomy. Since patients are the ones who experience suffering, surely they are in the best position to decide when it has become 'unbearable'; and since different individuals have different thresholds of tolerance with regard to different kinds of suffering, it is necessary that the concept of 'unbearable suffering' be very loosely defined.

That there might be something to be said for this is suggested by traditional moral reasoning, which allows patients the freedom to refuse life-sustaining treatment that they consider too burdensome. Why should this freedom not be extended from the refusal of treatment to the request for euthanasia or assistance in suicide? The reason is that what appears to be a straightforward extension of a certain freedom from one set of circumstances into another, would in fact involve the granting of a morally different kind of freedom altogether. Traditional moral thinking permits me to refuse life-prolonging treatment because I prefer a shorter life in which I can prepare to die – and discharge my remaining responsibilities – to a longer one in which all my energies are consumed in the struggle to stay alive. This limited permission falls a long way short of the freedom to intend death with a view to ending 'unbearable suffering'.

It is true that the law (at least in England) is more permissive than morality, since it permits the refusal of treatment even when it appears suicidal. However, this does not mean that the law is indifferent to suicide. Rather, recognising the limit to which it is possible to see into the hearts of other people and discern their intentions, and also the difficulty of forcing someone to carry on living against his will, it has decided to leave the moral responsibility in the hands of the patient.[135] Why should this legal freedom not be extended to those who, suffering intolerably, wish to be helped to die? After all, as we have argued, there are circumstances when it can be morally right to adopt a suicidal intention and to cooperate in suicide or commit euthanasia. Why should responsibility for this decision, too, not be left in the hands of the patient?

The answer is that we have recognised suicide, assistance in suicide, and euthanasia as morally permissible only in extreme circumstances: namely, either where human beings lack the possibility of responsible life because they are permanently bereft of the physical preconditions of consciousness, or where they lack the prospect of responsible life because of intense suffering that cannot be adequately relieved. The presence of these circumstances can be sufficiently determined by third parties with the appropriate medical expertise. No peering into the mysteries of another's heart is required.

Moreover, to permit assisted suicide or euthanasia on a ground so indefinite as that of 'unbearable suffering without prospect of improvement' is to undermine society's general affirmation of the high value of the life of the human individual. This affirmation is compatible with taking such life *in extremis*, when the possibility of responsible life has been forever lost; but it is not compatible with taking it in less severe circumstances. To leave it to patients to decide when their suffering has become unbearable and hopeless, and to permit others to cooperate in killing them at their request, implies far too casual a regard. Human life normally involves adversity of one kind or another, and many of us at some point contemplate suicide in the face of its more oppressive forms. Experience shows, however, that most adversity is worth enduring, either because of the prospects that lie beyond it, or because of what it teaches, or out of love for other people. Therefore our ordinary duty – the duty that respect for the exceptional value of individual human life ordinarily entails – is to help each other endure. Such a duty will involve precisely *not* taking at face value 'autonomous' requests to be killed or aided in suicide, and yielding to them. In most cases, what the patient really wants is not death at all, but rather that excessively burdensome life-prolonging treatment cease, that pain or other discomfort be controlled through palliative care, and that those around him affirm his continuing value.[136] To a very considerable extent, our 'autonomous' wishes are socially determined. Whether or not I want to go on living often depends on my self-esteem, and that in turn depends on my perception of how others view me. 'The picture that someone gains of himself', writes Eberhard Schockenhoff, 'depends not least on who he is in others' eyes. The estimation that he makes of the value of his own life always represents a reaction, one way or another, to the esteem he meets in the judgement of other people.'[137] Therefore it is not enough to satisfy ourselves that a patient's request to die is 'voluntary' or 'autonomous' in the sense of being well considered and persistent. For, as Emmanuel Hirsch puts it:

> [i]n the field of the choice between life and death, therefore, resort to the notion of individual autonomy is in part an illusion. [A] patient [whose physical and mental faculties are deteriorating] may truly want to die, but this desire is not the fruit of his freedom alone. It may be – and most often is – the translation of the attitude of those around him, if not of society as a whole which no longer believes in the value of his life and signals this to him in all sorts of ways. Here we have a supreme paradox: someone is cast out of the land of the living and then thinks that he, personally, wants to die.[138]

Our ordinary duty to those who suffer, then, involves our countering their poor self-esteem and confirming their worth precisely by our loyalty and care. Only in extraordinary circumstances ought we to help them escape – and then, not from a false sense of worthlessness, but only from a life that can never achieve or recover responsibility. To render help in escaping too soon or too readily – even if that's what they 'really want' – amounts to an act of abandonment. Accordingly, a high esteem for human life can only be affirmed by forbidding consensual killing in all but extreme cases. To permit it more liberally – for example, in the case of someone who is chronically depressed by grief or who finds life unbearable because avaricious relatives regard him as a nuisance – is not the mark of a humane society, but of one where carelessness is allowed to masquerade as respect.[139]

Therefore, because the elasticity of the condition of 'unbearable suffering without prospect of improvement' is incompatible with an esteem for human life that all but rarely expresses itself in support for fellow humans in enduring suffering, we judge its expansion of the circumstances in which euthanasia may be practised to constitute a morally deleterious slide.

We agree with John Keown, then, that the practice of euthanasia in the Netherlands during the period 1984–95 does show evidence of a morally objectionable deterioration; but we differ from him somewhat in our understanding of its nature. Keown objects primarily to the very fact of a shift from voluntary to non-voluntary euthanasia and this is where the main focus of the debate about the Dutch project has lain. We do not, however, regard this as the crucial moral issue, since we believe that there are extreme cases where it makes good sense to presume that another person would want to be killed, and where such a wish would be reasonable. Our main objection is to the liberal expansion of the range of cases in which it is deemed permissible to make such a grave judgement beyond those involving patients who have been set irrevocably beyond responsible life either by brain damage or by pain that cannot be relieved. Here, of course, we rejoin Keown in his criticism of the virtually infinite elasticity of the condition of 'unbearable suffering'.

Our agreement with Keown on this crucial issue ultimately sets us at odds with John Griffiths. On the one hand, Griffiths admits that current Dutch arrangements are not satisfactory. He acknowledges that there are abuses, that some doctors have reason to conceal what they have done, and that the self-reporting procedure does not provide adequate regulation. On the other hand, the solution that he proposes hardly suggests a serious concern about abuse. The removal of the threat of criminal prosecution from medical conduct that shortens life might well encourage innocent doctors who cannot stomach even the risk of criminal proceedings to report their life-shortening activity, and to do so more candidly, but it is hardly likely to encourage their law-breaking colleagues to do so.[140] To propose to solve a problem by means of encouraging candid self-reporting implies that the problem itself does not concern acts that really deserve to be hidden. However, our main complaint against

Griffiths is not just that he is equivocal in his concern about abuse, but also that he fails to see anything in current Dutch arrangements that actually fosters it. He denies that liberalisation in the Netherlands has presided over any moral slide, and he betrays no unease at all with the elasticity of the condition of 'unbearable suffering' and the carelessness it engenders.

So what do we conclude from the Dutch experience about the possibility of formulating and policing a law that permits euthanasia and assisted suicide only under certain conditions, and without precipitating any slide down slippery slopes to morally unacceptable situations? According to our reading, the data from the Netherlands for the period 1984–95 offer no support to those who see the realisation of such a possibility as unproblematic.[141] After all, here we have an unprecedented project of legal liberalisation that has been steadily and carefully developed over two decades (as Griffiths proudly avers), but which has nevertheless failed to stem a two-fold moral slide. This failure we have attributed crucially to the adoption of far too relaxed a set of criteria.

It is true that there is no reason *in principle* why these criteria could not be tightened or why another such project could not decide to adopt a stricter set from the beginning. Further, there is evidence that the criteria can be tighter *in practice* than they were in the Netherlands during the period under debate between Keown, Griffiths, and others. Recent legal developments there have involved a significant measure of retreat back up the Dutch slope. Responding to unease in medical and political circles over the Sutorius case[142] that the judgement of the Haarlem court (that being tired of life could constitute 'unbearable suffering without prospect of improvement') stretched the bounds of legitimate euthanasia too far, the public prosecution service subsequently launched an appeal in order to establish jurisprudence. In December 2001 an Amsterdam appeal court overturned the defendant's earlier acquittal on the ground that doctors have no expertise to judge 'existential' suffering, resulting from loneliness, emptiness, and fear of further decline.[143] Sutorius then appealed to the Supreme Court to quash his conviction. In December 2002 the court refused to do this in a judgement that underlined the appeal court's stipulation that 'unbearable suffering without prospect of improvement' must be linked to a recognisable medical or psychiatric condition.[144]

We must wait to see whether Dutch law now settles around this judgement, or whether the controversy that it has aroused leads eventually to its reversal. However, even if the Supreme Court's judgement does stick, it will still permit the practice of euthanasia and assisted suicide in a more relaxed range of cases than we think compatible with a humane society's commitment to support its hindered members in living responsible lives. Moreover, there are three reasons for being sceptical that sufficiently tight restrictions can ever be imposed, whether in the Netherlands or in any other part of the increasingly westernised world: the difficulty of achieving a democratic consensus on where to draw the line, with the consequence that it is drawn liberally; the predominant position of the value of individual autonomy in cultural common sense; and the influence of an expanded interpretation of the vocation of medicine that raises its sights beyond the mere promotion of physical health to the Promethean, utilitarian ambition of eliminating human unhappiness.[145] Therefore, while it is conceivable that laws could be formulated and enforced which severely restrict the practice of euthanasia and assisted suicide, practical success in so doing would require far more than a dose of clear, enlightened thinking untrammelled by the irrational prejudices of the past. It would take the taming and retraining of some powerful cultural prejudices.[146]

Fourth objection: physician-assisted suicide, which by definition involves the request of a competent adult, would avoid the feared slippage from voluntary into non-voluntary euthanasia

Fifth objection: the effects of permitting physician-assisted suicide would be no worse than those of permitting the refusal of life-sustaining treatment, since patients can be manipulated as easily into the latter as into the former; and since their number – and so the scope for abuse – would be smaller in the case of assisted suicide than in that of refusing treatment

These two objections have already been undermined by our response immediately above. They both presuppose that the morally crucial slippery slope issue is how to stop the slippage from voluntary to non-voluntary killing; and this, they argue, can be done by permitting physician-assisted suicide instead of voluntary euthanasia. By definition, assisted suicide cannot take place without the patient's express request and decisive action; and while it is true that patients could be manipulated by other people into making 'free' requests, their exposure to this manipulation would be no greater than it already is. In itself, this argument seems cogent. Since we already cede patients the legal freedom to refuse life-saving treatment, and since this is open to manipulation, permitting physician-assisted suicide would introduce no novel forms of abuse. It would, of course, expand the circle of the vulnerable; but data from the Netherlands suggest that the number of patients who would be involved in acts of assisted suicide, and so vulnerable to abuse, is only between 12 and 13 per cent of those already involved in the withdrawing or withholding of treatment.[147]

Yet this is all beside the point. We have argued that the deliberate killing of people in what we presume to be their best interests can be morally justified in some extreme circumstances, and that therefore the crucial issue is *not* the slippage from voluntary to non-voluntary euthanasia after all. The crucial issue is the slippage from very tight to relaxed conditions; and although physician-assisted suicide is more restrictive than voluntary euthanasia, it can still be extended to a far wider range of cases than we consider compatible with a humane society.

Sixth objection: the claim to be relieved of terrible suffering is stronger than the claim to be protected against unwanted pressure to choose to die

Dworkin admits that to establish a right to assisted suicide is bound to expose some patients to unwelcome pressure to avail themselves of it. The same could be said of the legalisation of voluntary euthanasia. Dworkin defends his proposal partly by arguing that more people would gain from this than lose; and, given that he is talking about the limited pool of patients with terminal or incurable (physical?) illness, he may be right. However, his argument falters at the point where, in utilitarian mode, he blithely asserts that the magnitude of the benefit of being spared great suffering exceeds that of the harm of being made to feel guilty about going on living or of being pressured into ending a miserable existence. The quantitative language ('magnitude') here implies a straightforwardness of comparative measurement that does not withstand a moment's reflection. Is it really clear that the terrible physical suffering from which I would be set free is a greater harm than your being driven to suicide by being made to feel worthless – and that therefore relieving me of the former is 'worth' your being made to suffer the latter? Not at all.[148] Further, when Dworkin seeks to bolster his argument by asserting that, while terminally or incurably ill patients have a stringent claim to be able to avoid needless pain and misery, they have no claim at all to be relieved of facing pressures on their choices, we must dissent. Our affirmation of the ordinary duty to help one another endure adversity implies that others do have a claim to expect such support from us; and one form that our support might well take is that of faithfully contradicting those voices that tell those who suffer that their lives have lost all value.

Margaret Battin's line of argument is superficially similar to Dworkin's. She argues that our duty to protect the vulnerable is not as strong as our duty to respect the right to die; but she does so on the ground that to withhold such respect from those for whom death has become 'rational' – that is, from those 'in the most unfortunate circumstances of us all' – is 'particularly cruel'.[149] Since she does not recognise any '*a priori* checks on the breadth of . . . extensions of the concept of rational suicide', she leaves its determination to the individual: suicide is rational whenever someone decides not 'to live in circumstances which *for him* are unacceptably or intolerably painful, physically or emotionally, or which are destructive of his most deeply held values'.[150] What she finds cruel, then, is not compelling someone to continue to endure, say, the intolerable physical pain of a life rapidly drawing to a close, but the thwarting of *any* will to die, for reasons medical or otherwise. For her, much more than for Dworkin, the moral issues reduce to that of the singularly fundamental moral imperative of respect for the individual's exercise of autonomy. Battin makes no move to justify the alleged supremacy of the legal right[151] to autonomy over the disposal of one's life; she merely asserts it. What she asserts, we deny – and for this reason: the granting of an untrammelled legal right to commit suicide is not compatible with the maintenance of a high social esteem for the exceptional value of the lives of human individuals; nor, therefore with the fostering of a common sense of the ordinary duty to help those who suffer to endure, perchance in their enduring to flourish.

Cahill's version of this objection is complex. One part argues that we should not tolerate the present evil of gross, pointless suffering out of fear that, should we act to end it, the future evil of the moral corruption of medical institutions might result. We have a greater responsibility to deal with evil that is certain than to worry about evil that is not.

To this we respond that comparative consideration of the certainty of two evils needs to be balanced by consideration of their gravity. While it would be imprudent to put up with an evil that is certain for the sake of avoiding a remote one of the same order, it would not be imprudent to suffer a certain evil for the sake of preventing a greater one which, while uncertain, is nevertheless highly possible or even probable. In this case, Cahill thinks that the remote evil of institutional corruption is not very certain at all, since she is sanguine that it can be prevented by prescribing 'relatively objective' conditions for the carrying out of euthanasia – for example, that candidates must be 'in the dying process' and in pain, or else lacking 'relational consciousness'.[152] It cannot be said, however, that our examination of the data from the Netherlands supports such optimism.

The second, anti-utilitarian part of Cahill's argument rather implies that the consequential considerations of the first part are beside the point. For here she maintains that the moral rightness or wrongness of what I do now cannot depend on what others might do later in response to it.[153] Since there are other responsible agents in the world than I, they too must have their own primary sphere of responsibility (namely, for their own choices), and where those begin mine must end. This is a more formidable point. It holds most obviously in the classic, paradigmatic case where you threaten to perpetrate a gross atrocity – the slaughter of my hostage family – unless I commit a murder. This I should not do, partly because I cannot be certain that you will follow through with your threat; more so because the atrocity would be your responsibility and not mine; but most of all because once I accept such utilitarian logic, there is nothing on earth that I would not be willing to do, should the circumstances suit. For these reasons, what you might do in response to my action cannot be a sufficient ground for my committing an injustice.

However, as we noted in Chapter Three,[154] the duty not to do an injustice is generally more stringent than the duty to do good or to promote welfare. This is because it is invariably possible for us to refrain from injury – by not opening our mouths, not raising our hands, not flicking the switch – whereas it is not always possible for us to confer a benefit – because we lack the resources or the means, or because we have an equal or stronger obligation to benefit other people, or because conferring this particular benefit is simply not our responsibility. The crucial question that presents itself, then, is this: Is it strictly unjust for me to refuse to kill someone who is dying without prospect of recovery and in pain that is beyond effective palliation, or is it merely a not-doing-good? Certainly it is not unjust in the sense that obtains in the classic case of the malevolent killing of a responsible person who threatens no harm. There the killing is an unambiguous evil; here the refusal to kill is not – because it refrains from doing harm to a living human being, albeit a non-responsible one, even if at the same time it refuses to confer the benefit of pain-relief. Further, to kill here will – and should be – a subjectively terrible experience for an agent who has been well formed to respect and treat with awe the exceptional value – the 'sacredness'[155] – of the responsible human individual, who only appears in bodily form. Further still, because of this sacredness the burden of proof should always lie much more heavily upon those who kill than upon those who refrain from killing. For these reasons, therefore, it is inappropriate to say of someone who refuses to kill a terminally ill and grossly suffering patient that they are committing an injustice. They cannot be held to have a duty to kill. Nor can a patient be said to have a right to be killed. Such killing may be morally permissible, but it is not obligatory.

If the refusal to kill in this case is not an injustice, then, *pace* Cahill, it could be warranted as necessary to meet the claims of strong obligations – for example, the duty, not only to protect patients against unfair pressure to ask for aid in suicide or for euthanasia, but also to foster care throughout society for all suffering and hindered human beings. So, if a respectable case can be made that the relaxation of the legal prohibition of the taking of innocent human life, in order to confer an ambiguous benefit on relatively few patients in extremis, might prove resistant to effective limitation; that this might jeopardise not only other classes of patient, but more broadly the humane (as distinct from laissez-faire) liberal ethos of society as a whole; and that these grave effects are at least highly possible; then the refusal to relax that prohibition could claim to be proportionate. We believe that such a case can be made, and we have presented our reasons.

One final remark remains to be made at this stage. At the end of Chapter Three, we raised the question of whether a patient's refusal to ask for voluntary euthanasia or for assistance in suicide could be considered a beneficial service to others. The argument in the paragraphs above brings us now to an affirmative answer. There is a strong obligation to foster a humane social commitment to help hindered and afflicted human beings flourish in responsible life as far as the limits of their suffering allow. This is stronger than the obligation to relieve human beings of suffering that permanently precludes any such flourishing. To permit such relief by voluntary euthanasia or assisted suicide would be to jeopardise society's humane ethos. Therefore, in refusing to add their voices to the clamour for the relaxation of the law against intentional killing of the innocent, patients can be said to exercise responsibility by performing a beneficial service to others. What is more, they thereby open their own suffering to the grace of meaning.

Conclusion

We hold that anxieties about the possibility of containing the deliberate killing of patients, or even deliberate cooperation in suicide, deserve to be taken seriously. Without exception, the critics of the traditional moral and legal prohibition of such killing and cooperation whom we have encountered in this chapter display a complacency about the security of humane and liberal values that the history of the twentieth century does not warrant.[156] Margaret Battin, for example, avers (with the virtually audible sigh of the morally self-assured) that '[a]fter Hitler, we are, I trust, beyond extermination of unwanted or dependent groups'.[157] One wonders who the happy 'we' are. Certainly not Cambodians or Rwandans or Iraqis. Maybe she just means 'westerners' or 'modern' people. But then with Srebrenica and 'ethnic cleansing' in Kosovo, the Serbs have stuck an awkward fly in that ointment. It takes someone who stands more directly in the shadow of the Nazi experience than naïve Anglo-Saxons to draw the humbler lesson: 'The veneer of civilisation,' writes the moral philosopher Dieter Birnbacher, 'is perhaps thinner than we allow ourselves to imagine.'[158]

Peter Haas confirms Birnbacher's more sober moral. Instead of seeing the Holocaust as the result of the mysterious irruption of evil, Haas reads it as the fruit of a gradual change of ethical sensibility in Germany to the point where many people considered it morally *right* to exterminate certain groups of human beings, because they were deemed evil or worthless or socially burdensome.[159] Although there may be more to be said for metaphysical evil than Haas supposes,[160] his interpretation has the advantage of helping to explain the participation in (what we deem) murder of so many ordinary, non-ideologically motivated citizens. It also prevents us from thinking that 'we' have nothing to learn from the Holocaust: for the lesson, according to Haas, 'is that people's moral inhibitions are easier to overcome than we might hope'.[161]

The realisation of the Nazi programme of the forcible killing of the mentally ill and handicapped fits Haas's reading. Notwithstanding its status as part of the stock-in-trade of opponents to the legalisation of euthanasia – and indeed notwithstanding a certain tendentiousness – the argument deployed by Leo Alexander during the Nuremberg Doctors' Trial remains cogent in its basic point:

Whatever proportion these [Nazi] crimes finally assumed, it became evident to all who investigated them that they had started from small beginnings. The beginnings at first were merely a subtle shift in emphasis in the basic attitude of physicians. It started with the acceptance of the attitude, basic in the euthanasia movement, that there is such a thing as life not worthy to be lived. This attitude in its early stages concerned itself merely with the severely and chronically sick. Gradually the sphere of those to be included in this category was enlarged to encompass the socially unproductive, the ideologically unwanted, the racially unwanted and finally all non-Germans. But it is important to realize that the infinitely small wedged-in lever from which this entire trend of mind received its impetus was the attitude toward the non-rehabilitable sick.[162]

While one might want to quarrel with this last statement – the Nazi inclination to exterminate the mentally ill or handicapped was impelled by *more* than just the single factor of the notion that some human life is unworthy to be lived – the point that the Nazi programme was nourished by developments in psychiatric thinking that preceded Hitler's accession to power is correct. As the historian of the Third Reich, Michael Burleigh, writes:

Long before the National Socialist government appeared on the scene, some psychiatrists advocated, or countenanced, killing . . . [the therapy-resistant chaff that comprised a] permanent reminder of the limits of their own therapeutic capacities and a permanent burden upon the nation's scant resources . . . [M]ost of the policies of the Nazi period were more or less apparent in the Janus-faced, and crisis-ridden, health and welfare apparatus of the Weimar Republic.[163]

The fertile soil in which Nazi policy grew was not simply medical, then. The urgent need to cut health-care costs was determined by general economic straits. And this was not the only non-medical factor. There was also the Nazi fetish-making of 'the mindless and narcissistic activism of youth [which] almost axiomatically entailed the neglect of the elderly and frail, let alone the mentally ill or physically disabled'.[164] And then there was widespread support among overburdened parents of the handicapped for the carrying out of euthanasia on their children: a survey conducted in 1925 of 162 parents of backward juveniles revealed that 73 per cent would approve 'the painless curtailment of the life of [their] child if experts had established that it is suffering from incurable idiocy'.[165]

The relevance of the events in Nazi Germany to contemporary debates about the legalisation of euthanasia is, of course, disputed. Lucy Davidowicz, for one, has indicated several points of disanalogy: the Nazi programme was fuelled by the motive of racial purity or health, not compassion, and it involved involuntary killing.[166] In each respect, however, the disanalogy is not as strong as she thinks. The desire for racial health is not clearly distinct from the desire for social utility, as Milton Himmelfarb has pointed out;[167] and Peggy Steinfels has observed that the concern for health and purity need not be racist in order to produce a prejudice against the infirm.[168] In addition, it cannot be taken for granted that compassion would motivate the practice of euthanasia in contemporary liberal societies, where the freedom for individualist consumerism vies with a commitment to humanity, and regard for other people is as much determined by laissez-faire carelessness as by anything more humane.

Moreover, our argument here can tolerate a measure of disanalogy, since it does *not* seek to establish that any permission of euthanasia *must* usher in a repeat of the Nazi project. What finally decided that, after all, was preparation for the launching of an aggressive war.[169] Our more modest point is that the record of Germany in the Weimar and Nazi periods warns of how medical frustration at impotence, economic pressures, the cultural worship of youth and physical health, and the natural desire of those who care for the incurable to have their burden lifted – all factors perfectly familiar to contemporary Western societies – can combine to create an impatience with the handicapped, the chronically ill, and the dying that undermines the commitment to support their more limited forms of personal life.

Neither from Germany's experience of Nazism nor from the Netherlands' experience of liberalisation do we conclude, as some are inclined to,[170] that any breach of the prohibition of the intentional killing of the innocent is *bound* – either logically, psychologically, or sociologically – to undermine society's solidarity with its hindered and ailing members. We can imagine a society where voluntary, and even non-voluntary, euthanasia is permitted, but where it is also recognised that this permission must be strictly confined to extreme cases, in order to maintain a general esteem for the 'sacredness' of personal life and to affirm the ordinary duty to support its hindered forms. Such recognition, however, would require something quite other than modern, Enlightenment optimism. It would take a sober reckoning with the power of the familiar forces that tend to erode solidarity with the weak, and the concomitant dislodging of dominant cultural illusions about the simplicity of individual autonomy and the moral sufficiency of individual rights.

At the very least, it cannot be said that success in achieving such salutary disillusionment is assured. Yes, there are growing signs of discontent with liberal naïvety about the autonomy of the individual, but those are mainly confined to academic and intellectual circles. What impact such unease will eventually come to have upon popular or common sense, on the media and the commercial forces that shape it, and on the terms of political debate that tend to follow it, is not clear. Certainly, the obsession of popular media with attention-grabbing narrative form, and their consequent inclination to focus on the dramatic story and the graphic distress of individuals, and to stir moralistic demands for instant relief, makes it very hard to win a hearing for other, less emotionally immediate, more morally complex, but arguably weightier considerations.[171]

However, even if the cultural battle were to be won, and public recognition secured for the need to confine strictly any permission of deliberate killing, a further problem would remain: how to settle where to draw the line? In this book I have argued that, wider social considerations apart, it could be morally permissible to take the lives of patients, if they were set irrevocably beyond responsibility either by brain damage or by intolerable suffering that cannot be relieved. There might be some extreme cases where the presence of such a condition would command all but universal agreement. But there would certainly be other, closely analogous cases where the definitions of 'responsible life' and of 'intolerable suffering', and the determination of the effects of brain-damage, would all be matter for vigorous and interminable controversy. While there might be good, clear reasons for drawing the line conservatively, there would be no strong, indisputable ones for drawing it precisely in one place rather than another. Therefore, because a conservative line is likely to be both somewhat arbitrary and very controversial, democratic deliberation would tend by default to draw a liberal one. *On Dying Well*, the Church of England's report, makes this point eloquently. Commenting on a stipulation by the Voluntary Euthanasia Bill presented to the Parliament of the United Kingdom in 1969 that an eligible patient must be suffering from 'a serious physical illness or impairment reasonably thought in the patient's case to be incurable and expected to cause him severe distress or to render him incapable of rational existence', it says:

> The expression 'physical illness' is presumably intended to rule out mental illness as a ground for euthanasia, but it could plausibly be argued, and almost certainly would be argued, that most, if not all, mental illnesses have a physical basis. It is very difficult to believe that the restriction to 'physical illness' as commonly

understood could be made effective, and this would
result not from any failure in rationality, or good faith,
but from the inherent difficulty of drawing a clear line
in such a case. The same problem might be expected to
arise in connection with 'severe' distress and 'incapable
of rational existence'. These are matters of degree, and
whereas there are extreme cases in which there can be
no doubt as to the applicability of such terms there is
no clear line of demarcation between these and more
disputable ones . . . Those who favour the widest possible extension would quite properly endeavour to
secure the most liberal possible interpretation of the
law . . . and the resulting pressure, because of the
inevitable imprecision of the key expressions, would be
extremely hard to resist.[172]

To give this prediction empirical substantiation, the report
appeals to the effects of the liberalisation of English law on
abortion in 1967. Elsewhere, Paul Badham supplies the
detail:

. . . Christian support for Abortion Law reform . . .
thought solely in terms of 'hard cases'. Christians could
see a justification for abortion when the mother's life
was in serious peril, or when there was a real risk of
gross abnormality in the foetus. What was never foreseen was that legislation to allow abortion in such cases
would lead to 170,000 legal abortions a year. Moreover,
a briefing paper . . . sent to the Diocesan Bishops on 14
April 1997 shows that since the 1967 Abortion Act only
0.004 per cent of abortions have actually been carried
out to save the life of the mother, and only 1.5 per
cent have been performed to prevent 'serious foetal
handicap'.[173]

Were we to need more recent and directly relevant substantiation of the claim that any relaxation of the law on
euthanasia is likely to result in a morally unacceptable

extension (if not quite 'the widest possible'), then recent Dutch experience would provide it. While this does not (yet) support fear of a slide to the point of mercy-killing on demand,[174] it certainly confirms doubts that the deliberate taking of the lives of patients can be confined so as not to threaten society's general esteem for the lives of human individuals, together with its humane affirmation of the ordinary duty to help the suffering to endure.

Therefore, on the decisive issue of whether any relaxation of the law can avoid sending both medical institutions and wider society down a slippery slope to morally unacceptable destinations, I finally side with McCormick and Ramsey against Cahill. I certainly doubt that such a slide can be avoided under current cultural conditions. And I can see no grounds for confidence that those conditions will ever be sufficiently different.

A methodological coda

By this point some readers might have begun to suspect that my argument has reduced itself to essentially pragmatic considerations. (Certainly, some listeners to early oral presentations of it did.) They might even have begun to suspect it of being consequentialist. Allow me, then, a defensive moment to try to dispel both suspicions.

It is true that my final judgement has turned on the consideration of a set of practical and empirical questions: How possible is it to settle the limits of permissible euthanasia or assisted suicide? What might be the consequences of limits that are too relaxed? How likely are these consequences? The answers that I have given to these questions have indeed been decisive in my argument. Nevertheless, it would be a mistake to infer from this that the latter is reducible to practical and empirical considerations. These have only arisen on the back of a prior set of moral ones, which have issued in the affirmation of one moral principle and two moral rules:

the principle that the lives of responsible human individuals are exceptionally valuable; the rule that one ought never to take such life intentionally or to accept its taking without proportionate reason, unfairly, or unfaithfully; and the rule that society ought to form its members into the kind of people who are predisposed to help each other flourish in such responsible life as defect or injury or pain allow. Only within a context already structured by these moral assertions has there arisen the practical and empirical issue of whether it is possible to establish a further, legal rule for the taking of human life bereft of any capacity for the exercise of responsibility, without realising deleterious consequences that might impair society's commitment to the second rule.

Obviously our response to this question has involved (inevitably crude) attempts to estimate possible consequences and their probability. It has not involved, however, any utilitarian pseudo-calculation, any spurious 'weighing up' of 'amounts' of different kinds of human unhappiness against each other (e.g. severe physical pain against a socially induced sense of personal worthlessness). Nor has the consideration of consequences been either the only or the primary kind of consideration. It has therefore not been consequentialist.

Conclusion

The end of all our exploring has been to arrive where we started, but knowing the place far better. At the beginning of this book I declared that I was setting off with conservative prejudices, and here at the end of it I have reached a conservative conclusion: that there should be no relaxation of the law that prohibits euthanasia and assisted suicide. The effect of this study, then, has been to confirm initial prejudices. But some prejudices are wiser than they can say and this book has also had the effect, I hope, of testing and explaining the wisdom of these particular ones.

Succinctly put, the explanation is this. The special value of the lives of human individuals is best understood in terms of their being dignified by the opportunity and obligation to respond to a call of God to play an inimitable part in the maintaining and promotion of the welfare of the world. This theological concept of responsibility secures the *value* of the individual better than ethically subjectivist celebrations of arbitrary self-assertion or self-expression. It also secures the value of the *individual* better than modern philosophical appeals to a generic rationality. Not all human beings, however, are capable of responsibility. Some are so irremediably hindered by physical injury or defect, or so consumed by unrelievable physical suffering, that any kind of response to 'external' stimuli is forever beyond their power. For this reason it makes sense to distinguish between life that is 'biographical' and that which is merely 'biological'. However, the concept of responsibility acts here to push the boundaries of 'biographical' life out, so that they embrace those hindered humans whose 'rationality' (narrowly conceived) might be in question, but whose capacity for showing due appreciation for what is good and bearing prophetic witness to what is true, is not.

Biographical human life is 'sacred'. No one should want to damage or destroy it. Everyone should always regard it with care. Nevertheless, there are tragic situations where the proportionate defence or pursuit of some good is not possible without taking such life. Here, it is permissible to cause death so long as one 'accepts' rather than 'intends' (wants) it, and provided that this acceptance is characterised by a reluctance that is genuine and therefore active. However, human life that is forever beyond responsibility may be taken intentionally, and even non-voluntarily – all other social considerations apart. At the end of Chapter Three, therefore, we concluded provisionally that the rule against the intentional killing of the innocent is not applicable to all cases.

Provisionally: for it might be that the effects of a legal relaxation of this rule would be so grave, and the possibility sufficiently high, as to justify keeping the prohibition unconditional. The grave effects that are feared here are the exposure of responsible patients to manipulation and abuse, and the undermining of society's high esteem for responsible human life and so of a common sense of the ordinary duty to support its many hindered and suffering forms. The history of the development of the Nazi policy of involuntary euthanasia indicates that such effects are indeed a possibility that even contemporary liberal societies must reckon with. The intrinsic difficulty of defining 'extreme cases' and confining candidates for euthanasia to them heightens that possibility. Widespread and deeply entrenched cultural assumptions, together with the practices of the popular media, compound the difficulty and heighten the possibility further. The recent failure of the Netherlands adequately to confine eligible cases pushes the possibility onto the verge of probability. Since the relief of suffering is not a strict duty, while the protection of the innocent against life-threatening manipulation and abuse is a stricter one, the requirements of the latter can justify refusing the former. Therefore, given that the feared effects of relaxing the law are very grave, and given that their possibility is high, we judge that the unconditional prohibition of euthanasia and assisted suicide should be maintained.

What does this conclusion imply for the treatment of extreme cases? Does it mean that patients who are consumed with severe pain that cannot be effectively managed must simply be left to endure it? Not at all. There is no such thing as pain that cannot be relieved, insofar as permanent sedation can always be used as a last resort; and provided that this is strictly ordered to the provision of pain-relief, there would be no moral objection to it, even if it were to result in the shortening of life.

A more awkward set of cases is that of patients in persistent vegetative state (PVS). Here the brain stem remains alive, with the result that the patient is able to breathe and digest unaided and is capable of reflex movement, including response to painful stimuli. However, because the brain's cortex is dead, he lacks cognitive function and can neither see nor hear, nor feel pain[1] and emotion, nor communicate. In other words, he is irrevocably bereft of the possibility of responsible life. (In Tony Bland's case the irrevocable nature of the loss is underscored by the fact that his cortex had liquefied.[2]) Are we obliged to support this form of human life? Or may we withdraw treatment, including artificial nutrition and hydration,[3] and withhold the use of antibiotics to combat infection?

It is morally permissible for a competent patient to refuse treatment because he would rather expend his limited energy on living as well and responsibly as possible than on striving to fend off death. Here the doctor's acquiescence in the patient's refusal through the withholding or withdrawing of treatment expresses a readiness to accept death, not a desire for it. The rationale of the decision to withdraw tube-feeding and withhold antibiotics from a patient in PVS, however, seems different. This rests on the judgement that human life that is forever bereft of a capacity for responsible life is not worth the costs of sustaining it;[4] and here the costs are not those of the patient, who is beyond suffering of all kinds, but the emotional burden borne by the family and the economic costs to the community. I believe that this judgement is correct. However, a familiar problem arises at this point; for if we permit the withdrawal or withholding of treatment in the case of a patient in PVS, because we consider this form of human life not worth sustaining, will we be able to draw a convincing line between this kind of case and other ones where the lack of responsible life is more ambiguous? If it were possible, I would support it, but I am not convinced that it is. John Keown observes that two years after the English legal system finally permitted the withdrawal of tube-feeding from Tony Bland (March 1993), the Irish Supreme Court permitted the same withdrawal from a patient who was not in PVS and 'retained some cognitive function' (May 1995).[5] Then, four years after that, the British Medical Association published influential guidance on the withholding and withdrawal of medical treatment, which endorses the withholding or withdrawal of tube-delivered food and water not only from patients in PVS, but also from other non-terminally ill patients such as those with severe dementia or serious stroke.[6] The conclusion to which this line of argument leads us is that, notwithstanding the fact that patients in PVS are irrevocably beyond responsible life, we should nevertheless persist in rendering them artificial nutrition and hydration and in using antibiotics to combat infection – so long as these are not medically disproportionate or futile.

This conclusion is consistent, but it is nevertheless odd. It is odd, since it commits us to prolonging the lives of incompetent patients who are in a far worse condition than those of competent patients whose decision to refuse treatment we deem morally permissible. We could try to mount an alternative line of argument, then: namely, that since it is morally permissible for competent patients who are capable of some responsible life to have treatment withheld or withdrawn, it is also morally permissible to withhold or withdraw treatment from incompetent patients in much worse conditions, on the assumption that they would ask for it if they had the power to do so. The problem with that, however, is that we cannot take our cue from the *morality* of treatment refusal, since that inspires a variety of opinions. We would have to take our bearings from the relevant *law*, and that is liberal to a fault: *any* treatment refusal by a competent patient must be respected. Reluctantly, therefore, I cannot see any consistent way of avoiding the conclusion that PVS patients should be sustained by proportionate and non-futile medical treatment.

Extreme cases, however, ought not to be allowed to dominate the horizon as we draw to a close. They are, after all, relatively few in number: as palliative care becomes ever more sophisticated, cases of suffering beyond adequate relief become ever rarer; and in a United Kingdom population of approximately sixty million there is a prevalence of 1500 cases of PVS.[7] For the overwhelming majority of patients who fear pointlessly prolonged or painful or lonely dying, the implication of our concluding judgement against relaxing the legal prohibition of euthanasia and assisted suicide is that much more needs to be invested in the development of palliative care. It would be the mark of a humane society's commitment to supporting its hindered members in adversity that it should make this its clear priority. (It is surely one of the most damning features of Dutch policy that it has pursued the relaxation of the prohibition of euthanasia and assisted suicide during a time when palliative care services in the Netherlands have been so rudimentary.) No doubt, the development of palliative care should involve an increase in the quantity of palliative resources – more hospice beds, more palliative care nurses, more specialist doctors. But, much more radically, it should also involve a change in the vision of the goals of health-care. Doctors – and other health-care professionals – need to learn to see professional success not only in terms of fending off death, but also in terms of helping patients to flourish in their dying. And that will require more than mere professional training. It will also require a certain spiritual formation, in which those who treat and care for the sick are formed into the kind of people who, when faced with death in the eyes of the dying, have the moral strength to resist the natural instinct of mortal human beings, and not to turn away.

Notes

Introduction

1. Jeremy Waldron, *God, Locke, and Equality: Christian Foundations in Locke's Political Thought* (Cambridge: Cambridge University Press, 2002), p. 20.
2. See 'Barthian' in the Glossary.
3. See my *The Hastening that Waits: Karl Barth's Ethics*, 2nd edition (Oxford: Clarendon Press, 1995), pp. 152–5.
4. ibid., p. 159.
5. The origins of a notion of responsible human individuality in the lonely witness of the biblical prophet are shrewdly identified by Oliver O'Donovan in *The Desire of the Nations: Rediscovering the Roots of Political Theology* (Cambridge: Cambridge University Press, 1996), pp. 73–81.
6. Richard Hays, *The Moral Vision of the New Testament: A Contemporary Introduction to New Testament Ethics* (Edinburgh: T. & T. Clark, 1996), Chapter 10.
7. ibid., pp. 298–304.

Chapter One

1. John Keown, *Euthanasia, Ethics, and Public Policy* (Cambridge: Cambridge University Press, 2002), pp. 58–9. My account of English law depends almost entirely on Keown.
2. ibid., p. 26.
3. ibid., pp. 11–12.
4. Quoted by Keown in ibid., p. 66.
5. ibid., p. 59.
6. ibid., p. 67. Keown argues that English law has recently fallen into serious inconsistency on this point, laying itself open to the interpretation that it requires doctors to assist in all refusals of life-saving treatment, even when they are clearly suicidal (pp. 67–8 and Part VI).
7. ibid., p. 58.
8. Michel Maret, *L'euthanasie: alternative sociale et enjeux pour l'éthique chrétienne* (Saint-Maurice: Éditions Saint-Augustin, 2000), p. 33.
9. See John T. Noonan, *Contraception: A History of its Treatment by the Catholic Theologians and Canonists* (Cambridge and London: Harvard University Press, 1965, 1986), Chapter IV, 'The Morals of the Manichees and St Augustine'.
10. See ibid., Chapter VI, 'The Canonists, the Cathars, and St Augustine'.
11. See Chapter Two, p. 42–5.
12. The Mennonites trace their origins back to Menno Simmons, a 16th century leader of Anabaptists in Holland. The Anabaptists were a

Notes 173

collection of religious dissidents who separated themselves from both Catholics and Protestants.

13. They recognise that the 'use of the sword' has been ordained by God but they deny that it is to be exercised by members of the Christian community. See the Schleitheim Confession (1527), Article 6 (John H. Leith [ed.] *Creeds of the Churches: a Reader in Christian Doctrine from the Bible to the Present*, rev. ed. [Atlanta: John Knox, 1973], p. 287).

14. See the gospels of Matthew, 22:34–40; of Mark, 12:28–31; and of Luke 10:25–28.

15. Augustine, *Against Faustus*, 22.74; *Letters*, 138.9 (to Marcellinus), 189.2, 6, 7 (to Boniface).

16. Augustine, *On Free Will*, Book I, ch.5.12; *Against Faustus*, 22.74–5; *Letters*, 47 (to Publico).

17. Augustine, *Letters*, 138.14 (to Marcellinus); *Letters*, 220.8 (to Boniface).

18. Augustine, *On Free Will*, Book I, ch.5.11–13.

19. *Summa Theologiae*, IIaIIae, q. 64, a. 7. More controversially, he goes on to argue that 'one is bound to take more care of one's own life than of another's' (ibid.).

20. See the first creation story in the book of Genesis in the Hebrew Scriptures (the Christian Old Testament), chapter 1 (e.g. 'And God saw everything that he had made, and behold it was very good').

21. The connection between right intention and proportion is made explicit by Aquinas in *Summa Theologiae*, IIaIIae, q. 64, a. 7.

22. Richard Shelly Hartigan, *The Forgotten Victim: A History of the Civilian* (Chicago: Precedent, 1982), pp. 31–3.

23. ibid., p. 43.

24. I rely here on Robert Regout's interpretation of Vitoria (*La doctrine de le guerre juste de Saint Augustin à nos jours*), as endorsed and reported by Hartigan, ibid., pp. 82, 142 n.6.

25. Francisco de Vitoria, *Commentary on the Summa Theologiae of St Thomas Aquinas, IIaIIae*, q. 40, a. 1.10 (quoted by Hartigan in *Forgotten Victim*, p. 84); *On the Law of War*, q. 1, a. 3.4 (quoted by Hartigan, p. 87).

26. Aquinas, *Summa*, IIaIIae, q. 64, a. 7.

27. Actually, Aquinas stipulates this only where someone is acting in a private capacity. Where the agent is acting with public authorisation – for example, as a soldier – he may intend to kill an aggressor, provided that he 'refers' this to – is motivated by – the public good.

28. Vitoria, *Commentary on the Summa*, q. 40, a. 1.10.

29. Augustine was the only Christian theologian to treat suicide at length until the 12th century, and his writing dominated Christian thinking after that (Alexander Murray, *Suicide in the Middle Ages*, vol. II: 'The Curse on Self-Murder' [Oxford: Oxford University Press, 2000], pp. 91, 101).

30. Augustine, *The City of God*, I.17.

31. ibid., I.22.

32. ibid., I.24.

33. ibid., I.17, 25.

34. ibid.

35. ibid., I.19.

36. ibid., I.21 (Augustine, *City of God*, ed. David Knowles [Harmondsworth: Penguin, 1972], p. 32).

37. ibid., I.26 (Augustine, *City of God*, p. 37). My initial interpretation of

Augustine on this point had him admitting divinely commanded suicide only as a theoretical possibility (for who can be *certain* about an ad hoc divine command?). A reading of Murray has convinced me otherwise (Murray, *Suicide in the Middle Ages*, vol. II, pp. 119–20).
38. Aquinas, *Summa Theologiae*, IaIIae, q. 64, art. 5, reply, and reply to objection 2.
39. ibid., reply to objection 3.
40. Sacred Congregation for the Doctrine of the Faith, *Declaration on Euthanasia* (5 May 1980), in Stephen E. Lammers and Allen Verhey (eds), *On Moral Medicine*, 2nd edition (Grand Rapids, MI: Eerdmans, 1998), p. 651.
41. ibid.
42. For an account of recent legal developments in the Netherlands, the Northern Territory, and Oregon, see Keown, *Euthanasia, Ethics, and Public Policy*, chapters 8, 14, 15.
43. Maret, *L'euthanasie*, pp. 53–4.
44. My translation of Maret, ibid., p. 61: 'Il se trouve isolé, éloigné de sa famille, de ses proches, hérissé de tubes, entouré de machines, ne pouvant pratiquement pas avoir des relations avec le personnel (lumières violentes, bruit des appareils, agitation des soignants, perfusions, transfusions, électroencéphalogrammes, radiographes, trachéotomie . . .)'.
45. ibid., pp. 56–7.
46. Stuart Horner, 'Preface to the Second Edition', *On Dying Well: A Contribution to the Euthanasia Debate*, report of a working party of the Board for Social Responsibility of the Church of England, 2nd edition (London: Church House Publishing, 2000), p. xi.
47. Daniel Callahan, *The Troubled Dream of Life: In Search of a Peaceful Death* (Washington, DC: Georgetown UP, 2000), p. 190.
48. The Voluntary Euthanasia Society, *The Last Right: the Need for Voluntary Euthanasia* (London: Voluntary Euthanasia Society, 1992), p. 7.
49. See, for example, Derek Humphry and Ann Wickett, *The Right to Die: Understanding Euthanasia* (New York: Harper and Row, 1986), p. 50.
50. See, for example, ibid., pp. 193, 201.
51. 'The Right to Die', *The Economist*, 17 September 1994, p. 14.
52. 'The Right to Choose to Die', *The Economist*, 21 June 1997, p. 13.

Chapter Two
1. Battin's critique may be found in two main places. The first is in Chapter 1 of *Ethical Issues in Suicide* (Englewood Cliffs, New Jersey: Prentice Hall, 1982, 1995), entitled 'Religious Views of Suicide'. The second is in Chapter 11 of *The Least Worst Death: Essays in Bioethics on the End of Life* (New York and Oxford: Oxford University Press, 1994), entitled 'Prohibition and Invitation: The Paradox of Religious Views about Suicide'. The content of these two essays appears to be identical.
2. Battin, 'Prohibition and Invitation', p. 217. A theological version of this argument is made by J. Pohier: 'God does not half-give humans freedom while keeping back a "reserved sphere". It is almost blasphemous to think that God gives us life while forbidding us to dispose of it, for better or worse, as we judge fit.' My translation of: 'Dieu ne donne pas à moitié la liberté aux humains en se gardant un "domaine reserve". Il est presque blasphématoire de penser que Dieu nous a

donné la vie en nous privant d'en disposer, pour le pire et pour le meilleur, selon notre jugement.' (quoted by M. Horwitz, in 'L'euthanasie en débat', *Actualité Religieuse dans le monde*, 119 [15 February 1994], p. 26)

3. Battin, 'Prohibition and Invitation', p. 218.
4. ibid., p. 219.
5. ibid., p. 220.
6. ibid., p. 221.
7. ibid., p. 222.
8. ibid., p. 230.
9. James Rachels, *The End of Life* (Oxford: Oxford University Press, 1986), pp. 5, 25.
10. ibid., pp. 5, 64–5. Peter Singer is another who uses the distinction between biological and biographical life, identifying the latter as characterised by 'rationality, autonomy, and self-consciousness' (*Practical Ethics*, 2nd edition [Cambridge: Cambridge University Press, 1993], pp. 192, 182).
11. Rachels, *End of Life*, p. 2.
12. ibid., pp. 60–7.
13. ibid., p. 65. My italics.
14. ibid.
15. John Harris, 'Euthanasia and the Value of Life', in John Keown (ed.), *Euthanasia Examined* (Cambridge: Cambridge University Press, 1995), pp. 8–9.
16. ibid., p. 11.
17. ibid., p. 16.
18. ibid., p. 9.
19. ibid., p. 16. While the phrase 'the intrinsic, cosmic importance of human life itself' belongs originally to Ronald Dworkin, Harris explicitly endorses it.
20. Ronald Dworkin, *Life's Dominion: An Argument about Abortion and Euthanasia* (London: HarperCollins, 1993), p. 27.
21. ibid., pp. 92, 79, 76.
22. ibid., p. 79.
23. ibid., p. 205.
24. ibid., p. 199. A 'critical' interest is one that issues from an individual's *judgement* about what makes his life valuable (pp. 201–2).
25. ibid., p. 216.
26. ibid., p. 217.
27. ibid., p. 211.
28. Battin exemplifies the 'utilitarian, even hedonistic, presuppositions that characterise much secular antitheodicy' (Brian Hebblethwaite, 'The Problem of Evil', in *Keeping the Faith: Essays to Mark the Centenary of 'Lux Mundi'*, ed. Geoffrey Wainwright [London: SPCK, 1989], p. 58).
29. Battin, 'Prohibition and Invitation', pp. 219–21.
30. Hebblethwaite, 'The Problem of Evil', p. 68.
31. I note that in *God, Locke, and Equality*, Jeremy Waldron makes a similar argument from the conviction that human beings are basically equal – 'We take equality seriously . . .' (p. 235) – to ownership of the Christian theological foundations that make such a notion 'most coherent and attractive' (p. 236).
32. Among Hollywood directors, Malick has the distinction of being the

author of the standard English translation of Heidegger's *Vom Wesen des Grundes – The Essence of Reasons* (Evanston, Illinois: Northwestern University Press, 1969). His *The Thin Red Line* (1998) is not to be confused with the 1964 film of the same name.

33. Battin, 'Prohibition and Invitation', p. 220.
34. Helmuth James von Moltke, *Letters to Freya, 1939–45* (London: Collins Harvill, 1991), p. 412.
35. Battin, 'Prohibition and Invitation', p. 220.
36. Germain Grisez, *The Way of the Lord Jesus*, 3 vols, vol. 2: *Living a Christian Life* (Quincy, IL: Franciscan Press, 1993), p. 460.
37. ibid.
38. ibid., p. 464.
39. ibid., p. 467.
40. ibid., p. 464.
41. ibid., fn.8.
42. ibid., p. 461.
43. ibid., p. 462.
44. ibid.
45. ibid., p. 466. The affirmation of the intrinsic value of bodily life as an argument against distinguishing between forms of human life that are worthwhile ('rational', 'biographical') and those that are not, appears in Lutheran quarters as well as conservative Roman Catholic ones. In his discussion of euthanasia and by appeal to the bodily resurrection, Dietrich Bonhoeffer asserts that human life is essentially bodily and that human dignity attaches to the body and not just the mind (according to Uwe Gerrens in *Medizinisches Ethos und Theologische Ethik: Karl und Dietrich Bonhoeffer in der Auseinandersetzung um Zwangssterilisation und 'Euthanasie' im Nationalsozialismus*, Schriftenreihe der Vierteljahrshefte für Zeitgeschichte, vol. 73 [Munich: R. Oldenbourg Verlag, 1996], pp. 151, 182, 183). And Martin Honecker argues that Peter Singer's definition of the human person in terms of freedom and self-consciousness neglects the natural, bodily basis of humanity; and that since bodiliness is the basis of all human activity, its protection is fundamental ('Sterbehilfe und Euthanasie aus theologischer Sicht' in *Lebensverkürzung, Tötung und Serientötung – eine interdisziplinäre Analyse der 'Euthanasie'*, ed. Manfred Oehmichen [Lübeck: Schmidt-Römhild, 1996], p. 79).
46. Grisez, *Living a Christian Life*, p. 467. My emphasis.
47. That this line of argument might be problematic is hinted at by the fact that Grisez himself does not always stick to it. For example, on one occasion he admits that 'to call a human individual "a person" . . . is to say more than that he or she is a member of the species *homo sapiens*'. The word 'person', he tells us, connotes the intrinsic worth of a human being 'as a subject of rights and responsibilities' (ibid., p. 461). A little further on, he associates personhood – and the prohibition of the taking of human life – with being made in God's image; that is, with being 'intelligent and free . . . made for communion with one another, empowered to procreate, and given dominion over the rest of the material world' (ibid.).
48. John Finnis, 'A Philosophical Case against Euthanasia' in Keown, *Euthanasia Examined*, p. 31.
49. ibid.

50. ibid. Or, as he puts it later in 'The Fragile Case for Euthanasia: A Reply to John Harris' (Keown, *Euthanasia Examined*, p. 50): any 'organism of human genetic constitution normal enough to provide, at least the organic basis of some intellectual act'.
51. Finnis, 'The Fragile Case for Euthanasia'., p. 48.
52. Finnis, 'A Philosophical Case against Euthanasia', p. 31.
53. ibid., p. 33.
54. Tony Bland was among those injured on 15 April 1989 in the disaster at the Hillsborough football stadium in Sheffield, where almost 100 spectators were crushed to death. Bland survived but his lungs were crushed and punctured and the supply of oxygen to his brain was interrupted, causing irreversible damage to its higher, cortical centres. The condition in which he lingered for just under four years in hospital is known as 'persistent vegetative state' (PVS). Its distinctive features are that the brain stem remains alive and functioning, but not the brain's cortex. The former supports basic bodily functions; the latter supports consciousness. Accordingly, the PVS patient is able to breathe and digest unaided, and he is capable of reflex movement, especially in response to painful stimuli. However, lacking cognitive function, he can neither see nor hear nor feel pain and emotion nor communicate. Nor can he feed himself. In Bland's case the medical consensus was that, like most patients in PVS, he would never recover. After all, his cortex had liquefied. Both his parents and his doctor wanted to stop his artificial feeding (by tube through the nose) and the treatment of his infections by antibiotics, but were advised that in the event the doctor might be prosecuted for homicide. In order to obtain an authoritative legal ruling, the trust that ran the hospital then applied to the High Court for a declaration that the cessation of feeding and antibiotics would be lawful. The Official Solicitor opposed the application, eventually appealing to the highest court in England, the House of Lords. In 1993, the Law Lords finally dismissed the appeal. Bland's tube-feeding was stopped and he died a few days later on 3 March.
55. Finnis, 'Misunderstanding the Case against Euthanasia: Response to Harris's First Reply' in Keown, *Euthanasia Examined*, p. 69.
56. Finnis, 'A Philosophical Case against Euthanasia', p. 32.
57. ibid., p. 32; Finnis, 'Misunderstanding the Case against Euthanasia', p. 69.
58. See above, n. 53.
59. Here I find myself in rare agreement with John Harris, who raises a similar objection to according a one-cell zygote the status of person on the ground of its possession of the organic basis of intellectual activity. He writes: 'we are entitled to ask how a creature that has never possessed, and will never possess, the ability, the power (dare I say the capacity) to perform . . . [an intellectual] act, can be valuable solely in virtue of such a remote (unrealisable and forever unrealised) connection with such an act' ('Final Thoughts on Final Acts' in Keown, *Euthanasia Examined*, p. 60).
60. Oliver O'Donovan, *Begotten or Made?* (Oxford: Clarendon Press, 1984), pp. 51, 53. As will become clear below, O'Donovan's understanding of individuality as constituted by a calling from God is essentially the same as Karl Barth's.

61. ibid., p. 53.
62. ibid., pp. 53–4, 58.
63. ibid., pp. 50, 54; 'Again: Who is a Person?' in J. H. Channer (ed.), *Abortion and the Sanctity of Life* (Exeter: Paternoster Press, 1985), pp. 126, 129.
64. O'Donovan, 'Again: Who is a Person?', p. 128.
65. O'Donovan, *Begotten or Made?*, pp. 59–60.
66. O'Donovan, 'Again: Who is a Person?', pp. 136–7. My emphasis.
67. O'Donovan, *Begotten or Made?*, p. 60.
68. O'Donovan, 'Again: Who is a Person?', pp. 129–30.
69. ibid., pp. 133–4.
70. ibid., p. 130.
71. ibid., p. 16.
72. Alasdair MacIntyre, *After Virtue: a Study in Moral Theory* (Notre Dame: University of Notre Dame Press, 1981), chs 2, 3.
73. Harris, 'Euthanasia and the Value of Life', p. 11.
74. Onora O'Neill also observes how autonomy, conceived in 'postmodernist' terms as lawless, unprincipled independence, erodes social trust and issues in 'isolation' (*Autonomy and Trust in Bioethics* [Cambridge: Cambridge University Press, 2002], pp. 24, 93–4. However, she rejects the Aristotelian option (taken by Taylor and Finnis) of subordinating autonomy to an antecedently given moral framework comprising substantive principles drawn from some conception of human flourishing or the human good. This is because she reckons that the prospect of arriving at a convincing account of the complete human good, and of the proper ordering of its components, is an 'implausibly ambitious' fantasy (ibid., p. 77). Instead, she follows Kant in arguing that autonomy is bound only by 'principles of thought in general' – that is, by non-derivative 'reason' (ibid., p. 90). What this amounts to is that principled and responsible autonomy makes practical judgements that other people find 'accessible', 'intelligible', 'adoptable', 'followable', and so 'as having a general authority that would lead us to speak of them as *reasoned*' (ibid., p. 91). But does not this immediately fall foul of the classic complaint against the 'formalism' of Kantian ethics? Does it not complacently assume the stable social dominance of a substantive ethic that precludes the possibility that other people will find accessible, intelligible, adoptable, and followable a proposal to commit, say, genocide? Perhaps O'Neill would reply that autonomous judgements must appear reasoned and so authoritative to *everyone*. But is this any less of an implausibly ambitious fantasy?
75. Finnis, 'The Fragile Case for Euthanasia', pp. 52, 53.
76. Charles Taylor, *The Ethics of Authenticity* (Cambridge, Mass.: Harvard University Press, 1991), p. 39.
77. Karl Barth, *Church Dogmatics*, 4 vols., ed. G. W. Bromiley and T. F. Torrance (Edinburgh: T. & T. Clark, 1936–77), Volume III, 'The Doctrine of Creation', Part 4 (Edinburgh: T. & T. Clark, 1961), p. 579.
78. ibid., p. 329. The idea that an individual is constituted by a morally obligatory 'calling' also appears in the thought of Emmanuel Levinas. 'To utter "I", to affirm the irreducible singularity', he writes, ' . . . means to possess a privileged place with regard to responsibilities for which no one can replace me and from whom no one can release me' (*Totality and Infinity: An Essay on Exteriority* [Pittsburgh: Duquesne

Notes

179

University Press, 1969], p. 245). I cannot even release myself, because I do not choose my own responsibilities. Rather, they are given me by the Other who 'commands me and ordains me' (*Otherwise than Being, or Beyond Essence* [The Hague: Martinus Nijhoff, 1981], p. 11). Levinas' position appears to differ from Barth's – and therefore from our own – in two respects. First, Levinas emphasises the absoluteness of the individual's responsibility to and for the Other, not its finiteness; and in doing so he risks crippling human creatures with a burden for which only divine shoulders are fitted. Second, the Other to whom I am absolutely responsible is a fellow human creature, the infinity of whose moral claims upon me is denoted by the word 'God'. Here, then, 'God' seems to refer to a transcendent source of unconditional obligation – a Kantian Moral Law? – rather than a more-than-human agent in whose salvific work human creatures are called to play a finite part. My reading of Levinas here is largely second-hand, depending heavily on A. T. Nuyen, 'Levinas and the Euthanasia Debate', in *Journal of Religious Ethics*, 28/1 (Spring 2000), especially pp. 124–5, 132–3. Nevertheless, discussion of these points with an expert student of Levinas' ethics, Robert Gibbs, has not inclined me to revise my interpretation.

79. Barth, *Church Dogmatics*, III/4, p. 659.
80. David Pailin objects to accounts of human worth that proceed in terms of social contribution or usefulness, because, among other things, they fail to secure the value of the individual (*A Gentle Touch: From a Theology of Handicap to a Theology of Human Being* [London: SPCK, 1992], pp. 100–102). Instead, he proposes that we think of human worth as 'a product of being of worth to others' (p. 118) or of 'care by others' (p. 121); and that since everyone is loved by God, everyone therefore has 'intrinsic worth' (p. 121). Our account agrees with Pailin's in that we understand the worth of each human individual to derive from his being addressed and called by God to do something that only he can do in his space and time and in his inimitable manner; and since we assume that what God calls each of us to do is for our own good, we assume that call to be moved by love. Further, we reject a utilitarian notion of social contribution that thinks only in terms of material, quantitative, measurable goods, and we expand the notion of worthwhile service to include acts of sheer (and prophetic) appreciation of what is good and beautiful. The one point of discrepancy between our two accounts is that Pailin locates human worth simply in God's love, whereas we locate it in the *call* of God's love. Consequently, Pailin's reading seems to us too 'laissez-faire' – for example, when he tells us that individuals have worth 'as they actually are at the moment, and not for what they might become' (p. 148). It is true that he qualifies this by adding that such love is compatible with desiring the beloved to change (p. 148), but only at the price of then casting into doubt whether the beloved really is loved as she actually is.
81. For this reason Richard McCormick and, following him, Lisa Cahill represent an advance upon Rachels when they identify the capacity for personal love as the human value, above all others, from sustaining which 'biological' life draws its 'sacred' value. See R. A. McCormick, 'To Save or Let Die: the Dilemma of Modern Medicine' in *How Brave a New*

World? Dilemmas in Bioethics (London: SCM, 1981), pp. 345–8; and Lisa Sowle Cahill, 'A "Natural Law" Reconsideration of Euthanasia' in Lammers and Verhey, *On Moral Medicine*, pp. 445–53; absent from the 2nd edition (1998); reprinted from *Linacre Quarterly*, 44 (February 1977).

82. Jean-Dominique Bauby, *The Diving-Bell and the Butterfly* (London: Fourth Estate, 1997), pp. 77–8.

83. Frances Young, *Face to Face: A Narrative Essay in the Theology of Suffering* (Edinburgh: T. & T. Clark, 1990), p. 9.

84. ibid., pp. 20, 28.

85. ibid., pp. 109, 179, 180. Dietrich Bonhoeffer makes the cognate point that their condition gives the handicapped an insight into the basic vulnerability of human existence that is not afforded the healthy (*Dietrich Bonhoeffer: Gesammelte Schriften*, ed. Eberhard Bethge, vol. II: 'Kirchenkampf und Finkenwalde – Resolutionen, Aufsätze, Rundbriefe 1933–43' [Munich 1966], pp. 77f.; quoted by Gerrens in *Medizinisches Ethos*, p. 129). Likewise, Stanley Hauerwas: 'Prophetlike, the retarded only remind us of the insecurity hidden in our false sense of self-possession' ('Suffering the Retarded: Should we Prevent Retardation?' in *Suffering Presence: Theological Reflections on Medicine, the Mentally Handicapped, and the Church* [Notre Dame: Notre Dame UP, 1986], p. 169).

86. Pailin, *A Gentle Touch*, pp. 110–11.

87. Our Barthian theological account of the value of the life of the human individual, and our argument that it 'outnarrates' at least one atheistic philosophical alternative, finds significant echoes in Jeremy Waldron's study of John Locke's theory of the basic equality of human beings. Waldron argues that Locke's theory is fundamentally theological. According to Locke, (individual) human beings are all equal (in value) insofar as they 'have Light enough to lead them to the Knowledge of their Maker, and the sight of their own Duties' (from Locke, *An Essay Concerning Human Understanding*, Introduction; cited in *God, Locke, and Equality*, p. 79), in which case they are 'all the servants of the one Sovereign Master, sent into the World by his order, and about his business; they are His property, whose workmanship they are made to last during His, not one another's pleasure' (from Locke, *Two Treatises of Government*, Book II, Chapter II.6; cited in *God, Locke, and Equality*, pp. 80–1). Waldron comments: Lockean equality 'is a conception . . . that makes no sense except in the light of a particular account of the relation between man and God' (*God, Locke, and Equality*, p. 82). Further: 'I believe that Locke's mature corpus . . . is as well-worked-out a theory of basic equality as we have in the canon of political philosophy' (p. 1). Further still: 'Locke's religious premises help to make sense of or give shape to a certain cluster of human characteristics that might seem arbitrary, shapeless, even insignificant apart from the religious context' (p. 48). Even further: ' . . . I am inclined to believe . . . that a commitment to human equality is most coherent and attractive when it is grounded in theological truth, truths associated particularly with the Christian heritage' (p. 236). Furthest: 'I actually don't think that we – now – *can* shape and defend an adequate conception of basic human equality apart from some religious foundation' (p. 13).

88. Dworkin himself rather reinforces this point when he writes that '[t]he

literature of conservation is studded with ... personifications of nature as creative artist' (*Life's Dominion*, p. 76).

89. Dworkin, *Life's Dominion*, pp. 216–17.

90. ibid., p. 215.

91. Hans Küng, 'A Dignified Dying' in Hans Küng and Walter Jens, *A Dignified Dying: A Plea for Personal Responsibility* (London: SCM, 1995), pp. 9–16.

92. In Lammers and Verhey, *On Moral Medicine*, pp. 443, 444.

93. John Paul II, *Apostolic Letter on the Christian Meaning of Human Suffering* (Boston: St Paul Books & Media, 1984), sections 12, 21.

94. ibid., s. 26, p. 44.

95. ibid., s. 1.

96. ibid., s. 17.

97. ibid.; s. 18.

98. ibid., s. 18.

99. ibid., s. 19.

100. ibid., s. 24.

101. For further elaboration, see my article on 'Atonement' in *Dictionary of Ethics, Theology, and Society*, ed. Paul Barry Clarke & Andrew Linzey (London & New York: Routledge, 1996).

102. I discuss these matters at greater length in 'Forgiveness in the Twentieth Century: A Review of the Literature, 1901–2001' in Alistair McFadyen and Marcel Sarot (eds), *Forgiveness and Truth* (Edinburgh and New York: T. & T. Clark, 2001), esp. pp. 196–207, 215–17.

103. This restricted concept of redemptive suffering is supported by the New Testament where the 'suffering' by which Christians are united with Christ refers primarily to persecution. This John Paul inadvertently shows when he quotes from the Gospels in section 25 of *Salvifici Doloris*.

Chapter Three

1. James Rachels, 'Active and Passive Euthanasia' in *Killing and Letting Die*, ed. Bonnie Steinbock and Alastair Norcross, 2nd edition (New York: Fordham University Press, 1994), p. 115. Rachels' article was first published in the *New England Journal of Medicine*, 292 (9 January 1975).

2. ibid., p. 116.

3. ibid., pp. 113–14.

4. Michael Tooley, 'An Irrelevant Consideration: Killing Versus Letting Die' in ibid., pp. 103–4.

5. ibid., p. 107.

6. Peter Singer, *Practical Ethics*, 2nd edition (Cambridge: Cambridge University Press, 1993), p. 209.

7. R. G. Frey, 'Distinctions in Death' in Gerald Dworkin, R. G. Frey, and Sissela Bok, *Euthanasia and Physician-Assisted Suicide: For and Against* (Cambridge: CUP, 1998), pp. 27, 29, 36, 38, 41.

8. See Chapter One, p. 100

9. Joseph T. Mangan sj, 'An Historical Analysis of the Principle of Double Effect', *Theological Studies*, 10 [1949], p. 43.

10. Jonathan Glover, *Causing Death and Saving Lives* (London: Penguin, 1977), p. 88. James Rachels makes the same point (*The End of Life*, p. 93).

11. Blaise Pascal (1623–62) was, among many other things, the author of

a classic attack on the ethical sophistry of mid-17th century Jesuit moral theology (*Lettres provinciales*, 1656–57).

12. Rachels, *The End of Life*, pp. 92–4.

13. Rachels, 'More Impertinent Distinctions and a Defense of Active Euthanasia' in Steinbock and Norcross, *Killing and Letting Die*, pp. 141–2. This essay was originally published in *Biomedical Ethics*, Thomas A. Mappes and Jane S. Zembaty (eds) (New York: McGraw Hill, 1981). Much of it is incorporated into *The End of Life* (1986), pp. 92–100, 152–60.

14. Glover, *Causing Death and Saving Lives*, pp. 87–8.

15. ibid., p. 90. Peter Singer also argues that 'a consequentialist judgment lurks behind the doctrine of double effect' (*Practical Ethics*, p. 210).

16. Glover, *Causing Death and Saving Lives*, pp. 89–90. Jonathan Bennett shares Glover's doubts about the notion of an intrinsically bad act ('Foreseen Side Effects versus Intended Consequences' in *The Doctrine of Double Effect: Philosophers Debate a Controversial Moral Principle*, ed. P. A. Woodward [Notre Dame: University of Notre Dame Press, 2001], pp. 88–9. This chapter comprises an excerpt from Jonathan Bennett, *The Act Itself* [New York and Oxford: Oxford University Press, 1995], pp. 194–225).

17. Rachels, *The End of Life*, p. 72.

18. Harris, *The Value of Life*, p. 43.

19. *Euthanasia and Clinical Practice: Trends, Principles, and Alternatives* (London: Linacre Centre, 1982), pp. 34, 35; quoted in ibid., pp. 43–44.

20. Harris, *The Value of Life*, pp. 43–4.

21. Mary Warnock, *An Intelligent Person's Guide to Ethics* (London: Gerald Duckworth, 1998), p. 37.

22. ibid., p. 39.

23. ibid., pp. 38–9.

24. ibid., p. 39.

25. Singer, *Practical Ethics*, p. 210.

26. Warnock, *Intelligent Person's Guide*, pp. 41–2.

27. This point Glover attributes to Jonathan Bennett, 'Whatever the Consequences', *Analysis*, 26/23 (1966); reprinted in Steinbock and Norcross, *Killing and Letting Die*, as Chapter 10.

28. Glover, *Causing Death and Saving Lives*, pp. 88–9.

29. Tom L. Beauchamp and James F. Childress, *Principles of Biomedical Ethics*, 5th edition (New York: Oxford University Press, 2001), pp. 142–3.

30. Callahan, *Troubled Dream of Life*, p. 79.

31. Arthur Dyck, *Life's Worth: The Case Against Assisted Suicide* (Grand Rapids, MI: Eerdmans, 2002), p. 38.

32. 'Life-sustaining treatment' is an ambiguous term. It can mean either treatment designed to sustain life or treatment actually effective in doing so. In this case, we assume that the treatment in question actually could sustain life further in some form; for if it had lost the power to do so, then its withdrawal could not be held to cause death at all.

33. Grisez, *The Way of the Lord Jesus*, vol. 1: *Christian Moral Principles* (Chicago: Franciscan Herald Press, 1983), p. 234 (9.C.4–6); *Living a Christian Life*, p. 478 (8.B.3.c).

34. Wolbert concludes cautiously that to hold that there is no general moral distinction between killing and letting die based simply on the

different causal relations between the 'agent' and death, 'appears not to contradict the Magisterium of the church' ('scheint dem kirchlichen Lehramt nicht zu widersprechen' in *Du sollst nicht töten: Systematische Überlegungen zum Tötungsverbot*, Studien zur theologischen Ethik, 87 [Freiburg, Switzerland: Universitätsverlag; Freiburg-im-Breisgau: Herder, 2000], p. 126; see also pp. 123–7).

35. Tooley perceives that there may be reasons other than the mere distinction between acts and omissions that establish a moral distinction between killing and letting die. He acknowledges that one reason why letting someone die is generally preferable to killing them is that saving them 'may involve considerable risk to the agent, or a very large expenditure of society's resources', while '[t]his will rarely be true of refraining from killing someone' (Tooley, 'An Irrelevant Consideration', pp. 103–4). Philippa Foot develops this point into the principle that the negative duty of avoiding doing someone an injury is generally more stringent than the positive one of bringing them aid, because whereas we are usually free to avoid causing harm, we are often not free to bring aid – whether because we lack the resources or because we are subject to moral constraints (e.g., against committing murder in order to obtain food for one's starving children) (Philippa Foot, 'The Problem of Abortion and the Doctrine of Double Effect' in Steinbock and Norcross, *Killing and Letting Die*, pp. 273–5; originally published in the *Oxford Review*, 5 [1967]. Foot reaffirms her position in 'Killing and Letting Die', in Steinbock and Norcross, *Killing and Letting Die*, pp. 284–5; originally published in Jay L. Garfield and Patricia Hennessey [eds], *Abortion and Legal Perspectives* [Amherst: University of Massachusetts Press, 1984]).

36. Paul Ramsey, 'On (Only) Caring for the Dying' in *The Patient as Person: Explorations in Medical Ethics* (New Haven: Yale UP, 1970), p. 151.

37. Norvin Richards, 'Double Effect and Moral Character', *Mind*, XCIII (1984), p. 386.

38. Rachels, 'More Impertinent Distinctions', pp. 141–2.

39. For example, the mid-17th century Salmanticenses Scholastici in their *Cursus Theologicus* (Parisiis, Bruxellis, 1877), t. [vol.] 7, tr. 13, disp. 10, dub. 6, n. 214–47, as quoted by Joseph Mangan SJ in 'An Historical Analysis of the Principle of Double Effect', p. 57; and Jean Pierre Gury SJ in his *Compendium Theologiae Moralis* (Lugduni, 1850; Ratisbonae, 1874), t. [vol.] 1, 'De actibus humanis', c. 2, n. 9, as interpreted by Alan Donagan in *The Theory of Morality* (Chicago and London: University of Chicago Press, 1977), pp. 159–60.

40. Donagan interprets Gury's version of the doctrine of double effect as ruling out the use of lethal force in self-defence (*Theory of Morality*, p. 162); Grisez reads 'some classical moralists' (among whom he includes Gabriel Vasquez and John de Lugo [*Living a Christian Life*, p. 472 n. 21]) as considering all directly and voluntarily caused deaths to be intentional (*Living a Christian Life*, p. 472 (8.B.1.d).

41. Again, this is how Donagan reads Gury (*Theory of Morality*, p. 160).

42. Germain Grisez, 'Toward a Consistent Natural Law Ethics of Killing', *The American Journal of Jurisprudence*, 15 (1970), pp. 88, 90; quoted with approval by Donagan in *Theory of Morality*, p. 160.

43. Grisez, *Living a Christian Life*, p. 472 (8.B.1.d).

44. Grisez, *Christian Moral Principles*, p. 239 (9.F.1, 2): 'We are responsible

for more than just what we aim at and choose . . . [O]ne can bear
responsibility for foreseen consequences that are no part of one's
proposal.'

45. For this reason, Grisez thinks it best to drop the language of 'directness' altogether (*Living a Christian Life*, p. 473 [8.B.1.f]).
46. Henry Sidgwick, *Methods of Ethics*, 7th edition (London: Macmillan,
1907; Indianapolis: Hackett, 1981), p. 202. My emphasis.
47. See Donagan, *Theory of Morality*, 2.2 (pp. 37–52).
48. ibid., p. 124.
49. *Euthanasia, Clinical Practice, and the Law* (London: Linacre Centre for
Health-Care Ethics, 1994), p. 39. Book One of this volume comprises
Euthanasia and Clinical Practice: Trends, Principles, and Alternatives,
which is the report of the Linacre Centre's Working Party that was first
published in 1982. See above, no. 19.
50. As reported by Donagan in *Theory of Morality*, p. 125.
51. ibid.
52. Grisez, *Christian Moral Principles*, 9.F; *Living a Christian Life*, pp. 471–2
(8.B.1.d).
53. G. E. M. Anscombe, 'War and Murder' in Woodward, *Doctrine of Double
Effect*, p. 257; reprinted from Walter Stein (ed.), *Nuclear Weapons: A
Catholic Response* (New York: Sheed and Ward, 1962).
54. Donagan, *Theory of Morality*, p. 125.
55. ibid., p. 164. Beauchamp and Childress make the same mistake when
they opt for a concept of intentionality 'based on what is *willed* rather
than what is *wanted*. On this model, intentional actions and intentional effects include any action and any effect specifically willed in
accordance with a plan, including tolerated as well as wanted
effects . . . Under this conception . . . the distinction between what is
intended and what is merely foreseen in a planned action is not viable'
(*Principles of Biomedical Ethics*, p. 131). However, under this conception
a mother who wills or chooses to interpose herself between a grizzly
bear and her child, intending to protect the latter but foreseeing that
she herself will very probably be mauled in the process, must be held
also to intend her own mauling. This is misleading, insofar as it fails
to distinguish different qualities of willing, and so connotes a suicidal
desire on the part of the mother to be killed by the bear.
56. Donagan, *Theory of Morality*, p. 125.
57. ibid., p. 164.
58. Grisez, *Christian Moral Principles*, p. 239 (9.F.1).
59. ibid., p. 240 (9.F.4).
60. ibid., pp. 205–6, 211–13, 215–16 (8.A, E, G); *Living a Christian Life*,
pp. 482–3, 484–5, 486 (9.C).
61. Grisez, *Christian Moral Principles*, pp. 239, 240 (9.F.2, 3).
62. ibid., p. 239 (9.F.2).
63. See Philippa Foot, 'The Problem of Abortion', p. 268.
64. Bennett, 'Foreseen Side Effects', pp. 101–2.
65. ibid., p. 104.
66. ibid., pp. 115–16.
67. ibid., p. 100.
68. The example is Grisez's ('Toward a Consistent Natural-Law Ethics of
Killing', p. 90).
69. Bennett, 'Foreseen Side Effects', p. 89.

70. ibid., p. 92.
71. ibid., p. 112.
72. ibid., p. 112.
73. What sense does it make to describe someone as simultaneously 'glad' and 'reluctant' over the same thing?
74. Bennett, 'Foreseen Side Effects', p. 113.
75. ibid., p. 114.
76. A variety of counter-factual tests for what is to be counted as intended means have been formulated and criticised. For example, Alan Donagan proposes that '[a] good test of whether you intend a particular foreseen effect of an action is to suppose that, by some fluke or miracle, the action does not have the effect that you foresee, and to ask whether you then consider your plan carried out and your purpose accomplished' ('Moral Absolutism and the Double Effect Exception: Reflections on Joseph Boyle's "Who is Entitled to Double Effect?"', *The Journal of Medicine and Philosophy*, 16 [1991], p. 496). However, Donald B. Marquis criticises this proposal for permitting *any* means (or better: any unwanted effect of the chosen means) to escape from the realm of the intentional, 'if the means causes an unwanted effect and the means is the only means available to achieve a good end' ('Four Versions of Double Effect', reprinted from *The Journal of Medicine and Philosophy*, 16 [1991] in Woodward, *Doctrine of Double Effect*, p. 168 – see also p. 171). My complaint against the 'fanciful' version of the counter-factual question echoes Marquis' complaint against Donagan's.
77. Here, of course, we echo Anscombe's insistence that an intention is not a purely private phenomenon, knowable only to the agent upon interior reflection. Rather, it is usually visible to others in what the agent does ('Medalist's Address: Action, Intention, and "Double Effect"' in Woodward, *The Doctrine of Double Effect*, p. 57 – reprinted from *Proceedings of the American Catholic Philosophical Association*, 56 [1982]; 'War and Murder', p. 257) – including the measures he takes or fails to take to avoid or minimise the evil that he accepts. This is the implicit ground of A. J. Coates' salutary defence of the doctrine of double effect's traditional stipulation that attention should be paid to 'the act itself' – because this is an indispensable way of testing what purports to be the intention (*The Ethics of War* [Manchester: Manchester University Press], 1997, pp. 241–3).
78. For completeness' sake, we should point out that our line of reasoning also leads us to judge the Linacre Centre's analysis of the pot-holer case – on which Harris bases his discussion – to be erroneous. Provided that there really is no other way out, and all reasonable steps are taken to avoid or minimise harm to the pot-holer who is blocking the exit, it does not matter whether he is killed by having his head crushed or being blown up (unless one of these is reckoned likely to be less painful) because in neither case is his death intended.
79. Richard McCormick, 'Ambiguity in Moral Choice' in Richard McCormick and Paul Ramsey, *Doing Evil to Achieve Good: Moral Choice in Conflict Situations* (Chicago: Loyola University Press, 1978), p. 23.
80. Aquinas, *Summa Theologiae*, IIaIIae, q. 64, a. 2; a. 3, r. obj. 2, 3.
81. Later, he clearly implies that he considers it unproblematic for a public official to intend to kill someone who poses a public threat: 'But as

it is unlawful to take a man's life, except for the public authority acting for the common good . . . it is not lawful for a man to intend
killing a man in self-defence . . .' (ibid., IIaIIae, q. 64, a. 7).

82. ibid., IIaIIae, q. 64, a. 2, r. obj. 3. To his credit, Aquinas is not at all consistent on this point, for in the very next article, where he addresses
the question, 'Whether it is lawful for a private individual to kill a man
who has sinned?', he asserts that public authorisation is needed,
because sinners are not 'by nature' distinct from good men and so
equivalent to beasts (a. 3, r. obj. 2); and later on he confirms this by
saying that 'in every man, though he be sinful, we ought to love the
nature which God has made, and which is destroyed by slaying him'
(a. 6).

83. ibid., IIaIIae, q. 64, a. 7.

84. ibid., a. 6.

85. ibid., a. 7.

86. Grisez, *Christian Moral Principles*, pp. 215 (8.G.1), 216–17 (8.H.1).

87. In *Life and Death with Liberty and Justice*, Grisez (and Boyle) explicitly
distance themselves from Aquinas on this point, rejecting the subordination of the individual to 'the well-being of political society', and
arguing that this itself is but (one form of) one of the basic goods and
finds its justification in its 'contribution to the flourishing of these
goods in [individual] persons' (Germain Grisez and Joseph M. Boyle,
*Life and Death with Liberty and Justice: A Contribution to the Euthanasia
Debate* [Notre Dame and London: University of Notre Dame Press,
1979], pp. 398–9).

88. Grisez, *Christian Moral Principles*, Chapter 9, Question F; vol. 2: *Living a
Christian Life*, pp. 471–2 (8.B.1.d).

89. ibid., F.3; Grisez and Boyle, *Life and Death with Liberty and Justice*,
pp. 386, 388.

90. Grisez and Boyle, *Life and Death with Liberty and Justice*, pp. 382–3.

91. Grisez, *Living a Christian Life*, pp. 468–9. Grisez is not alone among
contemporary philosophers in recognising the crucial importance of
the quality of the will; nor is this recognition confined to Christians.
It was because she came to the conviction that 'what matters morally
is not only how someone *acts* . . . but also how his will is disposed' that
Philippa Foot recanted her earlier denial of the moral significance of
the distinction between 'direct and indirect intention' ('Morality,
Action, and Outcome' in Woodward, *The Doctrine of Double Effect*,
pp. 70, 81–2 n. 6; reprinted from *Morality and Objectivity: A Tribute to J.
L. Mackie*, ed. Ted Honderich [London and Boston: Routledge and
Kegan Paul, 1985]). Thomas Nagel gives expression to a similar concern when, defending the moral relevance of the strictly intentional,
he writes that 'to aim at evil, even as a means, is to have one's action
guided by evil . . . But the essence of evil is that it should *repel* us . . .
So when we aim at evil we are swimming head-on against the normative current . . . What feels particularly wrong about doing evil intentionally even that good may come of it is the headlong striving against
value that is internal to one's aim' ('Ethics' in *The View from Nowhere*
[New York: Oxford University Press, 1986], pp. 181–2).

92. Grisez, *Living a Christian Life*, p. 478 (8.B.3.e); *Christian Moral Principles*,
p. 215 (8.G.1).

93. Grisez, *Living a Christian Life*, p. 479 (8.B.3.e); *Christian Moral Principles*, pp. 216–17 (8.H.1).
94. It is 'the central defect' of 'proportionalism' and 'consequentialism' that, assuming what they cannot know (that one good 'outweighs' another), they subordinate rational judgement to emotion; and '[t]hat', says Grisez, 'is simply to abandon morality' (*Living a Christian Life*, p. 479 (8.B.3.e).
95. ibid., pp. 479 (8.B.3.e), 480 (8.B.4.a).
96. ibid., p. 480 (8.B.4.a).
97. ibid.
98. ibid., p. 479 (8.B.4).
99. ibid., p. 479 (8.B.3.e).
100. Grisez, *Christian Moral Principles*, p. 185 (7.F.2).
101. ibid., p. 132 (5.H.10).
102. ibid., pp. 188, 185–6 (7.F.9, 2).
103. ibid., pp. 185–6 (7.F.2).
104. ibid., p. 186 (7.F.3).
105. ibid., pp. 185 (7.F.2), 186 (7.F.4).
106. ibid., p. 151 (6.F.1).
107. So Jeremy Bentham, the founding father of utilitarianism.
108. This at least is what Grisez says of the proportionalists, whom he counts as a species of consequentialist (Grisez, *Christian Moral Principles*, pp. 143, 156–7, 158–9 [6.B.1, H.2, 4, 5, 6]).
109. ibid., p. 223 (8.I.3).
110. ibid., p. 188 (7.F.9).
111. ibid., p. 132 (5.H.9).
112. ibid., p. 479 (8.B.3.e).
113. ibid., p. 156 (6.H.1). *Pace* Jean Porter ('Basic Goods and the Human Good in Recent Catholic Moral Theology', *The Thomist*, 57/1 [January 1993], pp. 40–1), Grisez does not say that physical pleasure cannot be a worthy object of rational action. He admits that 'normally a person's outward behavior is . . . directed both toward sensible pleasure (or the avoidance of its opposite) and intelligible fulfilment (or the avoidance of its privation)', and that in many cases 'what is done brings about results which are both pleasant (the sensible good is experienced) and fulfilling (the intelligible good is served)' (*Christian Moral Principles*, p. 119 [5.B.3, 5]). What he does say is that pleasure (the satisfaction of an emotional desire) should never be an *independent* object of action, apart from the pursuit of an intelligible good (ibid., p. 225 [8, Summary.3]); and that when one is faced with a choice between an intelligible good (e.g. healthy, functioning teeth) and avoiding a sensible evil (e.g. painful dental treatment) – or enjoying a sensible good (e.g. eating sweets) – the first should override the second (ibid., p. 120 [5.B.7]). While this does betray a covert anthropology, as Porter rightly points out, it is less austerely Kantian than she supposes ('Basic Good and the Human Good', pp. 41, 42).
114. Grisez, *Christian Moral Principles*, p. 144 (6.B.3, 5).
115. ibid., p. 156 (6.H.1).
116. ibid., p. 151 (6.E.6).
117. ibid., p. 120 (5.B.7).
118. ibid., p. 156 (6.H.1).
119. ibid., p. 119 (5.B.2).

188

Notes

120. According to the controversial eighth 'mode of responsibility' (ibid., p. 216 [8.H.1]).
121. ibid., pp. 147–8, 151, 153 (6.D.3, E.6, F.8).
122. ibid., p. 147 (6.D.2).
123. ibid., pp. 211–12 (8.E).
124. ibid., pp 210–11 (8.D)..
125. ibid., pp. 641–2 (26.G.1).
126. Porter, 'Basic Good and the Human Good', p. 39.
127. Grisez, *Christian Moral Principles*, pp. 643–4 (26.G.8).
128. See Chapter Two, response to the twelfth objection.
129. ibid., p. 120 (5.B.7). My emphases.
130. Timothy Chappell, 'Natural Law Revived: Natural Law Theory and Contemporary Moral Philosophy' in Nigel Biggar and Rufus Black (eds), *The Revival of Natural Law: Philosophical, theological, and ethical responses to the Finnis-Grisez School* (Aldershot: Ashgate, 2000), pp. 35, 36.
131. Aquinas, *Summa Theologiae*, IIa IIae, q. 64, a. 6.
132. As Kenneth Kirk writes, 'Every [moral] principle is partially illuminated by the known instances in which it holds good; without such known instances it would remain a mere unmeaning formula endowed with all the terrors of the unintelligible . . . [E]very principle, to be morally operative must be accompanied by illustrations or examples . . .' (*Conscience and its Problems: An Introduction to Casuistry* [London: Longman, Green and Co., 1927]), p. 107.
133. Here I find myself aligned with R. A. McCormick: ' . . . the tradition . . . overlooks the fact that there can be instances where there is "innocence" (no injustice), yet killing would involve no *injuria*' ('The Consistent Ethic of Life: Is There a Historical Soft Underbelly?' in R. A. McCormick, *The Critical Calling: Reflections on Moral Dilemmas since Vatican II* [Washington, D.C.: Georgetown University Press, 1989], pp. 226–7). For a discussion of how moral reasoning proceeds and moral rules develop by means of the critical comparison of typical and untypical cases, see Nigel Biggar, 'A Case for Casuistry in the Church', *Modern Theology*, 6/1 (October 1989), pp. 41–4.
134. The classic theological expression of such Kantian Protestantism is Anders Nygren's *Agape and Eros*, first published in 1930.
135. James M. Gustafson, *Ethics from a Theocentric Perspective*, 2 vols., vol. 2: 'Ethics and Theology' (Chicago: University of Chicago Press, 1984), p. 214.
136. ibid., p. 213.
137. ibid., p. 214.
138. ibid., p. 209.
139. ibid., pp. 214, 215.
140. Joachim Fest, *Plotting Hitler's Death: The German Resistance to Hitler, 1933–45* (London: Weidenfield & Nicholson, 1996), pp. 289, 398.
141. ibid., pp. 289–90.
142. Alexander Murray observes that medieval Christian thought tended to stereotype the psychology of suicides, failing (for the most part) to distinguish between despair of maintaining or achieving temporal goods and despair of faith and hope in God (Murray, *Suicide in the Middle Ages*, vol. II, Chapter 11).
143. Gustafson, 'Ethics and Theology', p. 213.

144. Barth, *Church Dogmatics*, III/4, pp. 398, 402.
145. ibid., p. 401.
146. ibid., p. 405.
147. ibid., pp. 404, 408.
148. ibid., p. 407.
149. ibid., p. 410.
150. ibid., p. 402. My emphasis.
151. ibid.
152. ibid., p. 410.
153. ibid., p. 408.
154. ibid., p. 412.
155. ibid., p. 425.
156. ibid.
157. ibid., p. 427.
158. Donagan, *Theory of Morality*, pp. 63, 64–5, 164.
159. ibid., p. 64.
160. ibid., p. 77.
161. ibid., p. 76.
162. ibid., p. 79.
163. As Garth Hallett notes in *Greater Good: the Case for Proportionalism* (Washington, DC: Georgetown University Press, 1995), p. 80.
164. Donagan, *Theory of Morality*, p. 85. My emphasis: note the plural case. For help in developing my suspicions on this front I am indebted to Garth Hallett's *Greater Good*, Chapter 6, especially p. 82. As Hallett says, 'In *The Theory of Morality*, values [goods] determine respect more than respect determines values . . . Comparisons of disparate values (e.g. justice, life, convenience, cost, community, self-respect, enjoyment) repeatedly determine what is "respectful" . . .' (ibid., pp. 84, 85).
165. Richard McCormick, 'A Commentary on the Commentaries' in McCormick and Ramsey, *Doing Evil to Achieve Good*, p. 247.
166. To be precise, this is what he held by the time he had finished writing his 'Commentary'. It was not what he held earlier when he wrote 'Ambiguity' ('Commentary', pp. 263–4).
167. McCormick, 'Ambiguity', pp. 26, 28, 39–40; 'The Principle of Double Effect', Appendix to *How Brave a New World? Dilemmas in Bioethics* (London: SCM, 1981), p. 427.
168. McCormick, 'Commentary', pp. 224, 261.
169. McCormick, 'Ambiguity', p. 47; 'Commentary', p. 207.
170. McCormick, 'The Principle of Double Effect', p. 426.
171. ibid., pp. 426–7: 'such [preference] is clearly not possible where basic goods are concerned'.
172. McCormick, 'To Save or Let Die: The Dilemma of Modern Medicine' in *How Brave a New World?*, p. 345.
173. ibid., p. 347.
174. ibid., p. 349.
175. McCormick, 'The Consistent Ethic of Life', pp. 218–19.
176. McCormick, 'Ambiguity', pp. 47–8.
177. Cahill, 'A "Natural Law" Reconsideration', pp. 446–7.
178. ibid., p. 453n.35: Aquinas, *Summa Theologiae*, IIa IIae, q. 25, a. 7; a. 12, r. obj. 2; q. 26, a. 4.
179. Aquinas, *Summa Theologiae*, IIa IIae, q. 64, a. 5, r. obj. 3.
180. Cahill, 'A "Natural Law" Reconsideration', p. 450.

181. ibid.

182. Lisa Sowle Cahill, 'Respecting Life and Causing Death in the Medical Context' in J. Pohier and D. Mieth (eds), *Concilium*, 179 (1985): 'Suicide and the Right to Die', pp. 35, 37.

183. Cahill, 'A "Natural Law" Reconsideration', p. 449.

184. Rachels, 'More Impertinent Distinctions', p. 144.

185. Paul Ramsey, 'On (Only) Caring for the Dying', pp. 161–2.

186. ibid., pp. 162–3.

187. ibid., p. 162. Although Ramsey explicitly says this only of the comatose, he make it clear on the following page that he regards someone in 'undefeatable agony' as equally beyond the reach of care.

188. ibid., p. 164.

189. ibid., quoting Leo Alexander, 'Medical Science under Dictatorship', *New England Journal of Medicine*, 241/2 (14 July 1949), pp. 44, 45.

Chapter Four

1. John Griffiths, 'The Slippery Slope: Are the Dutch Sliding Down or Are They Clambering Up?' in David Thomasma, Thomasine Kimbrough-Kushner, Gerrit Kimsma, and Chris Ciesielski-Carlucci (eds), *Asking to Die: Inside the Dutch Debate about Euthanasia* (Dordrecht: Kluwer, 1998), p. 93.

2. ibid., pp. 93–4.

3. ibid., p. 94.

4. ibid., p. 95.

5. Alistair Campbell shares these concerns:
   '[the] most serious threat to justice comes from the synchronicity of debates about health care rationing, and debates about legalizing euthanasia. Because of the escalating costs of health care, the older age group, especially those with few material resources, are increasingly coming under threat by a society which emphasizes productivity and wealth creation . . . [I]n such a scenario the poorest and weakest members of a society will be the most likely to feel that 'voluntary' death is the only option, since the rich will still be able to purchase whatever care resources they need . . . Once the boundary is crossed and killing on request is legally permitted, it is hard to see how we could ever ensure that social and commercial pressures do not define the 'volunteers'.' ('Euthanasia and the Principle of Justice', in *Euthanasia and the Churches*, ed. Robin Gill [London: Cassell, 1998], pp. 94, 95)

6. New York State Task Force on Life and the Law, *When Death is Sought: Assisted Suicide and Euthanasia in the Medical Context* (Albany, NY: New York State Task Force on Life and the Law, May 1994), pp. xiii–xiv, 74. My account here relies entirely on Frey's report in R. G. Frey, 'The Fear of a Slippery Slope' in Dworkin, *Euthanasia and Physician-Assisted Suicide*, pp. 47–8, and Dworkin's report in R. Dworkin, 'Public Policy and Physician-Assisted Suicide' in ibid., pp. 66–7.

7. Dworkin, 'Public Policy', p. 67 and n. 4.

8. ibid., p. 68.

9. Frey, 'Fear of a Slippery Slope', pp. 46, 59–60, 63; R. Dworkin, 'Public Policy', p. 73.

10. Frey, 'Fear of a Slippery Slope', p. 51.

11. Dworkin, 'Public Policy', pp. 73–4.

12. New York State Task Force, *When Death is Sought*, p. 132; as reported in Dworkin, 'Public Policy', p. 72.
13. Dworkin, 'Public Policy', p. 73.
14. New York State Task Force, *When Death is Sought*, p. 132; as reported in Dworkin, 'Public Policy', p. 71.
15. Dworkin, 'Public Policy', p. 72.
16. The argument is to be found in David Velleman, 'Against the Right to Die', *Journal of Medicine and Philosophy*, 17 (1992), pp. 665–81. It is reported by Dworkin in 'Public Policy', pp. 74–6.
17. Dworkin, 'Public Policy', pp. 76–7.
18. ibid., p. 80.
19. ibid.
20. ibid., pp. 77–80.
21. Margaret Pabst Battin, 'Manipulated Suicide' in M. Pabst Battin and David J. Mayo (eds), *Suicide: the Philosophical Issues* (London: Peter Owen, 1981), p. 171.
22. ibid., pp. 178–9.
23. Cahill, 'A "Natural Law" Reconsideration', pp. 451, 450.
24. Keown, *Euthanasia, Ethics, and Public Policy*, p. 76.
25. ibid., p. 77.
26. ibid., p. 78.
27. ibid., pp. 77, 78.
28. Griffiths, 'The Slippery Slope', p. 95.
29. In his explanation of the 'logical' version of the slippery slope argument, Keown does not entertain this possibility (*Euthanasia, Ethics, and Public Policy*, pp. 76–9), although the contemporary phenomenon of involuntary euthanasia in the Netherlands comprises part of the evidence that he later adduces to show that the liberalisation of Dutch law has resulted in an horrendous slide (ibid., pp. 104–6).
30. ibid., p. 79.
31. See Chapter Two, pp. 22, 39–45.
32. My account of the legal arrangements in the Netherlands relies entirely on Keown, *Euthanasia, Ethics, and Public Policy*, chapter 8; and on Henk Jochemsen, 'Update: The Legalization of Euthanasia in the Netherlands', *Ethics and Medicine*, 17 (2001), pp. 7–12. I am indebted to Jan Jans for helping me to iron out certain wrinkles in my understanding of the Dutch legal situation.
33. Jochemsen's account implies that cases should proceed for assessment from the committee to the prosecutor as a matter of course (ibid., p. 9). The website of the Ministerie van Buitenlandse Zaken (Ministry of Foreign Affairs), however, says otherwise (www.minbuza.nl/default.asp?CMS_ITEM=MBZ413152, 17 July 2003). I am indebted to Theo Boer for pointing this out.
34. The law was passed by the Dutch parliament on 10 April 2001 (Keown, *Euthanasia, Ethics, and Public Policy*, pp. 134, 88).
35. John Griffiths, a major apologist for the Dutch project – at least in principle – is usually scathing about international criticism, which, he and his co-authors judge, seldom rises above the level of 'international mud-slinging' and is based on little more than 'anecdotes, uncontrollable generalities ... and surmises' (John Griffiths, Alex Bood, and Helen Weyers, *Euthanasia and the Law in the Netherlands* [Amsterdam: Amsterdam University Press, 1998, p. 22]). 'On the whole', he writes,

'the charges [against recent changes to Dutch law] have not been made in a way which invites serious response. Imprecision, exaggeration, suggestion and innuendo, misinterpretation and misrepresentation, ideological *ipse dixitism*, and downright lying and slander (not to speak of bad manners) have taken the place of careful analysis of the problem and consideration of the Dutch evidence' (ibid., p. 28). The work of Herbert Hendin, the American professor of psychiatry, comes under particularly heavy – and precise – fire from Griffiths (ibid, pp. 23 n. 15, 24). In Keown's case, however, he makes a 'partial exception' (ibid.), since 'unlike most other critics of Dutch practice he has taken the trouble to inform himself carefully about Dutch law and the results of Dutch research' ('The Slippery Slope', p. 95). Griffiths' estimation of Keown is based on the latter's article, 'The Law and Practice of Euthanasia in the Netherlands', in *Law Quarterly Review* 108 (1992), pp. 51–78, and his chapter, 'Euthanasia in the Netherlands: Sliding Down the Slippery Slope?' in Keown, *Euthanasia Examined*, pp. 261–96. Our presentation of Keown's analysis and evaluation, however, is drawn from his more recent work, *Euthanasia, Ethics, and Public Policy* (2002).

36. Keown, *Euthanasia, Ethics, and Public Policy*, p. 87.
37. ibid.
38. ibid., p. 87.
39. ibid., p. 88.
40. P. J. van der Maas, J. J. M. van Delden, and L. Pijnenborg, *Medische beslissingen rond het levenseinde. Het onderzoek voor de Commissie onderzoek medische praktijk inzake euthanasia* (The Hague: SDU Uitgeverij Plantijnstrat, 1991) (hereafter 'Survey 1'), p. 182; quoted by Keown in ibid., p. 94. This has been published in English as *Euthanasia and Other Medical Decisions Concerning the End of Life: An investigation performed upon request of the Commission of Inquiry into Medical Practice concerning Euthanasia*, Health Policy Monographs (The Hague: Elsevier, 1992).
41. Survey 1, p. 72, table 7.2 and p. 90, table 8.15; quoted by Keown in *Euthanasia, Ethics, and Public Policy*, p. 95. Henk Jochemsen presents a different figure for cases of withholding or withdrawing treatment with the explicit purpose of shortening life: 3600 instead of 4000 ('Euthanasia in Holland: An Ethical Critique of the New Law', *Journal of Medical Ethics*, 20 (1994), p. 213, table 1).
42. Keown, *Euthanasia, Ethics, and Public Policy*, p. 96, table 1. The survey disclosed that in one third (i.e. 450) of the 1350 cases in which medication was administered explicitly to shorten life, no explicit request had been made by the patient (Survey 1, p. 72; quoted by Keown in ibid., p. 98).
43. ibid., p. 104.
44. ibid., pp. 106, 96, table 1.
45. *Outlines Report Commission Inquiry into Medical Practice with Regard to Euthanasia* [sic] (no date) (hereafter 'Outline'), p. 3; quoted by Keown in ibid., pp. 104–5. The Outline is an English summary, produced by the Ministry of Justice, of the report of the Remmelink Commission (P. J. van der Maas, J. J. M. van Delden, and L. Pijnenborg, *Medische beslissingen rond het levenseinde. Rapport van de Commissie onderzoek medische praktijk inzake euthanasie* [Medical decisions about the end of

life. Report of the Commission on medical practice regarding euthanasia][The Hague: SDU Uitgeverij Plantijnstrat, 1991]).
46. Keown, *Euthanasia, Ethics, and Public Policy*, p. 105, citing Survey 1, p. 61, table 6.4.
47. ibid., p. 105; Griffiths provides different percentages for the first two reasons: 44 per cent (cp. Keown's 60 per cent) for no prospect of improvement, and 67 per cent (cp. 39 per cent) for the futility of therapy (*Euthanasia and the Law*, p. 227).
48. Survey 1, pp. 76, table 7.9, 77; quoted by Keown in *Euthanasia, Ethics, and Public Policy*, pp. 106, 108.
49. Survey 1, p. 77; referred to by Keown in ibid., p. 108.
50. G. van der Wal and P. J. van der Maas, *Euthanasie en andere medische beslissingen rond het levenseinde. De praktijk en de meldingprocedure* (The Hague: SDU Uitgeverij Plantijnstraat, 1996) (hereafter 'Survey 2'), tables 11.1 and 11.2; cited by Keown in ibid., p. 113. This has been published in English as *Euthanasia and other medical decisions concerning the end of life: practice and notification procedure* (The Hague: SDU Uitgeverij, 1996).
51. Survey 1, pp. 2, 48; cited by Keown in *Euthanasia, Ethics, and Public Policy*, p. 113.
52. Survey 1, p. 65; cited by Keown in ibid.
53. ibid., p. 114.
54. ibid., p. 115.
55. ibid., p. 123.
56. Survey 1, p. 58, table 6.1; cited by Keown in ibid., p. 116.
57. Outline, p. 3.
58. Keown, in ibid., p. 117.
59. ibid., p. 121.
60. ibid., pp. 121–2.
61. ibid., p. 120.
62. See n. 50 above.
63. ibid., p. 127.
64. Survey 2, table 5.5; cited by Keown in ibid., p. 127.
65. ibid.
66. Survey 2, table 6.2; cited by Keown in ibid.
67. Survey 2, table 6.5; cited by Keown in ibid.
68. ibid.
69. Survey 2, table 6.4.
70. Survey 2, table 6.6; cited by Keown in ibid., pp. 128–9.
71. ibid., p. 130.
72. Agnes van der Heide et al., 'Medical End-of-Life Decisions Made for Neonates and Infants in the Netherlands', *Lancet* 350 (1997), pp. 251, 253; cited by Keown in ibid., p. 131.
73. Survey 2, tables 11.1 and 11.2; cited by Keown in ibid., p. 132.
74. ibid.
75. ibid.
76. Survey 2, table 11.8, p. 225; cited by Keown in ibid.
77. The bill passed by the Dutch parliament on 10 April 2001 enshrined the view that it is lawful to practise voluntary euthanasia where the patient refuses treatment alternatives (ibid., p. 134). This came into force in April 2002.
78. ibid., pp. 134–5.

79. Griffiths, 'Slippery Slope', p. 96; cp. *Euthanasia and the Law*, p. 26.
80. Griffiths, *Euthanasia and the Law*, p. 26.
81. Griffiths records a decline from 3500 cases in 1990 to 3000 cases in 1995 ('Slippery Slope', p. 98).
82. See Griffiths, 'Slippery Slope', p. 98 and *Euthanasia and the Law*, Chapter 5.
83. Keown, *Euthanasia, Ethics, and Public Policy*, p. 96. Keown records that the number of cases of pain-relief administered with the explicit purpose of shortening life rose from 1350 in 1990 to 2000 in 1995, but he does not tell us whether the number of such cases without explicit request by the patient also rose (p. 126).
84. Griffiths, 'Slippery Slope', pp. 98–9.
85. ibid., p. 99.
86. Keown, *Euthanasia, Ethics, and Public Policy*, p. 129. Keown's figures here differ from Griffiths': instead of a rise from 8500 in 1990 to 13,000 in 1995, he records one from 2670 to 14,200.
87. Griffiths, 'Slippery Slope', p. 99.
88. This is also his major complaint against C. F. Gomez's argument in *Regulating Death: Euthanasia and the Case of the Netherlands* (New York: The Free Press, 1991). See *Euthanasia and the Law*, p. 25.
89. Griffiths, *Euthanasia and the Law*, p. 27, n 25.
90. H. Kuhse et al., 'End-of-life Decisions in Australian Medical Practice', *Medical Journal of Australia*, 166 (1997), pp. 191–6; cited by Griffiths in ibid., p. 27 n. 23.
91. Griffiths, *Euthanasia and the Law*, p. 27. Griffiths reports ('Slippery Slope', p. 100) that the Australian rate of the intentional termination of life without an explicit request is 3.5 per cent of all deaths, which is more than 'three times' the Dutch rate (0.8 per cent in 1990, 0.7 per cent in 1995). Actually, it is exactly five times the 1995 rate.
92. Keown, *Euthanasia, Ethics, and Public Policy*, p. 135 n. 41. Keown draws this point from Nicholas Tonti-Filippini et al., *Joint Supplementary Submission to the Senate Legal and Constitutional Legislation Committee Re: Euthanasia Laws Bill 1996*.
93. Griffiths, 'Slippery Slope', p. 100.
94. ibid., p. 102.
95. Griffiths, *Euthanasia and the Law*, p. 268. Another supporter of the Dutch project, J. J. M. van Delden, also (indirectly) confirms Keown's critique, when in a response ('Slippery Slopes in Flat Countries – a Response', *Journal of Medical Ethics*, 25 [1999] he 'nowhere sought to question the central criticism that the guidelines have been widely breached and have failed to ensure effective control' (Keown, *Euthanasia, Ethics, and Public Policy*, p. 143). Van Delden agrees that non-voluntary euthanasia is 'a very serious problem' ('Slippery Slopes in Flat Countries', p. 24; quoted by Keown in ibid., p. 143); he admits that there had been a 'shift' toward using voluntary euthanasia even when palliative care could have provided an alternative ('Slippery Slopes in Flat Countries', p. 23; quoted by Keown in ibid., p. 143); and he does not deny that the reporting procedure has failed to ensure effective control (Keown, ibid., pp. 143–4).
96. Griffiths, *Euthanasia and the Law*, p. 268.
97. ibid., p. 269.
98. ibid., pp. 245–6.

Notes 195

99. ibid., p. 236.
100. ibid., p. 238.
101. ibid., p. 253.
102. ibid., pp. 264, 274.
103. ibid., pp. 254–5.
104. ibid., p. 29; quoted by Keown in *Euthanasia, Ethics, and Public Policy*, p. 142.
105. Griffiths, 'Slippery Slope', p. 101.
106. ibid., pp. 102, 103.
107. Griffiths, *Euthanasia and the Law*, p. 270.
108. ibid., pp. 270–2.
109. ibid., p. 272.
110. ibid., p. 275.
111. ibid., p. 276.
112. ibid., pp. 276–8. At the time of writing (1998), Griffiths was sceptical that the introduction of a 'buffer' between the reporting doctor and the prosecutorial authorities in the form of an 'assessment committee' – or what has come to be known as a 'regional euthanasia review committee' – would make a positive difference to the rate of reporting. Doctors are 'not so innocent', he writes, 'that they will not soon enough notice that the grounds on which and the frequency with which they are prosecuted have not changed' (ibid., p. 280).
113. ibid., p. 282.
114. ibid., pp. 282–3.
115. ibid., p. 286.
116. ibid., pp. 286 n. 47, 288.
117. ibid., p. 289.
118. According to research conducted by G. van der Wal in 1992 (*Euthanasie en hulp bij zelfdoding door huisarten* [Euthanasia and Assistance with Suicide by Family Doctors] [Rotterdam: WYT Uitgeefgroep, 1992]), cited by Griffiths in ibid., p. 205; according to the 1996 survey, cited by Griffiths in ibid., p. 232; and according to both the 1991 and 1996 surveys, cited by Griffiths in ibid., p. 238.
119. ibid., p. 289.
120. ibid., pp. 291–2.
121. ibid., pp. 293–4.
122. M. Angell, 'Euthanasia in the Netherlands – Good News or Bad?', *New England Journal of Medicine*, 335 (1996), p. 1677.
123. Raanon Gillon, 'Euthanasia in the Netherlands', *Journal of Medical Ethics* 20 (1994), p. 3.
124. Keown, *Euthanasia, Ethics, and Public Policy*, p. 145 n. 41.
125. ibid., p. 146.
126. Jochemsen, 'Euthanasia in Holland', p. 212. Jochemsen refers here to data for 1990 supplied by the 1991 survey (2300 cases, 9000 requests: a ratio of 1 case to 3.9 requests). The ratio for 1995 is lower, but the difference still does not amount to euthanasia on demand: 1 case to 3 requests (3,200 cases, 9,700 requests) (Keown, *Euthanasia, Ethics, and Public Policy*, p. 126).
127. In discussion of his paper, 'After the Slippery Slope: Dutch Experiences on Regulating Active Euthanasia', at the meeting of the Society for Christian Ethics in Pittsburgh in January 2003, Theo Boer reported that many Dutch doctors known to him are discontented with playing

the role of instrument to their patient's will, and are moving away
from an 'autonomy' paradigm to a more paternalist 'beneficence' one.
This paper was published in the *Journal of the Society for Christian Ethics*,
23/2 (2003), pp. 225-42.

128. This kind of case may be classic, but it is not merely hypothetical. Nor
is it confined to the extraordinary circumstances of the battlefield. For
example, when in 1915 a train carrying troops to Liverpool crashed at
Quintinshill in Dumfriesshire and burst into flame, an officer 'went
about the scene shooting men trapped in the burning wreckage'
(Michael Simkins, 'The express hit us and then I lost all consciousness',
Guardian, 18 May 2001, G2, pp. 11–12). Nor is such a horrendous situation confined to military circumstances. In September 1991 police
in South Africa were reported to be hunting for a 'mercy killer' who
had shot dead a badly injured motorist trapped in a burning car
('Mercy killing', *Independent*, 4 September 1991).

129. *On Dying Well*, p. 10.

130. ibid., p. 23.

131. Griffiths, *Euthanasia and the Law*, pp. 226–7.

132. ibid. Actually, Griffiths only tells us ambiguously that these cases num-
bered '30–130 cases per year'. Since the data to which he is referring
concern only two particular years, I assume that the first figure relates
to 1990 and the second figure to 1995.

133. The only one of Griffiths' sub-categories that we have not mentioned
is the 'very small number' of long-term coma patients. Griffiths gives
us no figure, but tells us that this is '[a] fraction of some 100 long-term
coma cases per year' (ibid., p. 226 n. 81). Given that he describes other
sub-categories comprising 1 and 15 cases as 'a very small number', we
shall assume a generous figure of 15 cases of long-term coma for both
years. On this assumption, Griffiths has explained only 255 (25.5 per
cent) of 1990's 1000 cases, and 231 (25.7 per cent) of 1995's 900 cases.

134. Keown, 'Euthanasia in the Netherlands: Sliding Down the Slippery
Slope?' in Keown, *Euthanasia Examined*, p. 270; listed by Griffiths in
Euthanasia and Law, p. 363.

135. Beauchamp and Childress imply that the right to refuse treatment is
tantamount to a right to commit suicide, speaking as they do of 'the
strong rights of autonomy that allow persons in grim circumstances to
refuse treatment *so as to* bring about their deaths' (*Principles of Biomedical Ethics*, p. 147. My emphasis). However, as we have argued here, this
is not so in traditional moral thinking; nor need it be so in the eyes of
the law.

136. *On Dying Well*, pp. 10, 46; Maureen McLellan, 'Palliative Care: An
Ethical Approach' in Frank A. Huser (ed.), *Palliative Care and Euthana-
sia*, Papers from the 1993 London Symposium on Care for the
Seriously and Terminally Ill (Edinburgh: Campion Press, 1995), p. 22.

137. My translation of 'Das Bild, das ein Mensch von sich selbst gewinnt,
hängt nicht zuletzt davon ab, wer er in den Augen der anderen ist; die
Einschätzung des eigenen Lebenswertes stellt in der einer oder anderen
Richtung immer auch eine Reaktion auf die Wertschätzung dar, die er
im Urteil der anderen erfährt.' (Eberhard Schockenhoff, *Ethik des
Lebens: Ein Theologischer Grundriß* [Mainz: Matthias-Grünewald-Verlag,
1993], p. 330)

138. My translation of 'Le recours à la notion de liberté individuelle est

donc, en ce domaine du choix entre la vie et la mort, en partie illu-
soire. Tel malade désire vraiment mourir, mais ce désir n'est pas le fruit
de sa seule liberté: il peut être – il est le plus souvent – la traduction de
l'attitude de l'entourage, sinon même de la société tout entière qui ne
croit plus à la valeur de sa vie et le lui signifie par toutes sortes de mes-
sages. Suprême paradoxe: on rejette quelqu'un de la communauté des
vivants et il pense vouloir, personellement, la mort.' (*Partir: l'accompagnement des mourants*, Entretiens avec Emmanuel Hirsch [Paris, 1986],
p. 95; quoted by Maret in *L'euthanasie*, p. 175 n. 83)

139. On these grounds we strongly gainsay Beauchamp and Childress, who
'can conceive of no moral grounds for restricting the liberty of a competent individual to make . . . a request for aid-in-dying', provided that
the request is made on the basis of an 'autonomous' judgement that
death constitutes a personal benefit (*Principles of Biomedical Ethics*,
p. 148).

140. Hans Jochemsen makes this point in response to G. van der Wal's
advocacy of the decriminalisation of euthanasia on request: 'Apart
from the problem that then one profession would have the power to
terminate the lives of people without judicial control, why is it
thought that physicians would be any the readier to report cases of
euthanasia in which the guidelines were not followed?' ('Euthanasia in
Holland', p. 216 n. 19).

141. In May 2003 a third survey of the practice of euthanasia in the Netherlands – this time based on data gathered in 2001 – was published: G.
van der Wal, A. van der Heide, B. D. Onwuteaka-Philipsen and P. J. van
der Maas, *Medische Besluitvorming aan het einde van het leven: De praktijk
en de toetsingsprocedure euthanasie* (Medical decision-making at the end
of life) (Utrecht: Tijdstroom Uitgeverij, 2003). Early reports of the content of this survey have given me no reason to revise my thesis.
Another piece of research composed by a team including all of the
authors of the third survey, and published in June 2003, yields data
that could be read as lending prima facie support to those who oppose
the relaxation of the law: between 1995 and 2001 the percentage of
physicians who believe that people have the right to choose to decide
about their own life and death fell from 64 to 56 per cent; between
1990 and 2001 the percentage concerned that substantial economic
measures in health care will increase the pressure on physicians to provide assistance in dying rose from 9 to 15 per cent; and during the
same period the percentage who said that during the previous five
years they had become more permissive declined from 25 to 12 per
cent, while the percentage who said that they had become more
restrictive rose from 14 to 20 per cent (B. D. Onwuteaka-Philipsen, A.
van der Heide, G. van der Wal, Paul van der Maas, et al., 'Euthanasia
and other end-of-life decisions in the Netherlands in 1990, 1995, and
2001' in *The Lancet*, online, 17 June 2003 at image.thelancet.com/
extras/03art3297web.pdf, especially Table 4).

142. See above, pp. 126-7

143. Tony Sheldon, '"Existential" suffering not a justification for euthanasia', *British Medical Journal*, 323 (15 December 2001), p. 1384.

144. Tony Sheldon, 'Being "tired of life" is not grounds for euthanasia',
British Medical Journal, 326 (11 January 2003), p. 71. I am indebted to
Jan Jans for alerting me to the recent history of this case.

198   Notes

145. Gerald McKenny, following Charles Taylor, finds the roots of this conception of the vocation of medicine in the early modern 'Baconian' project 'to eliminate suffering and to expand human choice' (*To Relieve the Human Condition: Bioethics, Technology, and the Human Body* [Albany, NY: State University of New York Press, 1997], p. 2). Whereas McKenny (and Taylor) tend to characterise this project in terms of a simple repudiation of the ancient and medieval moral framework of a (God-)given hierarchy of ends or goods, I wonder whether it is not more accurately conceived as a ruthless narrowing down of those ends to two: physical survival (Thomas Hobbes) and sensible pleasure (Jeremy Bentham). So, for example, whereas Aquinas sees the natural law as resting on a wide range of ends (self-preservation, procreation, friendship, knowledge of the truth about God), Hobbes reduces that basis to self-preservation (*Leviathan*, Part I, chapter XIV, 'Of the first and second Natural Lawes, and of Contracts').

146. Here we differ from Schockenhoff, who claims to find in the very idea of euthanasia ('der Euthanasie-Idee') a self-subverting contradiction. In a humane society, he argues, direct killing should only be morally permissible when it is the *sole* effective way to aid a dying or severely suffering person – i.e. as a last resort; but once it has become a generally accepted feature of social life, it cripples the search for alternatives (*Ethik des Lebens*, p. 332). However, what becomes generally accepted is not the idea of euthanasia as such, but the idea of its practice under more or less strict conditions. What then erodes the search for alternatives is the fading from common awareness of the reasons why it has to be strictly limited, and so of the urgent need to avoid it if at all possible. This failure of memory is not a logically necessary feature of the idea of euthanasia, but the result of other factors such as the growth to cultural dominance of the unqualified value of individual autonomy.

147. This statement makes the assumption that all those who currently choose voluntary euthanasia would choose physician-assisted suicide, if that were their only option. Whereas 22,500 patients died as a result of non-treatment decisions in 1990, only 2700 (12 per cent) died as a result of assisted suicide (400) and voluntary euthanasia (2300); and whereas 27,300 patients died as a result of non-treatment decisions in 1995, only 3600 (13.2 per cent) died as a result of assisted suicide (400) and voluntary euthanasia (3200). See Keown, *Euthanasia, Ethics, and Public Policy*, p. 126, Table 2.

148. The cruder version of this argument that Peter Singer offers in favour of voluntary euthanasia (*Practical Ethics*, p. 197) is vulnerable to the same objection.

149. Battin, 'Manipulated Suicide', p. 179.

150. ibid., p. 178. My italics.

151. Battin is only concerned with 'the social freedom to control one's dying as one wishes' (ibid., p. 179) that a legal right would secure. The question of whether, within the sphere of legal freedom, one's moral freedom might be constrained, she does not address. She gives no evidence, however, of supposing that the individual's choices about the disposal of her own life take place within a context of moral responsibility.

152. Cahill, 'A "Natural Law" Reconsideration', p. 451.

153. ibid.

154. Chapter Three, n. 35.
155. By importing the language of 'sacredness' here, I am not reverting to the position that says that the life of a human individual should never be intentionally harmed. Rather, I am saying that it should always be regarded with the utmost care and respect, and only touched with a measure of fear and trembling.
156. I suspect that this is symptomatic of an intra-historical, progressivist optimism that drives liberal thinking, which, having taken leave of God, can no longer rest its hope in the Eschaton. Robert Song has noted the phenomenon in the thought of the doyen of contemporary liberal philosophers, John Rawls, whose faith that justice as fairness will always be common sense seems never to be disturbed by the thought that one day some *non*-liberal comprehensive doctrine might prevail, and with it a different concept of justice. Song writes: '. . . it is not hard to imagine how, in an increasingly individualized and deracinated culture, justice as fairness might come to seem a relatively weak attraction for some, compared with those comprehensive doctrines which look to, say, public implementation of the sharia law or to nationalist fascist doctrines for their inspiration . . . In general, we may say, the stability of the overlapping consensus concerning the principles of justice is more open to doubt than Rawls allows for: in the long term the content of the public conception of justice will be determined by the content of the various elements of the background culture.' (*Christianity and Liberal Society* [Oxford: OUP, 1997], p. 113)
157. Battin, 'Manipulated Suicide', p. 177.
158. Dieter Birnbacher, 'Das Tötungsverbot aus der Sicht des klassischen Utilitarismus' in Rainer Hegselman and Reinhard Merkel (eds), *Zur Debatte über Euthanasie* (Frankfurt am Main: Suhrkamp Verlag, 1991), p. 42: 'Die zivilisatorische Decke ist vielleicht dünner, als wir es uns träumen lassen . . .'. My translation.
159. Peter Haas, *Morality after Auschwitz: The Radical Challenge of the Nazi Ethic* (Philadelphia: Fortress, 1992), Introduction.
160. ibid., pp. 1–2.
161. ibid., p. 90.
162. From Alexander, 'Medical Science under Dictatorship', pp. 39–47; quoted by Michael Burleigh in 'The Nazi Analogy and Contemporary Debates on "Euthanasia"' in *Ethics and Extermination: Reflections on Nazi Genocide* (Cambridge: CUP, 1997), p. 147.
163. Michael Burleigh, 'Psychiatry, German Society, and Nazi "Euthanasia"' in *Ethics and Extermination*, pp. 116–17.
164. ibid., p. 117.
165. Ewald Meltzer, *Das Problem der Abkürzung 'lebensunwerten' Lebens* (Halle, 1925), p. 88; cited by Michael Burleigh in *Death and Deliverance: Euthanasia in Germany, 1900–1945* (London: Pan Macmillan, 2002), p. 23.
166. In *Biomedical Ethics and the Shadow of Nazism*, Hastings Center Report, Special Supplement (August 1976); cited by Burleigh in 'The Nazi Analogy', p. 146.
167. ibid.; cited by Burleigh in ibid., pp. 147–48.
168. ibid.; cited by Burleigh in ibid., pp. 148–49.
169. Burleigh, 'Psychiatry', p. 114.
170. E.g. Schockenhoff in *Ethik des Lebens*, p. 336.

171. Onora O'Neill has much to say about the British media's presentation of bioethics. Little of it is complimentary. See *Autonomy and Trust in Bioethics*, Chapter 8, pp. 174–92.
172. *On Dying Well*, pp. 12–13.
173. Paul Badham, 'Should Christians Accept the Validity of Voluntary Euthanasia?' in Gill, *Euthanasia and the Churches*, pp. 54–5.
174. Badham is correct here (ibid., pp. 55–6).

Conclusion

1. While it remains possible that patients in the vegetative state may be capable of experiencing pain, 'the available evidence suggests that this is not the case' (Royal College of Physicians [London], *Working Party Report on the Vegetative State* [London: RCP, 2003], p. 3).
2. See above, Chapter Two, n. 54.
3. The description of artificial hydration and nutrition – or 'tube-feeding' – as 'treatment' is controversial. Some argue that it should be classified as a form of 'basic care', and should therefore never be withheld or withdrawn (e.g. Keown, *Euthanasia, Ethics, and Public Policy*, pp. 219–21, 241–43). However, insofar as tube-feeding 'substitutes a lost physiological function – in this case the ability to swallow sufficiently effectively to maintain nutrition' (Jennett, 'Letting Vegetative Patients Die', p. 182; see also the British Medical Association [BMA], *Withholding and Withdrawing Life-Prolonging Medical Treatment. Guidance for Decision-Making* [London: BMJ Books, 1999; revised edition, 2001], 3.4), insofar as it requires an operation to insert the tube, and insofar as it requires medical expertise to monitor the content of the feeding (for the balance of electrolytes, the number of calories, etc.), it is surely rather more than just 'basic care'.
4. In this kind of case, at least, I think that James Rachels is correct in his criticism of Paul Ramsey's version of the distinction between 'ordinary' treatment, which a doctor is morally obliged to offer and a patient to accept, and 'extraordinary' treatment, which the former may withhold or withdraw and the latter may refuse. 'Ordinary' treatment is that which offers reasonable hope of benefit without involving 'excessive expense, pain, or other inconvenience'; and 'extraordinary' treatment is that which either offers no hope of benefit at all, or, if it does, only by way of excessive expense, etc. (Ramsey, *Patient as Person*, p. 135; quoted by Rachels, 'More Impertinent Distinctions', p. 144). To this, however, Rachels replies that the meaning of 'excessive' expense, and the meaning of 'benefit', both depend on a *prior* decision about 'whether it would be a good thing for the life in question to be prolonged':
'Is a cost of $10,000 excessive? If it would save the life of a young woman and restore her to perfect health, $10,000 does not seem excessive. But if it would only prolong the life of Ramsey's cancer-stricken diabetic a short while, perhaps $10,000 is excessive . . . For a person with a painful terminal illness, a temporarily continued life may not be a benefit. For a person in irreversible coma . . . continued biological existence is almost certainly not a benefit. On the other hand, for a person who can be cured and resume a normal life, life-sustaining treatment definitely is a benefit.' (Rachels, 'More Impertinent Distinctions', pp. 144–5)

Rachels concludes that the distinction, as Ramsey understands it, is practically idle since it presupposes what it purports to decide (ibid., p. 145). John Harris concurs with Rachels' opinion that the distinction between 'ordinary' and 'extraordinary' treatment hangs 'crucially' on a judgement about the value to the patient of staying alive under the circumstances (*The Value of Life*, p. 39).

5. Keown, *Euthanasia, Ethics, and Public Policy*, p. 226.
6. BMA, *Withholding and Withdrawing Life-Prolonging Medical Treatment*; cited by Keown in *Euthanasia, Ethics, and Public Policy*, pp. 239, 248.
7. Institute of Medical Ethics Working Party on the Ethics of Prolonging Life and Assisting Death, 'Withdrawal of Life-support from Patients in a Persistent Vegetative State', *The Lancet*, 337 (1991), pp. 96–8.

Glossary

Analgesic: pain-relieving, from the Greek *an* ('not') + *algeein* ('to feel pain'). Analgesic drugs – such as morphine – are one of the means at the disposal of palliative care.

Abelard, Peter: 1079–1142.

Abelardian: of or following Abelard. An Abelardian theology of the Atonement is characterised by an understanding of the atoning function of Jesus' passion and crucifixion in terms of a revelation of God's love, and by an emphasis on the power of that revelation to bring about the moral transformation of those who behold it.

Active euthanasia: euthanasia by commission ('intentional killing'), as distinct from euthanasia by omission ('intending death by letting die'). See also 'passive euthanasia'.

Anthropology: a theory of human nature and the human condition. This can be empirical, philosophical, or theological.

Aquinas, Thomas: 1225–74. The tradition of theological thought to which Aquinas gave rise goes by his first name: Thomism.

Aristotle: 384–322 BC.

Atonement: generally, the reconciliation of sinful human creatures with God; specifically, the role of the passion and crucifixion of Jesus in bringing that reconciliation about.

Autonomy: literally 'self-governing', from the Greek, *autos* ('self') + *nomos* ('law'). The Kantian concept of moral autonomy is not absolute. In determining what is right and wrong, the individual may be free from the 'external' constraints of society or tradition, but he is nevertheless beholden to the 'internal' and universal law of reason or consistency. In contrast, both the popular understanding of moral autonomy and some contemporary philosophical views see it as absolutely unconstrained and arbitrary.

Augustine: 354–430. Bishop of Hippo in North Africa, not to be confused with the sixth century Augustine of Canterbury.

Barth, Karl: 1886–1968.

Barthian: of or following Karl Barth. One of the salient characteristics of Barthian theology is its insistence that the Christian church be true to its own constitutive convictions, and that Christian theology should therefore base itself, above and before all else, on what has been revealed in Jesus Christ. This insistence leads at best (in Barth's own hands) to a critical sifting of non-Christian religious, philosophical, intellectual, and cultural resources; but at worst (in the hands of some of his disciples) to a premature dismissal of them.

Casuistry: from the Latin, *casūs* ('case'). The methodical process of interpreting a case or particular situation in the light of moral norms (principles or rules). Part of 'normative ethics'.

Glossary

203

Comatose: of or in a state of deep unconsciousness for a prolonged or indefinite period, especially as a result of severe injury or illness.

Consequentialism: a theory of normative ethics that holds that the rightness or wrongness of acts is determined entirely by their effects. Utilitarianism is a species of consequentialism.

Deontology: from the Greek, *dei* ('it is right'). A theory of normative ethics that holds – against consequentialism – that the rightness or wrongness of acts is determined by whether they are performed out of a sense of duty and in accord with the moral law. Kantian ethics are a prime example of deontological ethics.

Double effect, doctrine of: this holds that it is permissible to perform an act that has two effects, one good and the other evil, under certain conditions. Most notable among these is that the good effect must be intended, while the evil effect must only be accepted as a 'side-effect'. Adumbrated in the thought of Thomas Aquinas, the doctrine has since been developed in Thomist circles.

Eschatological: from the Greek, *eskhatos* ('last'). In Christian theology, the Eschaton is the moment of the final establishment of the transforming and liberating rule of God in the world. Hope that is eschatological draws its strength from this prospect.

Eschaton, the: see 'Eschatological'.

Eudaimonism: from the Greek, *eudaimōn* ('happy'). A meta-ethical theory that understands the rationale of moral obligations in terms of their promotion of human well-being or flourishing.

Euthanasia: see Basic Terms.

Intention: this is the goal that we seek to bring about in acting, as distinct from the motive that moves us to seek it.

Involuntary euthanasia: see Basic Terms.

Kant, Immanuel: 1724–1804.

Kantian: of or following Kant. Kantian ethics are characteristically deontological, not consequentialist. Kantian autonomy is not absolute, but subject to the requirements of the moral law of reason.

Meta-ethics: that division of reflection upon moral matters that considers questions about moral concepts (e.g. 'What is it about a moral obligation that gives it its authority or force?'), rather than questions about right and wrong conduct. Cp. 'normative ethics'.

Moral realism: the position that affirms that there is a moral reality or order that exists prior to human ethical construction and moral choosing. This given, fundamental moral reality may be held to take the form of a set of basic ends or goods or values (Thomism) or of a set of universal laws of reasoning (Kantianism).

Motive: this is what moves us to intend something. It can be an emotion or a reason.

Neonate: a new-born child. Sometimes in medicine, more strictly, an infant less than four weeks old.

Normative ethics: that division of reflection upon moral matters that considers questions about norms (principles or rules) that should govern conduct (e.g. 'Does the norm of respect for human life always exclude our taking it?'), and that interprets cases or situations in the light of those norms (e.g. 'May we intentionally take the life of a patient in PVS?'). This latter operation is 'casuistry'.

Non-voluntary euthanasia: see Basic Terms.

Ontic necessity: from the Greek, $\bar{o}n$ ('being'). A necessity is ontic when it is required by the nature of things: e.g. when orthodox Christians deny that evil arises naturally out of being as God created it, they are denying that evil is an ontic necessity. In contrast, a necessity is logical when it is required by the nature of certain concepts: e.g. if human will is morally 'free', then by definition there must be morally bad as well as morally good options.

Palliative care: the branch of health care devoted to the medical treatment of, and other kinds of care (e.g. nursing) for, the terminally ill and their families. The use of analgesic drugs is only one of its forms.

Passive euthanasia: this is wrongly equated with 'letting die' by utilitarians. By definition, euthanasia intends the death of the one killed by it. By not intervening or ceasing to intervene and letting someone die, we *might* be intending their death. But that need not be so. We might instead be recognising the futility of further treatment and allowing the dying person to turn their limited reserves of energy from striving to stay alive to living as well as possible in the time that remains.

Persistent vegetative state (PVS): a medical condition where the brain stem remains alive and functioning, but not the brain's cortex. The former supports basic bodily functions; the latter supports consciousness. Accordingly, the PVS patient is able to breathe and digest unaided, and he is capable of reflex movement, especially in response to painful stimuli. However, lacking cognitive function, he can neither see nor hear, nor feel pain and emotion, nor communicate. Nor can he feed himself.

Physician-assisted suicide: see Basic Terms.

Proportionalism: a contemporary school of Roman Catholic moral theology that holds that no act (e.g. intentional killing) is evil intrinsically or in itself; and that one commits no moral evil or wrong (e.g. murder) when one intends to bring about a pre-moral evil (e.g. someone's death), on condition that the act is 'proportionate' – or strictly ordered – to its intended, good end. So, for example, it is morally permissible for me to intend to kill you, so long as your death is strictly necessary for my self-defence. R. A. McCormick (1922–2000) was a leading proportionalist.

Side-effect: this is an effect that is beside or outside the intention of an act, and is therefore 'accepted' rather than 'intended'. See 'double effect, doctrine of'.

Theodicy: from the Greek, *theos* ('God') + *dikē* ('justice'). The vindication of orthodox Christian belief in an omnipotent and benevolent God, in spite of the presence of natural and moral evil in the world that he created and over which he presides.

Thomism: the theological tradition that takes its cue from Thomas Aquinas.

Utilitarianism: a species of consequentialist ethic that holds an act to be right that results in 'the greatest happiness of the greatest number' or 'utility'. Jeremy Bentham (1748–1832) pioneered it, and J. S. Mill (1806–73) developed it.

Voluntary euthanasia: see Basic Terms.

Further Reading

General discussions
The judicious *On Dying Well* (1975) was produced by an eminent and inter-disciplinary Church of England working party that included R. M. Hare, Basil Mitchell, and Cicely Saunders. Covering moral, theological, medical, and legal issues, it has stood the test of time remarkably well and was re-issued, with a little updating and a few additions, in 2000. Likewise, the working party that produced the Linacre Centre's more absolutist 1982 report counted in its ranks eminent members such as G. E. M. Anscombe, John Finnis, and Robert Twycross. This was republished as the first part of Linacre Centre (1994). Lammers and Verhey (1987, 1998) helpfully collect a wide range of theological essays relevant to the concerns of this book, especially in the chapters entitled 'Life and its Sanctity', 'Death and its (In)dignity', and 'Choosing Death and Letting Die'. Uhlmann (1998) contains 29 essays on the history of thought about suicide, and contemporary moral, theological, medical, and legal views of assisted suicide and euthanasia. Almost all of the material in these two collections is written by Americans.

The cultural context
Callahan (2000) reflects with insight on contemporary views of suffering and death, the passion for control, and the distorting focus of health care on technological solutions. Similarly, the utopian quest of modern medicine to eliminate human suffering through technology is the target of McKenny (1997), who engages at close quarters with Hans Jonas, Leon Kass, James Gustafson, and Stanley Hauerwas.

The value of human life
Both Glover (1977) and Rachels (1986) are early, classic, and readable critiques of the traditional view of the sanctity of human life and its attendant ethic. Keown (1995) contains a vigorous six-chapter debate between Harris and Finnis. O'Donovan (1984), in Channer (1985), and in Lammers and Verhey (1998) offers original and thoughtful resistance to the drawing of a distinction between 'biological' and 'biographical' life. He also proposes a theological conception of the significance of individual human life in terms of vocation – one that finds strong resonance in Barth (1961). On the other hand, Christian support for the drawing of a distinction can be found in McCormick (1981, 1989), Ramsey (1970), and Cahill in Lammers and Verhey (1987).

Acts and omissions
Again, both Glover (1977) and Rachels (1986) offer standard critiques of the traditional moral distinction between killing and letting die. Steinbock and Norcross (1994) contains 21 essays, all focussed on this topic and including

classics by Tooley, Rachels, Bennett, and Foot. The final three chapters of
Keown (2002) are devoted to discussion of the Tony Bland case and the
British debate about withholding or withdrawing treatment. Jennett and
Boyle in Keown (1995) discuss the issue in general of letting PVS patients
die.

The doctrine of double effect and the moral significance of intentions

For an analysis of the doctrine of double effect and a history of its development, Mangan (1949) is standard. Kaczor (1998) brings the story up to date,
among other things. Woodward (2001) is very helpful, offering a collection
that covers some of the same ground as Steinbock and Norcross (1994), but
includes classic essays by Anscombe, Foot, Bennett, and Walzer. Glover
(1977) offers a utilitarian critique and Donagan (1977) a Kantian one. For an
original defence, see Grisez (1983, 1993). Another collection, McCormick
and Ramsey (1978), contains very important, if demanding material, much
of it of a proportionalist bent. For an analytic history of proportionalism, see
Hoose (1987).

Autonomy

Harris gives an absolutist version in Keown (1995). Taylor (1991) lays clear
its inadequacies. In her 2001 Gifford Lectures O'Neill (2002) offers a principled, Kantian alternative.

Suicide

Battin (1982, 1995) mounts a wide-ranging critique of the traditional,
absolute prohibition. Barry (1994) appeals to the Bible, Augustine, and
Aquinas in defence of it. Hauerwas in Lammers and Verhey (1987) doubts
the 'rationality' of suicide in light of a Christian vision of life as a gift from
God. However, Barth's (1961) theological account just opens the door to the
possibility of morally right suicide. Gustafson (1981) pushes it wider, as does
Donagan (1977).

Slippery slopes

In discussions of slippery slopes, frequent reference is made to Lamb (1988).
Keown (2002) opposes the legalisation of voluntary euthanasia mainly on
the ground of an inevitable slide to non-voluntary euthanasia. Dworkin in
Dworkin, Frey, and Bok (1998) does his best to persuade that the legalisation
of physician-assisted suicide would solve that problem; and Cahill in Lammers and Verhey (1987) argues that remote fears of moral slides should not
be allowed to trump the immediate moral claims to relief of grossly suffering people.

Nazi policy, its precursors, and its relevance

Michael Burleigh is an eminent expert on Nazi eugenic policies, as well as a
popular historian of the Third Reich. Burleigh (2002) places Nazi policy in
the historical context of congenial cultural developments going back to the
beginning of the century. His essay, 'The Nazi Analogy and Contemporary
Debates on "Euthanasia"', in Burleigh (1997) is especially useful.

International legal developments

Keown (2002) provides critical surveys of legal developments in the Netherlands, Australia, and the United States.

International legal developments: the Netherlands

Keown (2002) is a rare critic of the Dutch project whose expertise and professionalism appears to have won the grudging respect of one of its major apologists, John Griffiths. Griffiths (1998) is a book-length defence of the relaxation of Dutch law, albeit with criticisms of its current form.

Palliative care

Ramsey's 'On (Only) Caring for the Dying' in Ramsey (1970) is a classic moral theological treatment of palliative care. In Keown (1995), Twycross, the world-renowned palliative care specialist, views euthanasia critically out of his experience of hospice work. Twycross also chaired the ecumenical working party that produced *Mud and Stars* (1991), which offers a useful theological introduction to the care of the dying. Fordham and Dunn (1994) provide a readable and comprehensive account of the complexity of pain and the varieties of its management.

Bibliography

Alexander, Leo. 'Medical Science under Dictatorship'. *New England Journal of Medicine*, 241/2 (14 July 1949), pp. 39–47.

Andrews, Keith; Murphy, Lesley; Munday, Ros; and Littlewood, Clare. 'Misdiagnosis of the Vegetative State: Retrospective Study in a Rehabilitation Unit'. *British Medical Journal*, 313 (1996), pp. 13–16.

Angell, M. 'Euthanasia in the Netherlands – Good News or Bad?'. *New England Journal of Medicine*, 335 (28 Nov. 1996), pp. 1676–8.

Anscombe, G. E. M. 'Medalist's Address: Action, Intention, and "Double Effect"'. Woodward, *The Doctrine of Double Effect*, pp. 50–66.

———. 'War and Murder'. Woodward, *The Doctrine of Double Effect*, pp. 247–60.

Aquinas, Thomas. *Summa Theologiae*. 60 vols. Edited by Thomas Gilby et al. London: Eyre and Spottiswoode; New York: McGraw-Hill, 1964–6.

Augustine. *Against Faustus*, Book 22.74–6. O'Donovan and O'Donovan, *From Irenaeus to Grotius*, pp. 117–19.

———. 'On Free Will', Book I.v.11–13. Augustine, *Earlier Writings*, pp. 118–20.

———. *City of God*. Translated by Henry Bettenson. Edited by David Knowles. Harmondsworth: Penguin, 1972.

———. *Earlier Writings*. Edited and translated by J. H. S. Burleigh. Library of Christian Classics. London: SCM; Philadelphia: Westminster Press, 1953.

———. *Letters*. 6 vols. Translated by Sr Wilfrid Parsons. Fathers of the Church. Washington, DC: Catholic University of America, 1951–89.

———. *Political Writings*. Edited by E. M. Atkins and R. J. Dodaro. Cambridge Texts in the History of Political Thought. Cambridge: Cambridge University Press, 2001.

Badham, Paul. 'Should Christians Accept the Validity of Voluntary Euthanasia?'. Gill, *Euthanasia and the Churches*, pp. 41–58.

Barry, Robert L. *Breaking the Thread of Life: On Rational Suicide*. New Brunswick and London: Transaction, 1994.

Barth, Karl. *Church Dogmatics*. 4 vols. Edited by G. W. Bromiley and T. F. Torrance. Edinburgh: T. & T. Clark, 1936–77. Volume III, 'The Doctrine of Creation', Part 4 (1961).

Battin, Margaret Pabst. *Ethical Issues in Suicide*. Englewood Cliffs, NJ: Prentice Hall, 1982, 1995.

———. *The Least Worst Death: Essays in Bioethics on the End of Life*. New York and Oxford: Oxford University Press, 1994.

———. 'Manipulated Suicide'. Battin and Mayo, *Suicide: the Philosophical Issues*, pp.169–82.

Battin, Margaret Pabst; and Mayo, David J. (eds). *Suicide: the Philosophical Issues*. London: Peter Owen, 1981.

Bauby, Jean-Dominique. *The Diving-Bell and the Butterfly*. London: Fourth Estate, 1997.

Beauchamp, Tom L. (ed.) *Intending Death: the Ethics of Assisted Suicide and Euthanasia*. Upper Saddle River, NJ: Prentice Hall, 1996.

Beauchamp, Tom L.; and Childress, James F. *Principles of Biomedical Ethics*. Fifth edition. Oxford: Oxford University Press, 2001.

Bennett, Jonathan. 'Foreseen Side Effects versus Intended Consequences'. Woodward, *The Doctrine of Double Effect*, pp. 85–118.

_____. 'Whatever the Consequences'. Steinbock and Norcross, *Killing and Letting Die*, pp. 167–91.

Biggar, Nigel. 'A Case for Casuistry in the Church'. *Modern Theology*, 6/1 (October 1989), pp. 29–51.

_____. 'Atonement'. Paul Barry Clarke and Andrew Linzey (eds). *Dictionary of Ethics, Theology, and Society*. London and New York: Routledge, 1996.

_____. 'Forgiveness in the Twentieth Century: A Review of the Literature, 1901–2001'. McFadyen and Sarot, *Forgiveness and Truth*, pp. 181–217.

_____. *The Hastening that Waits: Karl Barth's Ethics*. Second edition. Oxford: Clarendon Press, 1995.

Biggar, Nigel; and Black, Rufus (eds). *The Revival of Natural Law: Philosophical, Theological, and Ethical Responses to the Finnis-Grisez School*. Aldershot: Ashgate, 2000.

Birnbacher, Dieter. 'Das Tötungsverbot aus der Sicht des klassischen Utilitarismus'. Hegselmann and Merkel, *Zur Debatte über Euthanasie*, pp. 25–50.

Board for Social Responsibility of the Church of England (report of a working party). *On Dying Well: A Contribution to the Euthanasia Debate*. Second edition. London: Church House Publishing, 2000.

Boer, Theo. 'After the Slippery Slope: Dutch Experiences on Regulating Active Euthanasia'. *Journal of the Society for Christian Ethics*, 23/2 (2003), pp. 67–83.

Boyle, Joseph. 'A Case for Sometimes Tube-feeding Patients in PVS'. Keown, *Euthanasia Examined*, pp. 189–99.

_____. 'Sanctity of Life and Suicide: Tensions and Developments within Common Morality'. Brody, *Suicide and Euthanasia*, pp. 221–50.

_____. 'Toward Understanding the Principle of Double Effect'. *Ethics*, 90 (July 1980), pp. 527–38.

British Medical Association. *Withholding and Withdrawing Life–Prolonging Medical Treatment: Guidance for Decision–Making*. London: British Medical Journal Books, 1999; revised edition, 2001.

Brody, Baruch A. (ed.). *Suicide and Euthanasia*. Dordrecht: Kluwer, 1989.

Burleigh, Michael. *Death and Deliverance: Euthanasia in Germany, 1900–1945*. London: Pan Macmillan, 2002.

_____. *Ethics and Extermination: Reflections on Nazi Genocide*. Cambridge: Cambridge University Press, 1997.

_____. 'The Nazi Analogy and Contemporary Debates on "Euthanasia"'. Burleigh, *Ethics and Extermination*, pp. 142–52.

_____. 'Psychiatry, German Society, and Nazi "Euthanasia"'. Burleigh, *Ethics and Extermination*, pp. 113–29.

Cahill, Lisa Sowle. 'Bioethical Decisions to End Life'. *Theological Studies*, 52 (1991), pp. 107–27.

_____. 'A "Natural Law" Reconsideration of Euthanasia'. Lammers and Verhey, *On Moral Medicine*, pp. 445–53.

_____. 'Respecting Life and Causing Death in the Medical Context'. Pohier and Mieth, 'Suicide and the Right to Die', pp. 29–38.

Callahan, Daniel. *The Troubled Dream of Life: In Search of a Peaceful Death.* Washington, DC: Georgetown University Press, 2000.

Campbell, Alastair. 'Euthanasia and the Principle of Justice'. Gill, *Euthanasia and the Churches*, pp. 83–97.

Channer, J. H. (ed.). *Abortion and the Sanctity of Life.* Exeter: Paternoster Press, 1985.

Chappell, Timothy. 'Natural Law Revived: Natural Law Theory and Contemporary Moral Philosophy'. Biggar and Black, *The Revival of Natural Law*, pp. 29–52.

Clarke, Paul Barry; and Linzey, Andrew (eds). *Dictionary of Ethics, Theology, and Society.* London and New York: Routledge, 1996.

Coates, A. J. *The Ethics of War.* Manchester: Manchester University Press, 1997.

Davis, Nancy. 'The Doctrine of Double Effect: Problems of Interpretation'. Woodward, *The Doctrine of Double Effect*, pp. 119–42.

Donagan, Alan. 'Moral Absolutism and the Double Effect Exception: Reflections on Joseph Boyle's "Who is Entitled to Double Effect?"'. *The Journal of Medicine and Philosophy*, 16 (1991), pp. 495–509.

_____. *The Theory of Morality.* Chicago and London: University of Chicago Press, 1977.

Dworkin, Ronald. *Life's Dominion: An Argument about Abortion and Euthanasia.* London: HarperCollins, 1993.

_____. 'Public Policy and Physician-Assisted Suicide'. Dworkin et al., *Euthanasia and Physician-Assisted Suicide*, pp. 64–80.

Dworkin, Gerald; Frey, R. G.; and Bok, Sissela. *Euthanasia and Physician-Assisted Suicide: For and Against.* Cambridge: Cambridge University Press, 1998.

Economist, 17 September 1994: 'The Right to Die'.

_____, 21 June 1997: 'The Right to Choose to Die'.

Fest, Joachim. *Plotting Hitler's Death: The German Resistance to Hitler, 1933–45.* London: Weidenfeld & Nicolson, 1996.

Finnis, John. 'Final Thoughts on Final Acts'. Keown, *Euthanasia Examined*, pp. 56–61.

_____. 'The Fragile Case for Euthanasia: A Reply to John Harris'. Keown, *Euthanasia Examined*, pp. 46–55.

_____. 'Misunderstanding the Case against Euthanasia: Response to Harris's First Reply'. Keown, *Euthanasia Examined*, pp. 62–71.

_____. 'A Philosophical Case against Euthanasia'. Keown, *Euthanasia Examined*, pp. 36–45.

Foot, Philippa. 'Killing and Letting Die'. Steinbock and Norcross, *Killing and Letting Die*, pp. 280–9.

_____. 'Morality, Action, and Outcome'. Woodward, *The Doctrine of Double Effect*, pp. 67–82.

_____. 'The Problem of Abortion and the Doctrine of Double Effect'. Steinbock and Norcross, *Killing and Letting Die*, pp. 266–79.

Fordham, Morva; and Dunn, Virginia. *Alongside the Patient in Pain: Holistic Care and Nursing Practice.* London: Ballière Tindall, 1994.

Frey, R. G. 'Distinctions in Death'. Dworkin et al., *Euthanasia and Physician-Assisted Suicide*, pp. 17–42.

_____. 'Fear of a Slippery Slope'. Dworkin et al., *Euthanasia and Physician-Assisted Suicide*, pp. 43–63.

Gerrens, Uwe. *Medizinisches Ethos und Theologische Ethik: Karl und Dietrich Bonhoeffer in der Auseinandersetzung um Zwangssterilisation und 'Euthanasie' im Nationalsozialismus*. Schriftenreihe der Vierteljahrshefte für Zeitgeschichte, 73. Munich: R. Oldenbourg Verlag, 1996.

Gill, Robin (ed.). *Euthanasia and the Churches*. London: Cassell, 1998.

Gillon, Raanon. 'Euthanasia in the Netherlands'. *Journal of Medical Ethics*, 20 (1994), pp. 3–4.

Glover, Jonathan. *Causing Death and Saving Lives*. London: Penguin, 1977.

Gomez, C. F. *Regulating Death: Euthanasia and the Case of the Netherlands*. New York: The Free Press, 1991.

Griffiths, John. 'The Slippery Slope: Are the Dutch Sliding Down or Are They Clambering Up?'. Thomasma et al., *Asking to Die: Inside the Dutch Debate about Euthanasia*, pp. 93–104.

Griffiths, John; Bood, Alex; and Weyers, Helen. *Euthanasia and the Law in the Netherlands*. Amsterdam: Amsterdam University Press, 1998.

Grisez, Germain; 'Toward a Consistent Natural Law Ethics of Killing'. *The American Journal of Jurisprudence*, 15 (1970), pp. 64–96.

_____. *The Way of the Lord Jesus*, 3 vols. Vol. 1: *Christian Moral Principles*. Chicago: Franciscan Herald Press, 1983.

_____. *The Way of the Lord Jesus*. 3 vols. Vol. 2: *Living a Christian Life*. Quincy, IL: Franciscan Press, 1993.

Grisez, Germain; and Boyle, Joseph M. *Life and Death with Liberty and Justice: A Contribution to the Euthanasia Debate*. Notre Dame and London: University of Notre Dame Press, 1979.

Gustafson, James M. *Ethics from a Theocentric Perspective*. 2 vols. Vol. 2: *Ethics and Theology*. Chicago: University of Chicago Press, 1984.

Haas, Peter. *Morality after Auschwitz: The Radical Challenge of the Nazi Ethic*. Philadelphia: Fortress, 1992.

Hallett, Garth. *Greater Good: the Case for Proportionalism*. Washington, DC: Georgetown University Press, 1995.

Harris, John. 'Euthanasia and the Value of Life'. Keown, *Euthanasia Examined*, pp. 6–22.

Hartigan, Richard Shelly. *The Forgotten Victim: A History of the Civilian*. Chicago: Precedent, 1982.

Hastings Center. *Biomedical Ethics and the Shadow of Nazism*. Special Supplement. Hastings Center: August 1976.

Hauerwas, Stanley. 'Rational Suicide and Reasons for Living'. Lammers and Verhey, *On Moral Medicine*, pp. 671–8.

_____. *Suffering Presence: Theological Reflections on Medicine, the Mentally Handicapped, and the Church*. Notre Dame: Notre Dame University Press, 1986.

_____. 'Suffering the Retarded: Should we Prevent Retardation?'. *Suffering Presence*, pp.159–81.

Hays, Richard. *The Moral Vision of the New Testament: A Contemporary Introduction to New Testament Ethics*. Edinburgh: T. & T. Clark, 1996.

Hebblethwaite, Brian. 'The Problem of Evil'. Wainwright, *Keeping the Faith*, pp. 54–77.

Hegselmann, Rainer; and Merkel, Reinhard (eds). *Zur Debatte über Euthanasie: Beiträge und Stellungnahmen*. Frankfurt am Main: Suhrkamp, 1991.

Hirsch, Emmanuel. *Partir: l'accompagnement des mourants,* Entretiens avec Emmanuel Hirsch. Paris, 1986.

Hobbes, Thomas. *Leviathan.* Edited by C. B. Macpherson. Harmondsworth: Penguin, 1968.

Honecker, Martin. 'Sterbehilfe und Euthanasie aus theologischer Sicht'. Oehmichen, *Lebensverkürzung, Tötung und Serientötung,* pp. 67–84.

Hoose, Bernard. *Proportionalism: The American Debate and its European Roots.* Washington, DC: Georgetown University Press, 1987.

Horner, Stuart. 'Twenty-five Years On: Introduction to the Second Edition'. *On Dying Well: A Contribution to the Euthanasia Debate,* pp. ix–xv.

Horwitz, M. 'L'euthanasie en débat'. *Actualité Religieuse dans le monde,* 119 (15 February 1994), pp. 19–35.

Humphry, Derek; and Wickett, Ann. *The Right to Die: Understanding Euthanasia.* New York: Harper and Row, 1986.

Huser, Frank A. (ed.). *Palliative Care and Euthanasia.* Papers from the 1993 London Symposium on Care for the Seriously and Terminally Ill. Edinburgh: Campion Press, 1995.

Independent, 4 September 1991: 'Mercy killing'.

Institute of Medical Ethics Working Party on the Ethics of Prolonging Life and Assisting Death. 'Withdrawal of Life-support from Patients in a Persistent Vegetative State'. *The Lancet,* 337 (1991), pp. 96–8.

Jennett, Bryan. 'Letting Vegetative Patients Die'. Keown, *Euthanasia Examined,* pp. 169–88.

Jochemsen, Henk. 'Euthanasia in Holland: An Ethical Critique of the New Law'. *Journal of Medical Ethics,* 20 (1994), pp. 212–17.

———. 'Update: The Legalization of Euthanasia in the Netherlands'. *Ethics and Medicine,* 17 (2001), pp. 7–12.

John Paul II. *Apostolic Letter on the Christian Meaning of Human Suffering.* Boston: St Paul Books & Media, 1984.

———. *Euthanasia.* Declaration of the Sacred Congregation for the Doctrine of the Faith (May 5, 1980). Lammers and Verhey, *On Moral Medicine,* pp. 441–4.

Kaczor, Christopher. 'Double-effect Reasoning from Jean Pierre Gury to Peter Knauer'. *Theological Studies,* 59 (1998), pp. 297–316.

Kass, Leon R. *Life, Liberty, and the Defense of Dignity: The Challenge for Bioethics.* San Francisco: Encounter Books, 2002.

Keown, John. *Euthanasia, Ethics, and Public Policy: An Argument against Legalisation.* Cambridge: Cambridge University Press, 2002.

——— (ed.). *Euthanasia Examined: Ethical, Clinical, and Legal Perspectives.* Cambridge: Cambridge University Press, 1995.

———. 'Euthanasia in the Netherlands: Sliding Down the Slippery Slope?'. Keown, *Euthanasia Examined,* pp. 261–96.

———. 'The Law and Practice of Euthanasia in the Netherlands'. *Law Quarterly Review,* 108 (1992), pp. 51–78.

Kirk, Kenneth. *Conscience and its Problems: An Introduction to Casuistry.* London: Longman, Green and Co., 1927.

Kuhse, H. et al. 'End-of-life Decisions in Australian Medical Practice'. *Medical Journal of Australia,* 166 (1997), pp. 191–6.

Küng, Hans. 'A Dignified Dying'. Küng and Jens, *A Dignified Dying: A Plea for Personal Responsibility,* pp. 1–40.

Küng, Hans; and Jens, Walter. *A Dignified Dying: A Plea for Personal Responsibility.* London: SCM, 1995.

Lamb, David. *Down the Slippery Slope: Arguing in Applied Ethics*. New York: Croom Helm, 1988.

Lammers, Stephen E; and Verhey, Allen (eds). *On Moral Medicine: Theological Perspectives in Medical Ethics*. Grand Rapids: Eerdmans, 1987, 1998.

Leith, John H. (ed.). *Creeds of the Churches: a Reader in Christian Doctrine from the Bible to the Present*. Revised edition. Atlanta: John Knox, 1973.

Levinas, Emmanuel. *Otherwise than Being, or Beyond Essence*. The Hague: Martinus Nijhoff, 1981.

_____. *Totality and Infinity: An Essay on Exteriority*. Pittsburgh: Duquesne University Press, 1969.

Linacre Centre. *Euthanasia and Clinical Practice: Trends, Principles, and Alternatives*. London: Linacre Centre, 1982.

_____. *Euthanasia, Clinical Practice, and the Law*. London: Linacre Centre, 1994.

Lockwood, Michael (ed.). *Moral Dilemmas in Modern Medicine*. Oxford: Oxford University Press, 1985.

MacIntyre, Alasdair. *After Virtue: a Study in Moral Theory*. Notre Dame: University of Notre Dame Press, 1981.

McCormick, Richard A. 'A Commentary on the Commentaries'. McCormick and Ramsey, *Doing Evil to Achieve Good*, pp. 193–267.

_____. 'Ambiguity in Moral Choice'. McCormick and Ramsey, *Doing Evil to Achieve Good*, pp. 7–53.

_____. 'The Consistent Ethic of Life: Is There a Historical Soft Underbelly?'. McCormick, *The Critical Calling*, pp. 211–32.

_____. *The Critical Calling: Reflections on Moral Dilemmas since Vatican II*. Washington, DC: Georgetown University Press, 1989.

_____. *How Brave a New World? Dilemmas in Bioethics*. London: SCM, 1981.

_____. 'The Principle of Double Effect'. McCormick, *How Brave a New World?*, Appendix.

_____. 'To Save or Let Die: the Dilemma of Modern Medicine'. McCormick, *How Brave a New World?*, pp. 339–51.

McCormick, Richard A.; and Ramsey, Paul. *Doing Evil to Achieve Good: Moral Choice in Conflict Situations*. Chicago: Loyola University Press, 1978.

McFadyen, Alistair; and Sarot, Marcel (eds). *Forgiveness and Truth*. Edinburgh and New York: T. & T. Clark, 2001.

McKenny, Gerald P. *To Relieve the Human Condition: Bioethics, Technology, and the Body*. Albany, NY: State University of New York Press, 1997.

McLellan, Maureen. 'Palliative Care: An Ethical Approach'. Huser, *Palliative Care and Euthanasia*, pp. 17–24.

Malick, Terrence. *The Thin Red Line*. Twentieth Century Fox Film Corporation, 1998.

Mangan, Joseph T. 'An Historical Analysis of the Principle of Double Effect'. *Theological Studies*, 10 (1949), pp. 41–61.

Maret, Michel. *L'euthanasie: Alternative sociale et enjeux pour l'ethique chrétienne*. Saint–Maurice: Editions Saint–Augustin, 2000.

Marquis, Donald D. 'Four Versions of Double Effect'. Woodward, *The Doctrine of Double Effect*, pp. 156–85.

Meltzer, Ewald. *Das Problem der Abkürzung 'lebensunwerten' Lebens*. Halle, 1925.

Moltke, Helmuth James von. *Letters to Freya, 1939–45*. London: Collins Harvill, 1991.

214 Bibliography

Mud and Stars: The Impact of Hospice Experience on the Church's Ministry of Healing. Oxford: Sobell Publications, 1991.

Murray, Alexander. *Suicide in the Middle Ages,* vol. II: 'The Curse on Self-Murder'. Oxford: Oxford University Press, 2000.

Nagel, Thomas. 'Ethics'. Nagel, *The View from Nowhere,* pp. 164–88.

_____. *The View from Nowhere.* New York: Oxford University Press, 1986.

New York State Task Force on Life and the Law. *When Death is Sought: Assisted Suicide and Euthanasia in the Medical Context.* Albany, NY: New York State Task Force on Life and the Law, 1994.

Noonan, John T. *Contraception: A History of its Treatment by the Catholic Theologians and Canonists.* Cambridge, MA and London: Harvard University Press, 1965, 1986.

Nuyen, A. T. 'Levinas and the Euthanasia Debate'. *Journal of Religious Ethics,* 28/1 (Spring 2000), pp. 119–35.

O'Donovan, Oliver. 'Again: Who is a Person?'. Channer, *Abortion and the Sanctity of Life,* pp. 125–37.

_____. *Begotten or Made?* Oxford: Clarendon Press, 1984.

_____. 'Keeping Body and Soul Together'. Lammers and Verhey, *On Moral Medicine* (1998), pp. 223–38.

_____. *The Desire of the Nations: Rediscovering the Roots of Political Theology.* Cambridge: Cambridge University Press, 1996.

O'Donovan, Oliver; and O'Donovan, Joan (eds). *From Irenaeus to Grotius: A Sourcebook in Christian Political Thought 100–1625.* Grand Rapids, MI: Eerdmans, 1999.

O'Neill, Onora. *Autonomy and Trust in Bioethics.* Cambridge: Cambridge University Press, 2002.

Oehmichen, Manfred (ed.). *Lebensverkürzung, Tötung und Serientötung—eine interdisziplinäre Analyse der 'Euthanasie'.* Lübeck: Schmidt–Römhild, 1996.

Onwuteaka-Philipsen, B. D.; Van der Heide, A.; Van der Wal, G.; Van der Maas, P. J. et al. 'Euthanasia and other end of life decisions in the Netherlands in 1990, 1995, and 2001'. *The Lancet,* online, 17 June 2003 at image.thelancet.com/extras/03art3297web.pdf

Outlines Report Commission Inquiry into Medical Practice with Regard to Euthanasia [sic]. The Hague: Ministry of Justice, 1990.

Pailin, David. *A Gentle Touch: From a Theology of Handicap to a Theology of Human Being.* London: SPCK, 1992.

Pohier, J.; and Mieth, D. (eds). 'Suicide and the Right to Die'. *Concilium,* 179/3 (1985).

Porter, Jean. 'Basic Goods and the Human Good in Recent Catholic Moral Theology'. *The Thomist,* 57/1 (January 1993), pp. 27–49.

_____. '"Direct" and "Indirect" in Grisez's Moral Theory'. *Theological Studies,* 57 (1996), pp. 611–32.

Rachels, James. 'Active and Passive Euthanasia'. Steinbock and Norcross, *Killing and Letting Die,* pp. 112–19.

_____. *The End of Life.* Oxford: Oxford University Press, 1986.

_____. 'More Impertinent Distinctions and a Defense of Active Euthanasia'. Steinbock and Norcross, *Killing and Letting Die,* pp. 139–54.

Ramsey, Paul. *Ethics at the Edges of Life: Medical and Legal Intersections.* New Haven: Yale University Press, 1978.

_____. '"Euthanasia" and Dying Well Enough'. Ramsey, *Ethics at the Edges of Life,* pp. 145–88.

_____. 'On (Only) Caring for the Dying'. Ramsey, *The Patient as Person*, pp. 113–64.

_____. *The Patient as Person: Explorations in Medical Ethics*. New Haven: Yale UP, 1970.

Regout, Robert. *La doctrine de le guerre juste de Saint Augustin à nos jours d'après les théologiens et les canonistes catholiques, etc*. Paris, 1935.

Richards, Norvin. 'Double Effect and Moral Character'. *Mind*, XCIII (1984), pp. 381–97.

Royal College of Physicians (London).*Working Party Report on the Vegetative State*. London: Royal College of Physicians, 2003.

Sacred Congregation for the Doctrine of the Faith. *Declaration on Euthanasia* (5 May 1980). Lammers and Verhey, *On Moral Medicine*, pp. 441–4.

Schockenhoff, Eberhard. *Ethik des Lebens: Ein theologischer Grundriß*. Mainz: Matthias–Grünewald–Verlag, 1993.

Scott, James Brown. *The Spanish Origin of International Law: Francisco de Vitoria and His Law of Nations*. Oxford: Clarendon Press; London: Humphrey Milford, 1934.

Sheldon, Tony. 'Being "tired of life" is not grounds for euthanasia'. *British Medical Journal*, 326 (11 January 2003), p. 71.

_____. '"Existential" suffering not a justification for euthanasia'. *British Medical Journal*, 323 (15 December 2001), p. 1384.

Sidgwick, Henry. *Methods of Ethics*. Seventh edition. London: Macmillan, 1907; Indianapolis: Hackett, 1981.

Simkins, Michael. 'The express hit us and then I lost all consciousness'. *Guardian G2*, 18 May 2001.

Singer, Peter. *Practical Ethics*. Second edition. Cambridge: Cambridge University Press, 1993.

_____. *Rethinking Life and Death: The Collapse of our Traditional Ethics*. Oxford: Oxford University Press, 1995.

Song, Robert. *Christianity and Liberal Society*. Oxford: Oxford University Press, 1997.

Steinbock, Bonnie; and Norcross, Alastair (eds). *Killing and Letting Die*. Second edition. New York: Fordham University Press, 1994.

Sullivan, Thomas D. 'Active and Passive Euthanasia: An Impertinent Distinction?'. Steinbock and Norcross, *Killing and Letting Die*, pp. 131–8.

Taylor, Charles. *The Ethics of Authenticity*. Cambridge, MA: Harvard University Press, 1991.

Thomasma, David; Kimbrough–Kushner, Thomasine; Kimsma, Gerrit; and Ciesielski–Carlucci, Chris (eds). *Asking to Die: Inside the Dutch Debate about Euthanasia*. Dordrecht: Kluwer, 1998.

Tonti–Filippini, Nicholas; Fleming, John I.; Fisher, Anthony; and Krohn, Anna. *Joint Supplementary Submission to the [Australian] Senate Legal and Constitutional Legislation Committee Re: Euthanasia Laws Bill 1996*. Submission no. 187.

Tooley, Michael. 'An Irrelevant Consideration: Killing Versus Letting Die'. Steinbock and Norcross, *Killing and Letting Die*, pp. 103–11.

Uhlmann, Michael M. (ed.). *Last Rights? Assisted Suicide and Euthanasia Debated*. Washington, DC: Ethics and Public Policy Center; Grand Rapids: Eerdmans, 1998.

Van Delden, J. J. M. 'Slippery Slopes in Flat Countries – a Response'. *Journal of Medical Ethics*, 25 (1999), pp. 22–4.

Van der Heide, Agnes; Van der Maas, P. J.; and Van der Wal, G. 'Medical End-

216   Bibliography

of-Life Decisions Made for Neonates and Infants in the Netherlands'. *Lancet*, 350 (1997), pp. 251–5.

Van der Maas, P. J.; Van Delden, J. J. M.; and Pijnenborg, L. *Medische beslissingen rond het levenseinde. Het onderzoek voor de Commissie onderzoek medische praktijk inzake euthanasia.* The Hague: SDU Uitgeverij Plantijn-strat, 1991. English translation: *Euthanasia and Other Medical Decisions concerning the End of Life: An investigation performed upon request of the Commission of Inquiry into Medical Practice concerning Euthanasia.* Health Policy Monographs. The Hague: Elsevier, 1992.

Van der Maas, P. J.; Van Delden, J. J. M.; and Pijnenborg, L. *Medische beslissingen rond het levenseinde. Rapport van de Commissie onderzoek medische praktijk inzake euthanasie* [Medical decisions about the end of life. Report of the Commission on medical practice regarding euthanasia]. The Hague: SDU Uitgeverij Plantijnstrat, 1991.

Van der Wal, G.; *Euthanasie en hulp bij zelfdoding door huisarten* [Euthanasia and Assistance with Suicide by Family Doctors]. Rotterdam: WYT Uitgeefgroep, 1992.

Van der Wal, G.; Van der Heide, A.; Onwuteaka-Philipsen, B. D.; and Van der Maas, P. J. *Medische Besluitvorming aan het einde van het leven: De praktijk en de toetsingsprocedure euthanasie* [Medical decision-making at the end of life]. Utrecht: Tijdstroom Uitgeveriij, 2003.

Van der Wal, G.; and Van der Maas, P. J. *Euthanasie en andere medische beslissingen rond het levenseinde. De praktijk en de meldingprocedure.* The Hague: SDU Uitgeverij Plantijnstraat, 1996. English translation: *Euthanasia and other Medical Decisions concerning the End of Life: practice and notification procedure.* The Hague: SDU Uitgeverij Plantijnstraat, 1996.

Velleman, David. 'Against the Right to Die'. *Journal of Medicine and Philosophy*, 17 (1992), pp. 665–81.

Vitoria, Francisco de. 'Commentary on the Summa Theologiae of St Thomas Aquinas, IIaIIae, Q.40'. Translated by Gwladys L. Williams. Scott, *The Spanish Origin of International Law*, Appendix F, pp. cxv–cxxxi.

――――. 'On the Law of War, Q.1'. Vitoria, *Political Writings*, pp. 293–306.

――――. *Political Writings*. Cambridge Texts in the History of Political Thought. Edited by Anthony Pagden and Jeremy Lawrance. Cambridge: Cambridge University Press, 1991.

Voluntary Euthanasia Society. *The Last Right: the Need for Voluntary Euthanasia*. London: Voluntary Euthanasia Society, 1992.

Wainwright, Geoffrey. *Keeping the Faith: Essays to Mark the Centenary of 'Lux Mundi'.* London: SPCK, 1989.

Waldron, Jeremy. *God, Locke, and Equality: Christian Foundations of Locke's Political Thought.* Cambridge: Cambridge University Press, 2002.

Warnock, Mary. *An Intelligent Person's Guide to Ethics*. London: Gerald Duckworth, 1998.

Williams, Bernard. 'Which Slopes are Slippery?' Lockwood, *Moral Dilemmas in Modern Medicine*, pp. 126–37.

Wolbert, Werner. *Du sollst nicht töten. Systematische Überlegungen zum Tötensverbot.* Studien zur theologischen Ethik, 87. Freiburg, Switzerland: Universitätsverlag; Freiburg-im-Breisgau: Herder, 2000.

Woodward, P. A. (ed.). *The Doctrine of Double Effect: Philosophers Debate a Controversial Moral Principle.* Notre Dame: University of Notre Dame Press, 2001.

Young, Frances. *Face to Face: A Narrative Essay in the Theology of Suffering.* Edinburgh: T. & T. Clark, 1990.

Index

Kant, Immanuel 18, 20, 107, 108, 109, 178 n74, 178-9 n78, 187 n113, 188 n134

Keown, John 121-4, 126-32, 133, 134, 140-1, 145, 149, 150, 169, 191 n29, 191-2 n35, 194 n83, n86, n95

Kirk, Kenneth E. 101, 188 n132

Kuhse, Helga 134

law: and euthanasia 1-4; and suicide 2-3; in Australia (Northern Territories) 14; in Belgium 14; in England 1-3, 146; on abortion (1967) 163; on suicide 172 n6; Tony Bland case 169; Voluntary Euthanasia Bill (1969) 162-3; in France 4; in Ireland 169; in the Netherlands 14, 124-51, 136-40, 193 n77; the Chabot case 126; the Sutorius case 126-7, 150-1; in the USA (Oregon) 14

Leenan, H.J.J. 130

legalisation, pressures in favour of 13-16

letting die 57-9, 65-7, 137-8, 183 n35; see also treatment, refusing, withholding, and withdrawing

Levinas, Emmanuel 178-9 n78

liberalism 199 n156

Linacre Centre 61-2, 185 n78

Locke, John 18, 20, 180 n87

McCormick, Richard 88, 109-11, 112, 164, 179-80 n81, 188 n133, 189 n166

Macintyre, Alasdair 40

McKenny, Gerald 198 n145

Malick, Terrence 28, 175-6 n32

Mangan, Joseph 59

Marquis, Donald B. 185 n76

media, the 161-2, 167-8, 200 n171

medical training 15, 171

medicine, 'Baconian' 198 n145

Mennonites 7, 172 n12, 173 n.13

Moor, David 1 - 2

Murray, Alexander 173-4 n37, 188 n142

Nagel, Thomas 186 n91

Nazism and 'euthanasia' 158-61, 167

Netherlands 14, 116, 124-51, 152, 155, 170, 194 n91; Remmelink Commission 129, 141; Royal Dutch Medical Association (KNMG) 125, 129, 130, 132, 141; van der Maas survey (1991) 116, 127-30, 192 n42; van der Maas and van der Wal survey (1996) 130-2; van der Wal et al. survey (2003) 197 n141; see also law, in the Netherlands

New York State Task Force on Life and the Law 116

non-maleficence and beneficence, duties of 155-6, 168, 183 n35

Northern Territories, Australia see law, in Australia (Northern Territories)

Nygren, Anders 188 n134

O'Donovan, Oliver 37-9, 172 n5

On Dying Well (1975) 143, 162-3

O'Neill, Onora 178 n.74, 200 n171

Oregon, USA see law in the USA (Oregon)

Pailin, David 47, 179 n80

pain see suffering

palliative care 67, 168, 170-1

Pascal, Blaise 59, 62, 181-2 n11